LOOKING WHITE PEOPLE IN THE EYE
GENDER, RACE, AND CULTURE IN COURTROOMS
AND CLASSROOMS

In this book Sherene Razack explores what happens when whites look at
non-whites, and in particular at non-white women. Many studies examining this encounter between dominant and subordinate groups focus on
how it occurs in films, books, and popular culture. In contrast, Razack
addresses how non-white women are viewed, and how they must
respond, in classrooms and courtrooms. Examining the discussion of
equity issues in the classroom and immigration and sexual violence cases
in the courtroom, she argues that non-white women must often present
themselves as culturally different instead of oppressed. Seen as victims of
their own oppressive culture who must be pitied and rescued by white
men and women, non-white women cannot then be seen as subjects. This
book makes clear why we must be wary of educational and legal strategies that begin with saving 'Other' women. It offers powerful arguments
for why it is important to examine who are the saviours and who are the
saved, and what we must do to disrupt these historical relations of power.

SHERENE H. RAZACK is an associate professor in the Department of Sociology and Equity Studies in Education at OISE/UT.

SHERENE H. RAZACK

Looking White People in the Eye: Gender, Race, and Culture in Courtrooms and Classrooms

UNIVERSITY OF TORONTO PRESS
Toronto Buffalo London

© University of Toronto Press Incorporated 1998
Toronto Buffalo London
Printed in Canada

ISBN 0-8020-0928-X (cloth)
ISBN 0-8020-7898-2 (paper)

Printed on acid-free paper

Canadian Cataloguing in Publication Data

Razack, Sherene
 Looking white people in the eye: gender, race, and culture in courtrooms
 and classrooms

 Includes bibliographical references and index.
 ISBN 0-8020-0928-X (bound)   ISBN 0-8020-7898-2 (pbk.)

 1. Minority women – Canada. 2. Racism – Canada. 3. Sex discrimination
 against women – Law and legislation – Canada. I. Title

 HQ1233.R39 1998   305.48'8'00971   C97-931802-5

University of Toronto Press acknowledges the financial assistance to its publishing program of the Canada Council for the Arts and the Ontario Arts
Council.

This book has been published with the help of a grant from the Humanities
and Social Sciences Federation of Canada, using funds provided by the Social
Sciences and Humanities Research Council of Canada.

Contents

Acknowledgments

This collection begins with two essays written while teaching at the Simone de Beauvoir Institute at Concordia University in Montreal, Quebec. There I benefited from the scholarly advice of my friend and colleague Homa Hoodfar, who continues to be an important influence and source of strength. When I came to the Ontario Institute for Studies in Education in Toronto, Ontario, I drew once again upon the enormous scholarly reserves and staunch support of Ruth Roach Pierson. My colleagues at OISE, including Kathleen Rockhill, Kari Dehli, and George Dei, helped me to refine my ideas. I often draw upon George's unwavering intellectual and political commitment to antiracism. Mary Louise Fellows came into my life during the writing of the last three essays of this book. Her intellectual gifts and generosity shaped my ideas about innocence and complicity and her shadow falls on many of these pages. Without a wider community of scholars of colour, I would have lost heart long ago. For their friendship and scholarly expertise, I am grateful to Yvonne Bobb Smith, Ramabai Espinet, Honor Ford-Smith, Richard Fung, and Narda Razack, and to my American friends and colleagues of the critical race theory workshops, including Laura Gomez, Frank Valdes, and especially Robert Chang, who is always forthcoming with ideas about maintaining connections with other scholars of colour.

If there is any overriding influence on my work, it would be the students at the Ontario Institute for Studies in Education. I have shamelessly relied on them for research assistance and found myself enriched and sustained by their intellectual talents and friendship. Those who contributed to specific chapters are listed in the endnotes of those chapters. I would also like to thank Honor Ford-Smith, Amina Jamal, Barbara Heron, Donna Jeffery, Jane Ku, Helle-Mai Lenk, Sheryl Nestel, and

Yvonne Bobb Smith for all the work they did on the overall production of this book and for taking it on as though it were their own. The two anonymous reviewers gave the manuscript extraordinary care and I found their suggestions and encouragement very valuable. Finally, I thank Jeanie Stewart who gave her meticulous attention to the computer production of the manuscript at a time when it was not easy for her to do so. The Social Sciences and Humanities Research Council supported my research for the last five years and I am grateful to them, the more so in this time of vanishing research grants.

Without my family, who give me strength and confidence, I could do very little. I thank my parents, Ishmile and Acclema, my siblings and their partners, and, most of all, Larry, Ben, and Ilya for all their love and support. This book is for the next generation of my family who know better than I how to be of many places, cultures, and races – my children, Ilya, and Ben; my nieces, Sherene, Satu, Natasha, Vanessa, Alisha, Yasmin, Sabrina, Corine, Sara, and Selena; and my nephews, Riza, Emir, Carlos, and Omar.

SHERENE H. RAZACK

LOOKING WHITE PEOPLE IN THE EYE

Introduction:
Looking White People in the Eye

And then the occasion arose I had to meet the white man's eyes. An unfamiliar weight burdened me. A real world challenged me. In the white world the man of color encounters difficulties in the development of his bodily schema. Consciousness of the body is solely a negating activity. It is a third-person consciousness. The body is surrounded by an atmosphere of certain uncertainty ... And I was battered down by tom-toms, cannibalism, intellectual deficiency, fetishism, racial defects ... I took myself far off from my own presence ... What else could it be for me but an amputation, an excision, a hemorrhage that spattered my whole body with Black blood.

Frantz Fanon, *Black Skin, White Masks*

Innocence and Eye Contact

The essays in this book explore, in a variety of ways, what happens in classrooms and courtrooms when dominant groups encounter subordinate groups. In the much quoted passage above, Fanon describes this encounter as it occurs in colonialism, from the point of view of the colonized Black male subject. Fanon's description of the profound depersonalization that marks the colonial encounter compels us to pay attention to how relations among unequals are powerfully shaped by the histories and contemporary realities of oppression. Although the encounter between colonizer and colonized changes in historically specific ways, and is always highly gendered, it remains a moment when powerful narratives turn oppressed peoples into objects, to be held in contempt, or to be saved from their fates by more civilized beings.

I was drawn to Fanon,[1] whom many have called the founding father of modern colonial critique,[2] to introduce this body of essays primarily because of a startling divergence between his views and those of many contemporary educators and legal practitioners on the issue of eye contact. Looking white people in the eye is an encounter for Fanon that is deeply psychically structured and sexualized, illuminating, as Homi Bhabha writes 'the madness of racism, the pleasure of pain, the agonistic fantasy of political power.' It is a moment when the 'white man's eyes break up the Black man's body and in that act of epistemic violence its own frame of reference is transgressed, its field of vision disturbed.'[3] The colonial encounter produces, in this way, both the colonizer whose eyes commit the act of violence, and the colonized who is erased by the colonial gaze. Both are depersonalized – the colonizer caught in a delirium of desiring what must not be desired, the colonized locked into showing that he is the human the colonizer says he is not: 'The Negro is not. Any more than the white man.'[4]

Asking 'What is the distinctive *force* of Fanon's vision?,' Homi Bhabha remarks that it is Fanon to whom we owe the insight that the madness of racism is the rule not the exception. It is the condition that *enables* the story of Western civil progress to be told, the bedrock upon which the emergence of bourgeois society is founded. Bhabha argues that Fanon's analysis of colonial depersonalization, written in a language of demand and desire, changes the direction of Western history and challenges 'the historicist idea of time as a progressive, ordered whole.' With Fanon's analysis, we are forced to confront the very meaning of the human subject, to question 'historical rationality, cultural cohesion, the autonomy of individual consciousness.' How can we explain colonial alienation, its violence, 'the febrile, phantasmic images of racial hatred that come to be absorbed and acted out in the wisdom of the West' without Fanon's psychoanalytic explanations of delirium, desire, and neurosis?[5]

Fanon's preoccupation with the look is not primarily a preoccupation with the white man in colonialism. As Stuart Hall points out, what preoccupies Fanon is 'the fact that the black man can only exist in relation to himself through the alienating presence of the white "Other."' He writes:

The subject to which Fanon addresses himself is historically specific. It is not racism as a general phenomenon but racism in the colonial relation which he dissects. His task was to unpack its inner landscapes – *to consider the conditions for the production of a new kind of subject* [emphasis added].[6]

This book is similarly concerned with identifying the conditions for the production of a new kind of subject. In opening with Fanon, I mean to emphasize that while this project begins with critically examining the extent to which relations between colonizers and the colonized are highly structured and overdetermined by racism, it ends, I hope, with a gendered version of Fanon's goal – the liberation of the woman of colour from herself, her release from the gaze and its consequences.

In this neocolonial age, in which the countries of the North still economically and militarily dominate those of the South and white supremacy remains securely in place, Fanon's description of the desire, delirium, and neurosis of the colonial encounter is still relevant. In her celebrated essay 'Eating the Other,' bell hooks echoes Fanon in her identification of 'those "nasty" unconscious fantasies and longings about contact with the Other embedded in the secret (and not so secret) deep structure of white supremacy.'[7] Emphasizing the gendered dimensions of the colonial encounter (which Fanon did not sufficiently do), hooks explores the contemporary desire not to reject but to eat the Other – to transgress racial boundaries. As she comments:

To make one's self vulnerable to the seduction of difference, to seek an encounter with the Other, does not require that one relinquish one's mainstream positionality. When race and ethnicity become commodified as resources for pleasure, the culture of specific groups, as well as the bodies of individuals, can be seen as constituting an alternative playground where members of dominating races, genders, sexual practices affirm their power-over in intimate relations with the Other.[8]

Thus the 'desire to make contact with those bodies deemed Other, with no apparent will to dominate, assuages the guilt of the past, even takes the form of a defiant gesture where one denies accountability and historical connections.'[9]

The desire for contact that underlies the commodification of otherness and contemporary preoccupation with difference takes a particularly gendered form. If, as hooks suggests, white men engage in sexual encounters with non-white women as a 'ritual of transcendence, a movement out into the world of difference,'[10] then for white women, contact with the non-white Other more often occurs with non-white women. For white women, contact with non-white women reinforces the imperial idea that white women are more liberated than their sisters in the South. The white woman as saviour of less fortunate women is, as Inderpal Grewal documents in *Home and Harem*, a narrative that is centuries old. Grewal examines how English feminists of the nineteenth century used the image of victimized Indian women 'to position themselves as English citizens when the notion of "citizen" was itself gendered.'[11] Some contemporary feminists, Grewal continues, including feminists of colour, re-enact this imperial relation through positioning themselves as modern, free, and enlightened.[12]

Today, newspaper descriptions of female genital mutilation (FGM) performed on African women, actual film footage of an FGM operation in progress playing throughout the day on CNN television network, and media reports of the brutalities of 'Islamic' and Asian states towards women reinforce the notion of a barbaric South and, by contrast, a civilized North. In these scripts, a more generalized narrative of Western superiority, the media version of which Edward Said detailed in his book *Covering Islam*,[13] meets up with a Western feminist script just as it did in the case of English feminists a century ago. If African and Asian women are victims of their cultures, Western women can rush in to save them and, in so doing, can affirm their own positional superiority.

Scholars play pivotal roles in sustaining these old colonial formulas. For example, in many legal texts (which I detail in chapter 4), both feminist and non-feminist scholars have actively participated in reproducing the binary of the civilized and liberated Western woman and her oppressed Third World sister. In articles on women seeking asylum, immigrants from the South are depicted as carrying within them the seeds of barbarism that can take root and ultimately contaminate our shores, unless they are controlled.[14] Legal scholars have been busy contributing to this internal policing, devising policies and regulations to prevent the spread of barbaric practices brought by immigrants. One has only to think of the energy so many scholars and legal activists have poured into the legal proscription of FGM *in North America* (in comparison with the energy directed to antiracist strategies) to recognize a preoccupation with scripts of cultural inferiority and an affirmation of white female superiority.

Female genital mutilation and the wearing of the veil, the two arch-symbols of Southern inferiority, undeniably oppress women. However, when these symbols are constructed as uncontested cultural practices and are oversimplified, and when they dominate the news and scholarship of the North, they function in similar ways to the tom toms and stories of racial defects (which continue to abound as well) in Fanon's description of the colonial encounter. That is, as markers of difference, they are stories that identify the bodies of Asian and African women, both in the

North and in the South, as bodies to be saved by benevolent and more civilized Europeans.

A message of Southern cultural inferiority and dysfunction is so widely disseminated that when we in the North see a veiled woman, we can only retrieve from our store of information that she is a victim of her patriarchal culture or religion. Few alternative images or more complex evaluations are possible. We find it difficult to compare the veil's restriction of women's movements to the wearing of high heels and tight skirts in the West.[15] Similarly, dangerous breast enlargement surgeries are seldom seen as comparable to female genital mutilation (as the language confirms), in part because Northern women are considered to choose these 'surgeries' while Southern women are thought to have their 'mutilations' inflicted upon them. In this way, we in the West are able, consciously or not, to congratulate ourselves on our good sense and ignore the oppression of women on our own turf. Not surprisingly, we seldom acknowledge African and Asian women's own strategies of resistance to oppressive practices. Typically, a Western legal scholar writing on female genital mutilation is then able to say: 'The practice of female genital mutilation is so ancient that it has become firmly ingrained into the cultural traditions of practising countries and has become almost impossible to eradicate.'[16] Inevitably, the conclusion is: 'Only a few women actually escape this predicament by fleeing from their homelands. United States asylum laws must serve as a refuge for those who escape.'[17]

The veil, images of FGM, and stories of Third World men's overall brutality towards women are merely a few contemporary examples of the othering and inferiorizing of people of colour in the North. Expressive of the desire and ambivalence so evoked by Fanon, these particular practices share the feature that enacts a sexism that is real and, simultaneously, enables racism and Northern hegemony. Focusing on women, these essays explore how the eyes of men and women of the dominant group see subordinate women in these complex, interlocking ways and consider the impact of this vision in the courtrooms and classrooms of the 1990s.

In stark contrast to understanding the encounters between dominant and subordinate groups as moments marked by ambivalence, desire, and the performance of domination, Crown attorney Rupert Ross (to take but one example) and the many legal practitioners and educators who endorse the views expressed in his popular book *Dancing with a Ghost* and its sequel *Returning to the Teachings* understand eye contact as simply an issue of managing diversity.[18] If one understood, Ross maintains, that in Aboriginal culture it is disrespectful to look figures of authority in the eye, one could begin to overcome the gulf that lies between an Aboriginal defendant and a white judge or lawyer. Intending to avoid communication mishaps in the courtroom, Ross advises:

The first step in coming to terms with people of another culture, then, is to acknowledge that we constantly *interpret* the words and acts of others, and that we do so subconsciously but always in conformity with the way which our culture has taught us is the 'proper' way. The second step involves trying to gain a conscious understanding of what those culture-specific rules might be.[19]

Equipped with the cultural rules of eye contact, all players can then proceed from a position of equality. According to Ross's conceptualization, the history of genocide and the relentless ongoing racism in Aboriginal peoples' lives do not affect *contemporary* relations between white and Aboriginal peoples, at least not to the extent that cultural differences do. A sensitivity to history merely produces a refined catalogue of cultural differences, for example, a detailed description of an Aboriginal healing circle, and the imperial relation remains undisturbed. Ross is still the anthropologist *cum* lawyer reporting on the characteristics of the Other and Aboriginal people remain merely different, rather than oppressed.

The title of this book,[20] *Looking White People in the Eye*, is meant to challenge the widely held view that relations between dominant and subordinate groups can be unmarked by histories of oppression, as so many cultural diversity theorists, educators, and legal practitioners presume. Without history and social context, each encounter between unequal groups becomes a fresh one, where the participants start from zero, as one human being to another, each innocent of the subordination of others. Problems of communication are mere technical glitches in this view, misunderstandings that arise because the parties are culturally, racially, physically, mentally, or sexually *different*. Educators and legal practitioners need only learn to navigate their way through these differences, differences viewed as unchanging essences, innate characteristics – the knowledge of which enables us to predict behaviour. In these essays, I contend the opposite. Encounters between dominant and subordinate groups cannot be 'managed' simply as pedagogical moments requiring cultural, racial, or gender sensitivity. Without an understanding of how responses to subordinate groups are socially organized to sustain existing power arrangements, we cannot hope either to communicate across social hierarchies or to work to eliminate them.

Increasingly, one sees the popularity of the cultural differences model in education. For example, researchers exploring the schooling issues of Asian children in Canada, the United States and Britain often attribute both their school achievements and failures to Asian cultural values and practices.[21] If Asians do well in school, it is because of their cultural attachment to education; if they do badly, it is because of their failure to 'acculturate' in the 'host' society. Teachers are then advised to become familiar with various cultural practices so that they might intervene appropriately. As Christine Sleeter and others have documented,[22] the adoption of apparently helpful 'cross-cultural' strategies does little to ensure that white teachers will view their Asian and Black pupils as capable of the same level of achievement and range of desires as their white students. Further, teachers are not pressed to examine whether the behaviour that is called cultural, for example passivity with authority figures, is in fact a response to an alienating and racist environment.

In the adult education classroom, a similarly technical view of the problems of communication across differences has prevailed. Educators 'challenged by diversity' consider that they can address differences through a variety of pedagogical tricks that accommodate culturally different or gender-specific styles of learning. At its worst, the 'management of diversity,' as such undertakings are usually called, entails an appropriation and misuse of the cultural practices of subordinate groups. White discussion groups that use an Aboriginal talking stick to pass from speaker to speaker or those that begin with healing circles and Native drums are examples of this kind.[23] More benignly, replacing traditional lectures for a more appropriate participatory style is another practice thought to enable us to bridge the gulf that lies between dominant and subordinate groups. Again, it is not necessary in this approach to consider the veils and the racial defects that haunt the imagination of both the colonizer and the colonized and that mark the encounter between them, our best intentions notwithstanding.

What makes the cultural differences approach so inadequate in various pedagogical moments is not so much that it is wrong, for people in reality are diverse and do have culturally specific practices that must be taken into account, but that its emphasis on cultural diversity too often descends, in a multicultural spiral, to a superficial reading of differences that makes power relations invisible and keeps dominant cultural norms in place. The strategy becomes inclusion and all too often what Chandra Mohanty has described as 'a harmonious, empty pluralism.'[24] Cultural sensitivity, to be acquired and practised by dominant groups, replaces, for example, any concrete attempt to diversify the teacher population. If

white teachers can learn the appropriate cultural rules, we need not hire
Black teachers, and we need not address racism. More important, pluralistic models of inclusion assume that we have long ago banished the
stereotypes from our heads. These models suggest that with a little practice and the right information, we can all be innocent subjects, standing
outside hierarchical social relations, who are not accountable for the past
or implicated in the present. It is not our ableism, racism, sexism, or heterosexism that gets in the way of communicating across differences, but
their disability, *their* culture, *their* biology, or *their* lifestyle. In sum, the
cultural differences approach reinforces an important epistemological
cornerstone of imperialism: the colonized possess a series of knowable
characteristics and can be studied, known, and managed accordingly by
the colonizers whose own complicity remains masked.

In this book, I wish to challenge this position of innocence by asking
questions about *how* relations of domination and subordination stub-
bornly regulate encounters in classrooms and courtrooms. My goal is to
move towards accountability, a process that begins with a recognition
that we are each implicated in systems of oppression that profoundly
structure our understanding of one another. That is, we come to know
and perform ourselves in ways that reproduce social hierarchies. Tracing
our complicity in these systems requires that we shed notions of mastering differences, abandoning the idea that differences are pre-given,
knowable and existing in a social and historical vacuum. Instead, we
invest our energies in exploring the histories, social relations, and conditions that structure groups unequally in relation to one another and
that shape what can be known, thought, and said. This does not mean that we
abandon sensitivity, that we throw up our hands in despair at the complexity of it all, nor reduce this complexity to the lament so often heard
that 'since I can never know what it feels like to be Black, I need not think
about race.' Instead, we need to direct our efforts to the conditions of
communication and knowledge production that prevail, calculating not
only who can speak and how they are likely to be heard but also how we
know what we know and the interest we protect through our knowing.

These pedagogical directions make it clear that education for social
change is not so much about new information as it is about disrupting
the hegemonic ways of seeing through which subjects make themselves
dominant. When we go about the business of subjecting these dominant
frames to scrutiny in the classroom or courtroom, we should be aware of
how deeply connected these ways of seeing are to identity. To disrupt
how a white judge views immigrants, for instance, as foreigners depen-

dent on the generosity of Canadians, is to call into question the judge's own sense of superiority as a benevolent man or woman. The denial of racism that is so integral to white Canadian identity was collectively in evidence at the time of the 1996 Summer Olympics. A national outcry arose (on radio and television and in newspapers) in response to Black Canadian Olympic athlete Donovan Bailey's reported statement that Canadians were as racist as Americans and displayed their racism in their responses to the achievements of Canada's Black athletes. Believing that a central part of Canadian identity was tolerance, many white Canadians were outraged by the suggestion that Canadians might be otherwise. Stories of racism and genocide are profoundly shocking, as Coco Fusco reminds us, because they deeply upset the dominant group's notion of self.[25]

White as the Colour of Domination

In working on how histories of oppression regulate what happens in classrooms and courtrooms, I have concentrated on narratives about culture, race, and gender. This leads me to use a language of colour to describe the politics of domination and subordination. White, as my title indicates, is the colour of domination. Two things need to be said about this language. First, it wraps my arguments in a mantle of race even while, simultaneously, I attempt to theorize how racial subjects come into existence through gender hierarchies and vice versa. Second, it leaves the impression that colour is what matters most, even when I am describing the very different histories and regulatory processes that affect Aboriginal peoples (chapter 3), Asians, and Africans (chapter 4) and women with developmental disabilities (chapter 5). The use of this language is in keeping with my emphasis on the physicality of the encounter between powerful and powerless groups and on the importance of the visible in colonial encounters – who and what is seen and not seen.

It has been difficult to find a language that captures the simultaneity of systems of domination and the many ways in which they mutually constitute one another.[26] My emphasis on capitalism, patriarchy, and white supremacy reflects the sites I have chosen to explore and the analytical path I have travelled. This book represents a five-year attempt to complicate the meaning of gender. I wanted to find a language for describing hierarchical relations among women, relations that meant that a working-class woman, for instance, experienced gender oppression in a different way from a middle-class woman. Interrogating the essentialist notion that all women are oppressed in the same way, I first tried to show that we do not come any closer to describing relations of domination and subordination when we move beyond an essentialist approach to an additive model of oppression (racism plus sexism produces a doubly oppressed woman). It tells us nothing, for example, about how systems of oppression work, how they sustain one another and how they come into existence in and through one another, to conclude that a white woman is always better off than a Black woman. Developing the picture further, by filling out the details so that we have a poor white woman and a rich Black one, still keeps us in the abstract realm of multiplying essences. Instead, it is vitally important to explore in a historical and site-specific way the meaning of race, economic status, class, disability, sexuality, and gender as they come together to structure women in different and shifting positions of power and privilege.

Pursuing the idea of interlocking systems of domination (with ample help from Patricia Hill Collins, Trinh T. Minh-ha, and many others),[27] I came to see that each system of oppression relied on the other to give it meaning, and that this interlocking effect could only be traced in historically specific ways. For instance, in nineteenth-century Britain, the cult of domesticity, which restricted white women's activities to the private sphere, not only structured male/female relations and the self-definition of the middle class but also was an indispensable element in the imperial enterprise, enabling imperial powers such as Britain to utilize the capital of the middle class, among other things, to colonize others.[28] Elaborating on the imperial project, Ann Stoler has shown how in Dutch colonies, a 'European family life and bourgeois respectability became increasingly tied to notions of racial survival, imperial patriotism, and the political strategies of the colonial state.'[29] Stoler has carefully elaborated, for instance, the importance of the construct of the vulnerable white lady in need of manly protection: 'A defense of community, morality, and white male power was achieved by increasing control over and consensus among Europeans, by reaffirming the vulnerability of white women, the sexual threat posed by native men, and by creating new sanctions to limit the liberties of both.'[30] This construct had great currency in the colonies and in the metropolis where, in Victorian England as well as elsewhere in Europe, it was an enduring plank in the doctrine of separate spheres and, consequently, in the maintenance of patriarchy and class exploitation.

For their part, European women, as Sara Suleri has written of Anglo-Indian women[31] and Reina Lewis[32] of English women painters of the nineteenth century, often viewed Other women through the lens of their own subordination, with historically specific and varying results. For example, Lewis writes of how the white women artists she studies under-stood themselves as simultaneously being beneficiaries of imperialism and inferior (owing to gender) in the world of European art. This dual consciousness, which Lewis reminds us cannot be separated from the actual material relations that enabled white women to displace gen-dered exploitation onto the colonial Other, resulted both in white women gaining their autonomy as cultural producers at the expense of the colonized Other and, contradictorily, in their uneven attachment to imperialism. These complex operations of hierarchies of gender and race point to contradictions and cracks in hegemonic systems and illustrate the central importance of understanding how various systems interlock to produce specific effects.

Analytical tools that consist of looking at how systems of oppression interlock differ in emphasis from those that stress intersectionality.[33] Interlocking systems need one another, and in tracing the complex ways in which they help to secure one another, we learn how women are pro-duced into positions that exist symbiotically but hierarchically. We begin to understand, for example, how domestic workers and professional women are produced so that neither exists without the other. First World policies of colonialism and neo-colonialism, which ultimately precipitated the debt crisis and the continuing impoverishment of the Third World and enabled the pursuit of middle-class respectability in the First World, were implemented in highly gendered ways. Cynthia Enloe vividly cap-tures this process:

The 'debt crisis' is providing many middle-class women in Britain, Italy, Singa-pore, Canada, Kuwait and the United States with a new generation of domestic servants. When a woman from Mexico, Jamaica or the Philippines decides to emi-grate in order to make money as a domestic servant she is designing her own international debt politics. She is trying to cope with the loss of earning power and the rise in the cost of living at home by cleaning bathrooms in the countries of the bankers.[34]

More recently, Abigail Bakan and Daiva Stasiulis have demonstrated that women's work in the home cannot be fully understood without address-ing the differences in citizenship status among members of households. As they forcefully argue: 'The increasing demand for in-home child care in developed capitalist states and the similarly increasing but highly regu-

lated supply of Third World migrant women together work to structure and mediate citizenship rights across and within national boundaries.'[35]

By understanding the connections between systems of oppression,
geographical regions and various groups of women, we might better
come to see why it has been so difficult for each one of us to see our privilege at the same time as our penalty. An interlocking analysis reminds us
of the ease with which we slip into positions of subordination (for example, the sexually vulnerable woman, the woman with sole responsibility
for child care, or the woman without access to managerial positions)
without seeing how this very subordinate location simultaneously reflects and upholds race and class privilege. In focusing on our subordination, and not on our privilege, and in failing to see the connections
between them, we perform what Mary Louise Fellows and I call 'the race
to innocence,'[36] a belief that we are uninvolved in subordinating others.
More to the point, we fail to realize that we cannot undo our own mar-
ginality without simultaneously undoing all the systems of oppression.

An analysis of interlocking systems of oppression and a feminist political project that proceeds with a wary eye for complicity in these systems
has increasingly guided the work presented here. For educators, there
are important implications of maintaining a critical gaze through the
tracing of relations of privilege and penalty. First and foremost, when we
consider what it is that limits seeing, we begin with subject position and
the assumption, as I have already noted, that power relations deeply
shape encounters. Second, in attending to how positions of power are
secured, that is through what mechanisms, we gain a sense of what is at
stake when we attempt to raise critical consciousness. In understanding,
for instance, how white supremacy is gendered, we begin to unravel the
resistance we sometimes see in white feminist classrooms to complicat-
ing the meaning of gender by talking about how women are raced. Confronted with white racial superiority, white women can deny their
dominance by retreating to a position of subordination – that is, since we
are oppressed as women, we cannot be oppressors of women of colour.
Finally, attention to interlocking systems of domination requires that we
move beyond essences and educational responses related to mastering
our knowledge of the subordinate groups, but not in order to claim that
we are all just human beings. To move beyond essences, we have to do
the work around how subjectivity is constituted and how systems of
domination are reproduced.

I have not illustrated here the interconnectedness of all systems of oppression nor shown how they operate at a wide number of sites. For example, I have barely explored race and sexuality. Given the sites I have chosen to work on, my analysis would have been immeasurably enriched had I examined, for example, in chapters 3 and 4, how a heterosexual norm shapes the refugee determination process or the legal determination of who has endured violence and who has not, and, further, how this norm intersects with the racialized and gendered norms I do discuss. For the most part, I have concentrated my efforts on how racist ideas are supported by certain essentialist notions of gender, and vice versa.

In chapter 5, I show how patriarchal and white supremacist ideas about violence against women combine with ableist notions of the meaning of disability to deny the violence in the lives of women with disabilities. In some ways, this small foray into an interrogation of ableism repeats the additive move of which I am deeply critical, namely that disability complicates or changes the stories of race, gender, and class that can be told in the courtroom. That is, I have tried to extend my analytical framework of race and gender through an examination of disability and not concentrated on how responses to disability itself are organized in ways that rely on race and gender hierarchies.

In the sites of law and education that I explore, the dominant group is clearly white, hence the title of this book. This hierarchy is evident in practice and in theory. Most educators in the school system, the university, and the informal sector are white, as are most judges, lawyers, and lawmakers. The theories in use in classrooms and courtrooms, for example theories about cultural diversity, are developed mostly by white theorists. This material fact does not exonerate those of us who are not white and who are also teaching and producing theory. I have not, however, directed my efforts to this subgroup, at the moment a very small percentage of the elites whose gazes I explore.

Like Mary Louise Pratt in her book *Imperial Eyes*, I have been preoccupied with the representational practices of Europeans, not only with the 'seeing man' – 'he whose imperial eyes passively look out and possess'[37] – but also with the seeing woman. Imperial eyes are clearly gendered. While it may be, as Reina Lewis argues, that the European woman's gaze in colonialism is less pejorative and less absolute owing to her own gender subordination,[38] one of my concerns in this book is how, in the context of feminist politics, the white female gaze often sustains rather than disrupts white supremacy, capitalism and patriarchy. Like Pratt, I am worried that in insufficiently exploring how white gazes are returned by subordinate groups,[39] I leave few openings to interrupt the totalizing moment that Fanon so directly describes. How do we resist imperial eyes? I do not ask, as Rey Chow does in her important work, What does the ethnic eye see?[40] In this omission I am in danger of repeating what Edward Said has noticed about Joseph Conrad. Conrad, Said writes, can see 'the West's wicked power' but he is largely unable to imagine that the peoples of 'India, Africa, and South America also had lives and cultures with integrities not wholly controlled by the gringo imperialists and reformers of this world.'[41] I do not want to leave the impression that subordinate groups are simply erased by the violence of the white gaze. Rather, the question What do the eyes of the dominant group see when they encounter subordinate groups? is raised both to name the epistemic violence of this vision *and* to interrupt its consequences. These essays were written from the premise that these deeply organized responses of dominant groups to subordinate groups can be disrupted and that education, which others have called education for critical consciousness, is central to this process. If we can name the organizing frames, the conceptual formulas, the rhetorical devices that disguise and sustain elites, we can begin to develop responses that bring us closer to social justice. That is, we can each begin to stop performing ourselves as dominant as well as better calculate how to return the gaze.

Rights Thinking, Essential Woman, and the Culturalization of Differences

The essays in this book trace some of the constructs that *enable* the suppression of histories of oppression, constructs I encountered over the last fifteen years of trade union, community, and university teaching. In my involvement with predominantly white workers in union education classes on human rights issues, I wanted to know what stories or explanations the participants in my classes told themselves in order to believe that racism did not exist in Canada. Similarly, in their own minds, how did white male judges account for violence against women? As an educator, I did not view these as broad conceptual questions but rather as urgent pedagogical challenges. How do we disrupt claims of innocence and moves of superiority in the specific context of a human rights course, a graduate seminar, or a trial – in effect, how do we build critical consciousness and achieve social justice?

Like most educators working in the area of issues of social justice, I experienced an increasingly predictable set of responses that inhibited the development of critical consciousness and blocked the actions necessary to change the world. These responses can be summed up as a denial of oppression. Thus, some of my white students would claim, for example, that there was no racism in Canada, that all immigrants had a hard time at first and later would enjoy better access to society's resources, or that Aboriginal people were killing each other before white men arrived. While some of these responses seemed simple enough to understand (and relatively archaic), others indicated that apparently progressive ideas were in fact *enabling* people to deny violence and oppression and their complicity in it.

In these essays, I trace three ideas or organizing constructs that most often enabled students to deny that oppression existed: rights thinking, essential woman, and the culturalization of differences. Each of these constructs masks relations of power and enables dominant groups to maintain their innocence, even while such constructs can simultaneously empower subordinate groups. I have arranged these essays in the order in which they were written so that the reader might trace some of the twists, turns, and reverses in my exploration of these constructs.

Beginning with rights thinking in chapter 1, I take up where I left off at the end of my first book *Canadian Feminism and the Law*[42] and ask, How do women speak about their realities in a court of law when the naming of those realities would force a confrontation over naming men, and white people, as oppressors? Underlying chapter 1 is the paradox of liberalism as articulated by David Goldberg:[43] race is irrelevant but all is race. That is to say, as Linda Alcoff has written in commenting on Goldberg's work, 'the universal sameness that was so important for the liberal self required a careful containment and taxonomy of difference. Where rights require sameness, difference must be either trivialized or contained in the Other across a firm and visible border.'[44] The problem that I explore is thus twofold: first, how can we talk about power and privilege using a concept – rights – that leaves no room for a discussion of histories of subordination? Rights thinking is based on the liberal notion that we are all individuals who contract with one another to live in a society where each of us would have the maximum in personal freedom. Starting from this premise, there then are no marginalized communities of people and no historical relations of power. Each man, and the prototype is male, makes himself anew. Second, when histories do enter the discussion, for instance when we examine how slavery and racism affected the freedom to engage in this contract, or when we consider how violence against women secured the freedom and autonomy of men, they implicate dominant groups and are thus strenuously resisted through the narrative that we are all just human beings.

One way in which critical educators and legal practitioners have worked with the paradoxes inherent in rights language is to counter the individualizing, dehistoricized features of rights thinking with stories of subordination. In chapter 2, reflecting on pedagogical moments in the courtroom as well as moments when human rights activists tried to thread their way through various histories of subordination in order to determine political action, I trace more specifically what is at stake for us when we are confronted with these stories of oppression. As Trinh insightfully suggests of these moments: 'The Man can't hear it the way she means it.'[45] How stories are heard and the voices we use to tell them are the two themes of this chapter. If we pay attention to the interpretive structures we use both to tell stories and to hear them, we quickly find ourselves having to thread our way through a number of relations at once. For example, in seeing ourselves as good human rights activists engaged in crucial issues of social justice, we can sometimes repeat an imperial civilizing move, and in so doing, fail to see how we oppress others. The challenge in radical education becomes how to build critical consciousness about how we, as subjects, position ourselves as innocent through the use of such markers of identity as the good activist.[46]

Such a challenge is overwhelming. How do we begin to theorize subjectivity and then to map the educational routes that would enable us to cut through the structures of dominance in which we are embedded? Generally, as chapters 3, 4, and 5 indicate, I have not found it useful to answer such questions in the abstract. Instead, I seek to explore the interpretive structures that limit what can be known, heard, and said in a court of law when the issue is violence against women. My choice of context originates in the relentless violence in women's lives, violence ranging from sexual violence in the home and on the street, to violence encountered in institutions, in employment, and in crossing borders. I felt strongly that a language restricted to what men do to women does not sufficiently account for the violence in the lives of Aboriginal women, women of colour, and women with disabilities. Indeed, it does not even account for the violence that white women suffer at the hands of white men. If the violence that all women encounter cannot be described with an analytical framework of gender abstracted from all other social relations, what language do we use to describe these various interlocking realities? Again, such a question remains impossibly abstract and must be pursued in the specific way suggested in chapter 2: What stories are told and how are they heard? How does gender interlock with race and disability to produce specific experiences of violence?

In cases of sexual violence involving Aboriginal women and immigrant women (chapter 3), the contexts of both the victims of violence and their attackers are often *culturalized*, that is, understood as cultural and frozen in time, rather than as dynamic, historical, and social. Cultural differences perform the same function as a more biological notion of race (for example, the idea that Black people have smaller brains) once did: they mark inferiority. A message of racial inferiority is now more likely to be coded in the language of culture rather than biology. What does it mean when a white judge takes the cultural contexts of Aboriginal men into account during a rape trial? It can mean, and it has, that the rapes are viewed as a kind of cultural practice: these people do these kind of things. In this instance, cultural difference, as inferiority, can be a mitigating factor in sentencing. Of course, the culturally different man has to fit this stereotype of primitive. In one of the cases discussed in chapter 3, the defendant could not manage to do so because he had bound his victim with a cord from a stereo, and was therefore clearly not primitive enough. These moments of overt inferiorizing of Aboriginal culture form one expression of the cultural approach. It is more common, however, to find in Canadian courts a relatively more refined version of cultural difference as pre-given and as a marker of inferiority. Canadian judges are now less inclined to rely on overt pronouncements about the inferiority of cultures (land claims disputes excepted – here overt inferiorizing is still *de rigueur*) and more interested in cloaking their opinions in a mantle of sensitivity to cultural differences. In such matters, the judge appears progressive and even anti-imperialist by displaying his or her familiarity with Aboriginal culture and history. A culturally sensitive judge might understand that colonization has wreaked havoc on Aboriginal communities, leaving a trail of alcohol abuse and a legacy of sexual abuse in residential schools. However, this history is not often taken into account to understand the victim – for example, to understand the impact that sexual assault would have on a woman for whom community is the only refuge against racism. More important, cultural considerations do not lead to an understanding of the current workings of white supremacy. A cultural differences approach is not a discussion of contemporary white/Aboriginal relations but a discussion of who Aboriginal people are. Colonization, when it is mentioned, achieves the status of a cultural characteristic, pre-given and involving only Aboriginal people, not white colonizers. We may know how colonization changed Aboriginal people, but do we know how it changed, and continues to change, white people?

Pursuing the process of culturalization in the refugee determination process (chapter 4) has strengthened my conclusion that we cannot go beyond essential woman without understanding that women's realities are simultaneously shaped by patriarchy, capitalism, and white supremacy. Patriarchal violence, understood in the simple frame as what men do to women, eclipses racial and economic violence, and more important, obscures how they constitute each other and inhibit women's means of resistance. When women from the South flee domestic violence and seek asylum in the North, our refugee determination process has required that they frame their realities as though colonialism and neocolonialism do not affect them. In the refugee determination process, as in sexual assault trails, the language of culture replaces the language of domination.

In the North, we will only save those whose plights do not implicate us. Asylum seekers who cannot present themselves as the victims of unusually patriarchal and culturally dysfunctional cultures are not granted asylum in Canada. Tracking the ways in which a narrative about what men do to women combines with one about the North saving the South, I ask questions in chapter 4 about how we might go about speaking about patriarchal and colonial violence in the same breath. It seems clear that our potential to do so begins with giving up our claims to innocence, claims that enable us in the North to cast ourselves as saviours of Third World women. Instead, tracing complicity and accountability, we must ask: How are we each implicated in the violence?

Moving beyond victims and their saviours requires the same tracing of accountability when the issue is violence against women with disabilities. Few legal scholars have bothered to theorize disability at all, although disability rights activists have done so for some time now.[47] Most legal scholars appear to think that disability is simply a special issue and one that does not enable us to say anything about race, gender, class, or sexuality. This is perhaps the underlying logic of what I have been calling claims of innocence. On the one hand if we understand the realities of groups subordinate to us as different or special, we plunge into hierarchy: we become saviours of less fortunate peoples. On the other hand, if we start from the premise that non-disabled people are implicated in what happens to women with disabilities, we might stand a better chance of detecting when we are simply re-establishing our superiority by noticing difference. The question for us – those of us in a dominant group – always has to be, 'What do I gain from understanding something in this way?'

On those rare occasions when we non-disabled scholars have thought about disability, we have done so on the basis of pity. Relying on additive analysis (where disability plus gender equals double oppression), we have been content to describe the situation of women with disabilities as one of double vulnerability. With the concept of vulnerability, we successfully manage to see disability as a condition that is pre-given, a biological essence or even a social condition, but one that simply is. We privatize the condition of being disabled and do not ask questions about the social relations that transform a physical and mental situation into one of great vulnerability. As Martha Minow has also articulated, when difference is thought to reside in the person rather than in the social context, we are able to ignore our role in producing it.[48]

What is most needed is a theory of difference that accounts for the violence in the lives of women and our complicity in it. As I have discussed throughout these essays, relying on the notion of an essential woman, the idea that all women share a core of oppression on to which can then be grafted their differences, has enabled a masking of how systems of domination interlock and thus how we, as women, are implicated in one another's lives. Tracing complicity thus begins with a mapping of relations among women. We can then critically examine those constructs that homogenize our differences or package them as innate, decontextualized, and ahistorical.

This collection ends with some misgivings expressed in chapter 6. Like many educators, scholars, and activists of colour, I have run headlong into the perils of both essentialism and anti-essentialism. Most of this book is about the ways in which essentialist constructs mask relations of power. In searching for a language to describe multiple relations of power, and thus to uncover complicity in these relations, I have not, however, arrived at a foolproof strategy to raise critical consciousness or to identify effective antisubordination practices. It is not clear, for instance, that talking about culture in an essentialist way is always a bad thing. As Aboriginal peoples, and more recently African Canadians[49] have shown, when one is thought to have a dead, dying, or dysfunctional culture, emphasizing cultural values and practices is an important oppositional strategy. In the courtroom, too, it has sometimes been possible to introduce histories of domination through a frame of cultural difference. For example, during the trial of Donald Marshall, focusing on Mi'kmaq ways of knowing created an opportunity (but perhaps one that was not wide enough) to recall the destruction of the Mi'kmaq by white society and the continuing impact of this genocide.[50] Thus, at least one misgiving I have is that in arguing for a focus on domination, I may have not attended to alternative strategies grounded in specific contexts unlike those discussed here.

A second important misgiving is my fear that anti-essentialism has of late been wielded as a weapon to undermine the struggles of people of colour. The cry is growing stronger that calls for the hiring of faculty of colour, Afrocentric schools, Aboriginal Centres of learning and the Arts, South Asian festivals, writers of colour conferences represent dangerous separatist and particularist moves to discriminate against white people. It is sometimes difficult to counter such charges and at the same time pay heed to the interlocking nature of systems of oppression. When negotiating how to be heard, sometimes we must speak in a language that belies this interconnectedness. We will need to find ways to understand where strategy ends and reinstatement of domination begins. In this quest for tools for critical thinking, I have suggested that we keep our eye on domination, and that we do so in a context-specific way that recognizes the interdependency of systems of oppression. As a friend of mine often asks, Could we have racism without sexism, heterosexism, ableism, and capitalism? Whichever way the question is asked, I hope that these essays promote the answer as no. The systems of oppression that regulate our lives sustain one another but we do not always see this interdependency.

In an introduction of this sort, I leave the impression of a coherence and order to my thoughts that I did not experience at the time each chapter was written. The chapters reflect both the gaps and the continuities in my thinking as well as the many times I have had to double back and refashion the conceptual tools with which I worked. At the end of this body of work, which has stretched over five years, I am left with one central thought that I continue to pursue. The gist of what I propose in the areas of critical pedagogy and the sociology of law is captured in the concept of innocence. As long as we see ourselves as not implicated in relations of power, as innocent, we cannot begin to walk the path of social justice and to thread our way through the complexities of power relations. Ending with Fanon, as I began, I would say that when we are in a dominant group we must remember the power relations that regulate why those in subordinate groups would not want to look us in the eye. Our pedagogy must begin here if we are to 'turn the world upside down, to stake out the right to imagine another.'[51]

1

'The Cold Game of Equality Staring'

The cold game of equality staring makes me feel like a thin sheet of glass: white people see all the worlds beyond me but not me. They come trotting at me with force and speed; they do not see me. I could force my presence, the real me contained in those eyes, upon them, but I would be smashed in the process. If I deflect, if I move out of the way, they will never know I existed.

Patricia Williams, *The Alchemy of Race and Rights*

Rights in law are fundamentally about seeing and not seeing, about the cold game of equality staring. Talking about women's lives in the language of rights is a cold game indeed, a game played with words and philosophical concepts which bear little relationship to real life. In spite of these doubts, the game is always enticing, perhaps because it seems to hold out the promise that something about the daily realities of oppression will eventually emerge from under the ice. Equality staring, however, as Patricia Williams poetically describes, feels like a no-win situation. The daily realities of oppressed groups can only be acknowledged at the cost of the dominant group's belief in its own natural entitlement. If oppression exists, then there must also be oppressors, and oppressors do not have a moral basis for their rights claims. If, however, we are all equally human, with some of us simply not as advanced or developed as others, then no one need take responsibility for inequality. Moreover, advanced, more civilized people can reconfirm their own superiority through helping those who are less advanced. Trinh T. Minh-ha writes:

The perception of the outsider as the one who needs help has taken on the successive forms of the barbarian, the pagan, the infidel, the wild man, the 'native,' and the underdeveloped. Needless to say, these forms whose meanings help-lessly keep on decomposing can only exist in relation to their opposites.[1]

Unlikely to acknowledge their oppressive practices, dominant groups merely deny that such practices exist. To insist on being seen, that is, to contest the dominant group's perception is – for an oppressed person – to be smashed in the process by a wall of denial that makes of one's exis-tence an illusion, an imagined story of unfairness and injustice.

The idea of rights, turning as it does on notions of individual freedom and autonomy, feeds the illusion that subordinate groups are not op-pressed, merely different and less developed. Rights rhetoric, beginning with the idea that each person is free to pursue his or her own interests, masks how historically organized and tightly constrained individual choices are. The individual who has failed has simply chosen badly. Fur-ther, the autonomous man or woman so dear to liberal thinkers has no defining connections to others. His or her freedom is not a relation; one man's freedom to choose his destiny is not seen to depend on another being compelled to live with the consequences of his choice. In one way, this chapter is yet another lament about these constricting features of rights discourse. This is where I begin with the question: What's wrong with rights? It is also, however, a preliminary exploration of how we might seek more fruitful ways to acknowledge the realities of women's oppression and of the legitimacy of their group-based claims for justice, themes that I pursue in the second half of this chapter.

What's Wrong with Rights?

I first came to think about rights as a human rights educator. Without a strong legal background, I was compelled none the less to talk about the problems of women and minorities within a framework of rights in law. My first workshops (and the manuals that emerged from them) consisted of squeezing the realities of daily life into a rights framework and realiz-ing somewhat belatedly that not only was it difficult to obtain a fit but any experience that could be taken up within a rights framework was hardly ever the one that was most relevant for evaluating claims for justice. Let me illustrate these early encounters.

Working with a paradigm which I now know to be common to many liberal thinkers but which I then knew from a booklet written by Alan Borovoy called *The Fundamentals of Our Fundamental Freedoms*,[2] I began with the notion that we all have rights as rational human beings. At the first level, we possess the right to pursue our own interests. As a woman of colour, I never found this autonomous existence to ring true for me but I usually played along with the game to level two – in the event that my interests collide with anybody else's, we are each entitled to equal consideration. Finally, at level three, no one can inflict harm on another and when harm cannot be avoided, the individual whose claim inflicts the least harm wins the right to assert her claim. In my classes with trade unionists and community human rights activists, we usually viewed this three-part model as impossibly abstract. What was harm? What was equal consideration? Even more fundamental, the idea that a human being was, above all else, a rational person entitled to pursue his or her own interests seemed unrelated to our daily lives.

In the activist classroom we would often debate some classic examples of conflicts in rights in an effort to make the 'model' work. Should the police have the right to bug the homes of the members of an allegedly violence-prone Black Panthers group in Nova Scotia? Even when the threat to national security was overemphasized in the example, most trade union and community activists introduced into the rights balancing process their scepticism of police allegations and their sense that to be Black in Nova Scotia was to be overwhelmingly disadvantaged at any point in the justice system. It made little sense to us to evaluate abstractly whose rights were most important in the example, given that neither the police nor the public they are meant to be protecting could be disentangled from the racism that we knew pervaded Canadian society. It was more important to us to identify how that racism limited what could be known about Black Panthers.

When my students tried to work out conflicts in rights involving groups, the bearing that existing relations of domination have on the rights balancing process became even clearer. For instance, in deciding whether or not Quebec's Bill 101, which limited the rights of individuals to attend English language schools, was justifiable in order to protect the francophone collectivity in Quebec, many English-speaking activists abandoned their characteristic sense of identification with the 'oppressed' group largely because they did not believe that French-speaking Quebecers were an oppressed group at risk of losing their language. English students would not grant collective language rights to French Canadians if they could not 'see' the oppression. Similarly, men (and some women) who rejected affirmative action for women and minorities did so on the basis that such groups were not oppressed. If there were few firemen of colour, the argument went, it was because there were few men of colour who could do the job. The same argument could be applied to the absence of women in traditionally male-dominated occupations. If there is no harm, then there need not be a remedy and we need not consider setting as a goal a racially and gender-balanced workforce.

The granting of special rights in the above examples turned on whether or not the collective realities of the groups in question were acknowledged to be under oppression. The subject position of those 'granting' special rights considerably affected how the realities of subordinate groups were perceived. Those who stood in a dominant position to the groups requiring special rights often had difficulty perceiving oppression. (See chapter 2 for further illustration of this point.) White men, for example, generally did not believe that men of colour, in particular Asian men, could fight fires as effectively as whites could. Their views of Asian men were, of course, nurtured by the prevailing Hollywood stereotypes of effeminate and physically weak Asians.[3]

I later came to review the exercises on rights conflicts in an academic context. I took the concerns of my activist students and used them to lay the basis for a critique of liberalism and of 'rights discourse.' I began, as most scholars do, with the limitations of liberalism, using Michael Sandel as well as several feminist scholars to make the point that the liberal self is a being without defining links to community – that is, someone who is not socially constituted. My complaints were that liberalism, as I understood it from John Rawls and Ronald Dworkin among others, isolated the individual from his or her various communities to the point that one could no longer see how group membership altered or constrained individual choices and opportunities. I wrote then of the difficulties that seemed to flow from this premise: I was bothered primarily by the individualized view of power relations that lurked within the concept of free, autonomous individuals:

In sum, the concept of an independent, decontextualized individual functions to suppress our acknowledgement of the profound differences between individuals based on their situation within groups and the profound differences between groups. Without a theory of difference, we also cannot make clear what the relationship is between groups or communities. Finally, what this notion most inhibits is our understanding of power as something other than the power of one individual to assert his or her claim over another's. It is difficult to explain oppression, that is the consistent dominance of the claims of one group over another with this one-dimensional and individualized view of power. Further, it is a framework that effectively shuts out opportunities to propose new relationships not predicated on the concept of individuals in competition for pieces of the pie.[4]

It is tempting, in making this critique of liberalism, to invent 'a liberalism eerily unified and unchanging over time, denuded of any ethical dimension or indeed of any ability at all to see beyond the virtues of self-interest.'[5] Even without straw men who are invented only to be knocked down, however, finding a way out from within liberalism is difficult. Theoretical efforts to contextualize individuals in their communities and thereafter to deal with their rights claims floundered for a number of reasons. First, Kenneth Karst (and others) tried to work from a premise of the interdependency of individuals, but this did not enable him to establish the boundaries to caring and thus to work out either the boundaries between self and community or the relationship between communities.[6] Second, communities have been oppressive places for women and we ignore at our peril what happens to individuals within communities. Third, feminist efforts to talk about the community of women encouraged a universalizing of women's experience that left unexamined the realities of women of colour, lesbians, and women with disabilities.[7]

Some liberals *have* thought carefully about the self's relationship to community, and what they have to say has been used to acknowledge the collective realities of some subordinated groups and thus to make a case for collective rights. For example, William Kymlicka has argued in *Liberalism, Community, and Culture* that even if one begins with the basic liberal premise that what is most important in a society committed to justice is that individuals enjoy the maximum in personal autonomy, one can still find the space to honour minority rights. Individuals have choices for which they are held responsible but if those choices are constrained by factors not of their own choosing, they are then entitled to special rights that correct the situation and effectively bring them to a point where they might be said to be exercising freedom of choice. Moreover, freedom of choice is important because it enables individuals to pursue what is most important to them.[8]

This argument has held great attraction for feminists articulating a basis for collective rights for women. Defenders of affirmative action use it to talk about bringing women up to a 'level playing field.' Scholars such as Martha Minow, Elizabeth Wolgast, and Ann Scales argue that special rights for women are simply a route to treating men and women equally.[9] Kymlicka himself proposes that such special rights are justifiable for two reasons: in the interest of equality and in order to honour historical agreements. Difficulties persist with justifying collective rights from within liberalism, however, that have to do with how constraints on choice are understood. The breakdown occurs in much the same way it did in the rights-balancing exercises in my classroom of activists. If the contexts in which individuals must make their choices are not carefully analysed, we easily deny rights to those whose realities we do not wish, or are ill-equipped, to acknowledge. For example, it is often argued that immigrant groups are not entitled to the same rights as the French and the English collectivities in Canada.[10] Co-existing with official state policy of multiculturalism is the paradoxical assumption that, in choosing to come here, immigrants relinquish their right to the conditions under which their cultural identities might flourish. Such an argument denies the conditions under which most of us become immigrants, and it side-steps the point that immigrants seek protection from oppression, a protection that can come from maintaining their own cultural practices. How much of a choice is it to flee poverty and starvation in lands ravaged by a global economy dominated by the First World? Who is ultimately responsible for such flight?

The question of when historical accountability begins – one that plagues Canada's constitutional struggles – must be confronted when we justify the granting of special rights based on bargains struck at an earlier time. The terms of the bargain become all-important, as Kymlicka and others recognize, but not only in the sense of determining who agreed to what. We have to examine such bargains on the basis that they were not only or even primarily rational agreements between equally free parties. Focusing on autonomy and freedom has the combined effect of detracting our attention from the terms and conditions under which many bargains are made – the historical conditions, that is, under which individuals and groups 'choose' their own destinies. In the case of immigrants from the South, for instance, their migration to the North came about largely in response to colonial and neocolonial economic conditions created by the North. Were we to pursue accountability to this extent, we would then conclude that Europeans are responsible for the flight of people of the South to the North. As a popular T-shirt slogan puts it: we are here because you were there.

Constraints on Choice and Women

What is and is not of our own choosing? In mapping out for a court's benefit women's group-based realities, feminists have found that many of their difficulties begin around the proof required to answer this question. For instance, when a male judge considers an incident of sexual harassment to be about the attraction of one individual to another, and takes lightly the consequences in the workplace of this so-called attraction, it may involve an enormous conceptual leap for him to grasp that what happens between individual men and women on the job has a great deal to do with their respective socialization and status in society as members of different and unequal groups. Women who argue this feminist position are often told that they could have exerted their individual agency and said 'no.' Individual choice is even further obscured in rape cases, where the meanings of consent and resistance change if one takes into account men's social power and the deeply sexualized forms of this power.

While it has certainly been possible – and the successes of the Women's Legal Education and Action Fund illustrate this[11] – to introduce context, hence to argue that women share a group-based oppression that alters their opportunities, such an approach has simply not worked when the group-based reality in question is too unseemly to stomach (for example the extent of violence against women) or too costly to acknowledge (domestic workers who do not enjoy the same employment and citizenship rights as others). In the end, group-based constraints on choice are simply not acknowledged in these situations, mainly, I think, because of the implications that this would have for fulfilling the requirements of justice. If we were to recognize domestic workers as being entitled to the same rights as other workers or other migrants, there would no longer be a plentiful supply of cheap domestic labour and a central foundation of middle-class respectability would be in jeopardy.

The complicity that gets in the way of dominant groups acknowledging the subordination of others was very much in evidence in January of 1992 when the media devoted considerable attention to a woman with a disability who wanted the right to die. The case of Nancy B., involving a woman paralysed from the neck down and living on a respirator, dominated the news for a few days and acted to remind me of what happens when individual freedom and autonomy are our starting points at the expense of what we know to be the deeply embedded ways in which choice is constrained. Nancy B.'s individual right to choose life or death precluded discussion of the circumstances under which she made her choice.[12] Few commentators pointed out that real societal constraints (such as lack of provision for full attendant care), not her physical condition itself, might have greatly influenced her wish to die. The able-bodied privilege that enabled many of us to see Nancy B.'s life as one not worth living was, in this instance, well-served by the liberal rhetoric around individual agency. Jenny Morris, commenting on similar American cases, notes: 'The question is, in such a context, is the wish to die a so-called rational response to a physical disability? Or is it a desperate response to isolated oppression? As Ed Roberts, head of the World Institute on Disability, said, "It's not the respirator, it's money." '[13] Would Nancy have wanted to live had she had the quality of attendant care necessary to live a better life? We do not know because we never asked. We, the able-bodied, preferred to talk about her courage and to mourn her death. That the concepts of freedom and autonomy can be so easily harnessed in the interests of dominant groups should serve as a powerful reminder to question their construction in the first place.

Scholars who have inquired into the origin and constructions of freedom, choice, and autonomy have invited us to consider whether we can use these constructs without immediately relying on their built-in relations of domination. For instance, Carole Pateman has taken issue with the original premise of the social contract at the heart of liberalism by arguing that the problem of political freedom has effectively foreclosed any discussion about domination. That is, the free, autonomous individual who acts in his or her own self-interest can only do so while standing on the back of someone else. That someone is usually a woman. She notes, too, that whites have stood on the backs of Blacks. As Pateman concludes: 'Contract always generates political right in the form of relations of domination and subordination.'[14] I take this statement to mean that in order to have your own way, you have to suppress someone else's: concretely, someone else takes care of the kids. To exercise their freedom to work outside the home, for example, parents require that another adult become responsible for taking care of the children. In the abstraction of contract theory, it is difficult to imagine the figure who can pursue his or her own interests, given the hierarchical relations that have ensured that, in the Western world, it is poorly paid women of colour who support the freedom of mostly white middle-class men and women to participate in the paid labour force. Developing the idea that in contract theory the individual is owner, Pateman outlines in ways more complicated than I suggest here how a sexual and a slave contract supports the whole notion of individual freedom. Thus, in any discussion of rights, it will be exceedingly difficult to introduce the notion of oppression of women by men (and whites by non-whites) because this oppression is the hidden cornerstone on which rests individual autonomy.

The Habit of His Power, the Absence of Her Choice

Patricia Williams, with whose words I began, is also concerned with the fiction of choice that lies at the heart of the social contract. She reminds us, as does Pateman, of the subtexts, the knowledge that is suppressed in contracts. The constraints on individual choice are in reality far more pervasive and deeply embedded than we realize. We would be wise to explore how constraints on individual choice shape what kind of contract is possible. Such an exploration helps to identify the hierarchical relations that make choice and freedom possible; it serves, in effect, to place the emphasis on domination.

To talk about constraints on individual choice within a framework of autonomous individuals and with an individualized view of power relations is difficult. For instance, to say we decide how to live our lives but that we do so within certain cultural and linguistic narratives is to avoid asking how those narratives are historically organized in the interests of some and not others. Women clearly have not enjoyed the same options as have men within these narratives, and people of colour have clearly not benefited from them as have white people. Without the ongoing genocide of Aboriginal peoples, non-Aboriginal North and South Americans would quite literally have no land from which to pursue freedom of choice. To understand where personal agency ends and the narratives take over is no easy task. Patricia Williams uncovers some of these deeper levels of constraints when she pursues the point that freedom is either a contradictory or meaningless concept given that one person's freedom is another's loss of freedom. She writes: 'In our legal and political system, words like "freedom" and "choice" are forms of currency. They function as the mediators by which we make all things equal, interchangeable. It is, therefore, not just what "freedom" means, but the relation it signals between each individual and the world. It is a word that levels difference.'[15]

Freedom, choice, autonomy are all concepts that impose a particular kind of order, a structure that violently suppresses those details that do not fit – in particular, the details surrounding the persistent domination of men over women, rich over poor, and whites over Blacks. When my students and I complained that the rational, autonomous individual seemed irrelevant, we were trying to identify what is not said: such an individual can only exist at the expense of the individual defined by responsibilities to Other, defined by emotion – defined in short, by all that cannot be expressed 'in the language of power and assertion and staked claims.'[16]

Considering her own family history, Williams makes concrete these ideas of absence-defining presence, ideas central to postmodern thinkers such as Foucault. Williams's great-great-grandmother was purchased at the age of eleven by her great-great-grandfather, a white slave owner. In examining the implications of this relation, Williams illuminates the meaning of freedom and autonomy:

I track meticulously the dimension of meaning in my great-great-grandmother as chattel; the meaning of money; the power of consumerist world view, the deaths of those we label the unassertive and the inefficient. I try to imagine where and who she would be today. I am engaged in a long-term project of tracking his words – through his letters and opinions – and those of his sons who were also lawyers and judges – of finding the shape described by her absence in all this.

I see her shape and his hand in the vast networking of our society, and in the evils and oversights that plague our lives and laws. The control he had over her body. The force he was in her life, in the shape of my life today. The power he exercised in the choice to breed her or not. The choice to breed slaves in his image, to choose her mate and be that mate. In his attempt to own what no man can own, the habit of his power and the absence of her choice.

I look for her shape and his hand.[17]

We must begin with the relationship that is the habit of his power and the absence of her choice, for this was not only the context in which the concepts of freedom and choice were developed (as Pateman shows). We ought to be aware that his habit of power depends on the absence of her choice. As Toni Morrison has argued, 'individualism is foregrounded (and believed in) when its background is stereotypified, enforced dependency.'[18]

The most obvious difficulty to emerge is how communities are going to recognize and make allowances for circumstances beyond an individual's or a group's choosing when to do so is to subject their own privilege to scrutiny. To force one's presence is to be smashed in the process. The discussion around rights will therefore remain where it began for my human rights students: Whose description of reality will be taken up and whose sense of self is at stake when oppressive practices are revealed? What is harm? What is equal consideration? Privilege will prove to be the major stumbling block, as critical educators have acknowledged in our work in the classroom. Women and minorities will simply not be seen to deserve collective rights. Their realities will not be admissible within the construct of rights.

This perspective is a bleak one and we must, if we are to find a practical way out of it (for hope is also tied to interest!), devise ways to interrogate ourselves about what we see and do not see. The major stumbling block to collective rights is not simply the failure of collective rights advocates to present their case within liberalism but the way in which the discussion is already regulated to obscure relations of domination. However, as many others have seen, it is not satisfactory to refuse to play rights games altogether simply because of their built-in limitations.[19] The games are in fact thrust upon us. In playing them, we can make use of the idea that they impose a particular kind of order and violence on experience. We can anticipate, then, that collective realities of oppressed groups will be barely visible for the simple reasons that they implicate dominant groups and are hidden under the layers of constructed meanings designed to suppress knowledge of their existence.

Knowing that the idea of rights regulates the discussion and hides 'the complex, multi-faceted structure of domination in modern patriarchy,'[20] what are we to do? One strategy is to insist on descriptions of the realities of oppressed groups that bring the relations of domination and submission to the surface, as feminists working in law have done. A second is to be ever mindful of what can be heard in any given context. A third is to use, advisedly, concepts such as rights in reference to such realities as violence against women and children and the genocide of a people. We shall need to find new concepts to talk about the way in which power works that can describe oppression – the consistent and organized domination of one group over another.

On Dispensing with Autonomy

Feminist thinkers remind us that women have only recently been thought to be the makers of their own fate; we ought, therefore, to think twice about dispensing with the value liberals place on freedom and autonomy. We may come to see women, as Jane Flax puts it, as 'acted upon beings,'[21] leaving little room for their resistance to oppression. Dwelling on the apparent contradiction between saying, on the one hand, that the concepts of individual freedom and autonomy presuppose relations of domination and, on the other, that women are oppressed because they do not have freedom and autonomy, I returned to Foucault's work. In 'Two Lectures' he elaborates on his understanding of how power works, noting, in language akin to Pateman's questioning of the concept of the individual as owner, that power is not something one 'possesses, acquires, cedes through force or contract.'[22] Instead, power is a relation of force. The system of right, which relies on the idea that individuals possess their autonomy, compels us to consider, then, the legitimacy of one claim over another rather than 'the methods of subjugation that it instigates.'[23] If, in fact, we turn our attention to methods of subjugation, we are taken back to Pateman's idea that a sexual and a slave contract underpins the whole notion of individual freedom. The individual, then, doesn't simply possess power but is constituted by a set of power relations cast like a net over how she or he sees and thinks. It is precisely these power relations that are obscured when we balance competing claims. The individual can, however, resist these relations at nodal points along the net.

Drawing on Foucault, as I have done, Valerie Walkerdine makes the important observation that when we work with a concept of liberation as personal freeing (from constraints), hence with a notion of power as a fixed possession, we focus on the lifting of those overt constraints we experience as repressive. Freedom becomes freedom from overt control, and our attention is taken away from the many covert ways in which we are regulated.[24] This has been my argument about understanding collective rights. Unless we come to terms with covert regulation, with power as an effect, we will be unable to determine who is being oppressed, by whom, and what should be done about it. Oppression, in liberalism, means the imposition of unjust constraints. When one departs from the notion of choice and freedom that is the beginning of this particular story – the 'contract-oppression scheme,' to use Foucault's words – and comes to see power as a net organizing how individuals are constituted in any one context, oppression becomes a story of 'struggle and submission,'[25] of how what is present is made possible by what is absent.

I believe this to be a useful political direction in which women might travel in our quest for justice: we might make use of the notion of autonomy and perhaps return to oppression as the absence of choice, as a matter of strategy so as not 'to make the question of women's oppression obsolete.'[26] In so doing, though, we ought to be aware that women could emerge as individuals 'further implicated in the patriarchal and logocentric tradition which proposes the bourgeois individual as guarantor of the new order.'[27] That is to say, autonomous women derive their autonomy on the backs of other women. A mesh of material relations surrounds our capacity to be autonomous – other women who are our babysitters, domestic workers, secretaries. Jennifer Nedelsky's proposal – that we consider autonomy not as an essence innate to us but as a capacity which must be nurtured through relationships with others – will not suffice if we forget to examine how nurturing is accomplished.[28] It is imperative to ask about how relationships are structured hierarchically. It becomes necessary, in other words, to put oppression back into the picture.

Jane Flax offered the following observations about the fourfold task of feminist theory:

We need (1) to articulate feminist viewpoints of and within the social worlds in which we live, (2) to think about how we are affected by these worlds, (3) to think about how our thinking about them may itself be implicated in existing power/knowledge relationships, and (4) to think also about the ways in which these worlds ought and can be transformed.[29]

Her advice applies equally well to those of us either theorizing or organizing for collective rights. We need to ground the discussion of collective rights in concrete social realities. We need to think about how those realities affect different women. We need to think especially about what we know and can know about these realities before we begin to evaluate claims for justice. These prescriptions amount, in my view, to a search for the patterns and consequences of domination, which begins with an acknowledgment that women live a collective reality of oppression in which their individual choices are seriously constrained in ways related to race, class, sexuality, and disability. We ought to use with care any rhetoric that does not begin there.

2

The Gaze from the Other Side: Storytelling for Social Change

Her (story) remains irreducibly foreign to Him. The Man can't hear it the way she means it. He sees her as victim, as unfortunate object of hazard. 'Her mind is confused,' he concludes. She views herself as the teller, the un-making subject ... the moving force of the story.

Trinh T. Minh-ha, *Woman, Native, Other*

For many of us who would describe ourselves as teaching for social change, storytelling has been at the heart of our pedagogy. In the context of social change storytelling refers to an opposition to established knowledge, to Foucault's suppressed knowledge, to the experience of the world that is not admitted into dominant knowledge paradigms. Storytelling is central to strategies for social change in two apparently different sites: law and education. In law, there is lively debate on 'outsider jurisprudence,' Mari Matsuda's useful phrase for 'jurisprudence derived from considering stories from the bottom.'[1] Storytelling is less new to critical educational theorists and practitioners, but the emphasis in critical pedagogy on voices silenced through traditional education is now being met with calls to interrogate more closely the construction of subjectivity. That is, the complex ways in which relations of domination are sustained, lived, and resisted call for a more careful examination of how we come to know what we know as well as how we work for a more just world across our various ways of knowing.

When we depend on storytelling, either to reach each other across differences or to resist patriarchal and racist constructs, we must overcome at least one difficulty: the difference in position between the teller and the listener, between telling the tale and hearing it. Being all about subjectivity, storytelling is often uncritically 'understood as sentimental, personal and individual horizon as opposed to objective, universal, societal, limitless horizon; often attributed to women, the other of man, and natives, the other of the west.'[2] When, for instance, the Canadian Advisory Council on the Status of Women collected and published the stories of immigrant women, one suspects that it was the sentimental, the personal, and the individual that were being sought after.[3] To what uses will these stories be put? Will someone else take them and theorize from them? Will they serve to reassure everyone that Canada really is diverse and full of folklore? Who will control how they are used? Will immigrant women tell a particular kind of story in a forum they do not control? Such dilemmas are evident wherever storytelling is used.

In this chapter, I propose to situate my introductory comments in the context of storytelling in law, leaving the central part for a consideration of storytelling and critical pedagogy. I want to suggest, from the perspective of a community educator who also works in academe doing legal research, that there are land mines strewn across the path wherever storytelling is used, that it should never be used uncritically, and that its potential as a tool for social change is remarkable, provided we pay attention to the interpretive structures that underpin how we hear and how we take up the stories of oppressed groups.

Storytelling in Law

Law relies on a positivist conception of knowledge. That is, there is a straight line between the knower and the known. In law, judges and juries are meant to discover the truth from the array of information put before them. There is only one objective truth and it is empirically provable. Reason features prominently and emotion is ruthlessly banished. The rule of law is 'the consistent application of prior stated rules,' a process theoretically uninformed by politics or ethics.[4] Storytelling in law, then, is an intellectual movement that is 'a rebellion against abstractions.'[5] Its purpose is to interrogate the space between the knower and the thing known; its function is one of putting the context back into law. Kim Lane Scheppele writes of the conceptual scheme of the observer that stands between him or her and the event. Storytelling is a theoretical attention to narrative, to the nature and consequences of this conceptual scheme. Concretely, it is an interrogation of how courts come to convert information into fact, how judges, juries and lawyers come to 'objectively' know the truth: 'Those whose stories are believed have the power to create fact.'[6]

Legal rules and conventions suppress the stories of outsider groups. The fiction of objectivity, for example, obscures that key players in the legal system have tended to share a conceptual scheme. Thus, judges who do not see the harm of rape or of racist speech are considered to be simply interpreting what is before them. They are not seen to possess norms and values that derive directly from their social location and that are sustained by such practices as considering individuals outside of their social contexts. Stories of members of marginalized groups must therefore 'reveal things about the world that we *ought* to know.'[7] These stories are 'a means of obtaining the knowledge we need to create a just legal structure.'[8] Matsuda argues forcefully that 'those who have experienced discrimination speak with a special voice to which we should listen.'[9] Stories, in the context of law, bring feeling back into jurisprudence, and they tend to work from experiential understanding.[10] How this happens in a courtroom is clear from feminist jurisprudence.

Feminists working in law describe for the court's benefit the nature of women's oppression and then make an argument that policies and practices that perpetuate that oppression ought to be declared illegal. (In Canada, section 15, the equality rights section of the Charter of Rights and Freedoms, is usually invoked in support.) The Women's Legal Education and Action Fund (LEAF), formed in 1985, is one of the major groups developing and making this argument in Canadian courts.[11] The challenge has been to bring details about women's daily lives into the courtroom, a forum constructed to negate or silence such realities. As I discussed in chapter 1, Western law functions on the basis of liberalism where the individual is thought to be an autonomous, rational self, essentially unconnected to other selves and dedicated to pursuing his or her own interests. To present an individual in her community, and further, to describe that community as LEAF has done as 'the disadvantaged, the disempowered, the marginalized' is to pose a fundamental challenge to legal discourse. The individual in her community is less empirically provable, and courts are inordinately fond of empirical proof.

Feminists working in law theorize on the nature of the challenge they pose to law's 'truth.' Robin West, for instance sees the process as one of telling women's stories. Thus, feminism applied to law consists of flooding 'the market with our own stories until we get one simple point across: men's narrative story and phenomenology is not women's story and phenomenology.'[12] An example of this kind of flooding is the defence mounted by the Federation of Women Teachers' Associations of Ontario (FWTAO) in 1987, when they found themselves in court defending their right to exist as a women-only teachers' union, a right entrenched in a by-law of the FWTAO establishing five separate teachers' unions united under the Federation's umbrella. Under the by-law, women elementary school teachers must belong to FWTAO, while men who are elementary school teachers must belong to the Ontario Public School Teachers' Federation. (Separate school teachers also have their own unions as do secondary school teachers and teachers in French language schools.) Margaret Tomen, an elementary school principal, protested the by-law that compelled her to pay dues to FWTAO. She argued that such a by-law contravened the Charter of Rights and Freedoms because it discriminated against her as a woman, forcing her to join FWTAO. Women teachers are free to join the men's teachers federation but only as voluntary members. At issue was whether the by-law establishing FWTAO could be justified as a special program for a disadvantaged group, women, an action justifiable under section 15 (2) of the Charter.[13]

The Federation argued that women were and are an oppressed group and that in this specific context, a mixed-sex union would only perpetuate that oppression. The men teachers' federation, which supported the challenge to the Federation's right to exist as an all-female institution, maintained that women teachers are equal in every way to men teachers; a mixed sex union would serve all teachers best. Whereas the side arguing for a mixed union only felt obliged to point to the collective agreement as proof of equality between men and women, the Federation enlisted the aid of over twenty women (experts in women's history, women's studies, women's unions, etc.) to deluge the court with information about the past and daily lives of women in general and women teachers in particular. For instance, Dale Spender was asked to testify on her research that men dominate in mixed-sex groupings. Joy Parr, a Canadian historian, gave evidence that historically Canadian women have had to fight to protect their rights. Management studies experts testified that 'the routines of inequality' blocked women's advancement. Principals, for instance, had to have training in curriculum studies – training which was only available after school hours when most women shouldered family responsibilities. At times, the tale became highly subjective, as when Sylvia Gold, then president of the Canadian Advisory Council on the Status of Women, testified that she felt that the Federation had directly influenced the creation of women leaders. At other times, details about women came into the courtroom in full scientific dress. Margrit Eichler, a sociology professor, quantified gender inequality for the court's benefit and then applied twenty indices of inequality to the Federation's work. Her conclusion: the Federation advanced women's equality interests.[14]

For subordinate groups, storytelling in law, as exemplified by the approach taken by FWTAO, is clearly necessary since their stories have not been told. The problem subordinate groups confront, however, is not simply one of exclusion. The stories of their lives are stories of oppression and they are largely being told to individuals who are members of the dominant group – mostly white men of the middle class and now, increasingly, white women of the middle class. How are the stories going to be received? As Trinh asks, 'Can the Man hear it the way she means it?' Patricia Monture-Angus has eloquently described the difficulties she, as an Aboriginal woman legal scholar, has in being heard when she attempts to describe to white people the racism inflicted on her community. Unwilling to face their own complicity, many white listeners simply reverse the pain, and the claim for justice:

When are those of you who inflict racism, who appropriate pain, who speak with no knowledge or respect when you ought to know to listen and accept, going to take hard looks at yourself instead of at me. How can you continue to look to me to carry what is your responsibility? And when I speak and the brutality of my experience hurts you, you hide behind the hurt. You point the finger at me and you claim that I hurt you.[15]

Canadian Native women in prisons, familiar with the denial and reverse onus claims of the dominant group, have wondered, as has Monture-Angus, if Aboriginal women's stories of oppression are even 'translatable' for the court's benefit.[16]

Storytelling as a methodology in the context of law runs up against the problem of the dominant group's refusal to examine its own complicity in oppressing others. The power of law's positivism and the legal rules that underpin it are willing accomplices in this denial of accountability. For example, the requirement of empirical proof of women's inequality can lead very quickly into dichotomies and generalizations about women as a group that make it difficult to describe the intersections of race, class, gender, sexuality, and disability. A woman's gender, uncontaminated by race, class, disability, or sexual orientation is the prism through which the court views her daily life; differences among women fit awkwardly into the story. When gender is constructed in its pure form, that is, uncontaminated by race or class or culture, Norma Alarcón has pointed out, the woman thus imagined names herself; her culture, race, or class do not name her. Thus, ironically, she remains the old, autonomous liberal self, only female; and as such, another abstraction.[17]

Moving beyond such abstractions through a more complex storytelling is difficult, however. Toni Massaro, reflecting on the consequences of an unproblematic call for stories and context, identifies one important difficulty with storytelling: in the end, law has to privilege one story over another. A judge has to choose and it is not so much his or her understanding that is required as an acceptable legal solution. Furthermore, given the fact that most judges continue to come from dominant groups, they are unlikely to be able to empathize with marginalized groups. In any event, in the area of discrimination, as Massaro points out, empathy is not the ultimate goal. It is not enough to try to find ways to communicate to the judge that discrimination is hurtful, as the women teachers' union tried to do. It is equally necessary to convince him or her that an action is morally wrong and requires legal censure. Massaro suggests that how we hear different stories is therefore dependent on the moral code with which we function.[18] While we experience many unpleasant things, only some are considered both morally reprehensible and 'actionable' in law. Justice is all about drawing the boundaries between wrong and right. I would add, however, that how we hear stories is also dependent on the interpretive structures on which we rely to come to a decision about right and wrong. In this respect, the interpretive structures of subordinate groups can differ, owing to their experiences of oppression.

Mari Matsuda's work on legal sanctions for racist speech provides a careful reflection on how we might evaluate the stories of victims from the basis of what we as a society consider to be morally wrong. Arguing that a 'legal response to racist speech is a statement that victims of racism are valued members of our polity,'[19] Matsuda grapples with the complexities of how we decide whose perspectives to take into account in determining the kinds of racist speech that require legal sanction. She notes, for instance, that the typical reaction of oppressed groups to an incident of racist propaganda is alarm and calls for redress, whereas the typical reaction of dominant groups is denial and dismissal of the incident as a harmless prank.[20] Denial of the impact of this form of racism helps to sustain the view that censorship of racist hate messages is a greater harm than the harm of the messages themselves. If we listened to the voices of those harmed by racist propaganda, however, basic principles would emerge that help us to assess the context in which racist speech occurs. Victims of racism are clear that racism must be fought on

all levels and that their lives would be improved by an explicit legal condemnation of racist speech.

One immediate criticism of the position that we ought to listen to the
voices of the oppressed in determining what is and is not just is, as Matsuda herself observes, the sorting out of who is oppressed and who is not.
Anticipating such critics, Matsuda directs us to examine such social indicators as wealth, mobility, comfort, health, and survival that tell us which
groups have status. She allows for the fact that oppressed groups participate in one another's oppression but claims that racist speech from a
member of a historically subjugated group is not to be judged as harshly
as racist speech from a member of a dominant group. The former's
racism 'is tied to the structural domination of another group.'[21] A member of a historically subjugated group forfeits this consideration when
she allies herself with the dominant group.[22]

Clearly, deciding which voices to privilege in law is enormously complicated and relies not only on our being able to thread our way through
historical domination but also on the clarity of our moral vision. The alternatives, however, are to ignore the voices of marginalized groups or to
accept them uncritically. This latter option would leave us with no way
of evaluating the difference between Zionism and generic white supremacy
(to use Matsuda's example), since we would have no guidelines for assessing the context in which stories originate.

Storytelling in Critical Pedagogy

In traditional educational theory, the existing arrangement of society is
taken as given and schools 'are seen as the means of rationally distrib-
uting individuals in what is conceived as a basically just society.'[23] In
contrast (and like outsider jurisprudence), critical educational theory
recognizes, as Henry Giroux has put it, that

ideology has to be conceived as both source and effect of social and institutional
practices as they operate within a society that is characterized by relations of
domination, a society in which men and women are basically unfree in both objective and subjective terms.[24]

Thus, a radical or critical pedagogy is one that resists the reproduction
of the status quo by uncovering relations of domination and opening up
spaces for voices suppressed in traditional education. How critical educators do so is once again through the methodology of storytelling. The

critical educator thus 'takes as central the inner histories and experiences of the students themselves,' seeking to foster critical reflection of everyday experience.[25] In this way, individuals who develop critical thinking can challenge oppressive practices.

As in outsider jurisprudence, storytelling for social change in an educational setting is more complicated than the phrase would indicate. In her work on how the school covertly regulates the production of self-regulating, autonomous individuals, Valerie Walkerdine stresses that those who are most targeted in the school system – the poor, the working class, and ethnic minorities – also resist and engage differently with the systems of domination in which they are enmeshed. As Walkerdine puts it, 'the constitution of subjectivity is not all of one piece without seams and ruptures.'[26] The voices of the oppressed are not simply left out of the system. Rather, the school regulates what a child is, and children of outsider groups (and all girls) respond in a number of contradictory ways, from various positions. The critical educator has to understand how 'particular children live those multiple positionings.' For example, Walkerdine writes:

How might a girl's docility in school produce both losses and gains? She might be denied in the status of 'active learner' and yet at the same time be enabled to maintain another site of power, for example by taking the position of mother. Yet she must experience pain and anxiety if the contradiction between those positions is not recognized and understood as an effect of the pathologizing process [i.e., where masculinity is the norm]. What, too, if that pathology operates in relation to different and contradictory assumptions of the normal? How then are the resultant splittings lived?[27]

The double strategy that Walkerdine recommends, 'one which recognizes and examines the effects of normative models, whilst producing the possibility of other accounts and other sites of identification,'[28] is an important reminder of the multiple and contradictory nature of subjectivity, hence of the complexities of working with the stories of outsiders to resist domination.

While critical educational theorists like Walkerdine begin here, popular educational theorists and practitioners often fail to theorize multiple and contradictory subjectivities. Paulo Freire's pioneering work[29] on the fostering of critical consciousness in oppressed groups continues to be applied relatively straightforwardly in North America, for instance in ways that often stop short of interrogating the category oppressed for the

North American context as opposed to the Latin American context, in which Freire's work originated. Although some questions have been asked about the exporting of Freirean pedagogy from the First World back to the Third World, in the guise of 'helping' the Third World achieve its social goals, there have been few critical analyses of, for example, white middle-class educators (primarily men) leading subordinate groups to which they do not belong into critical pedagogy.[30] The high consulting fees that often accompany such endeavours are also seldom discussed.

The North Americanization of Freire's work aside, there is a built-in tendency within the different practices of a pedagogy of the oppressed to discourage critical reflection of various hierarchical differences within oppressed groups. In Freire's work, as Charles Paine writes, a pedagogy that is radical, whether in the popular education or academic classroom, 'must help students transcend culturally imposed consciousness, allowing them to exit their circular, self-enclosed, and self-perpetuating "uncritical immersion in the *status quo*." '[31] Popular education, grounded in this theoretical approach, writes one practitioner,

stresses dialogue, group learning, and valuing the participants' experience as the foundation for further learning and knowledge. The educator is considered a facilitator of a collective educational process, someone who is able to question critically different perceptions of reality and custom, and to contribute to the formulation of *new knowledge* [emphasis added] that addresses the problems of poor communities and the actions those communities want to undertake.[32]

Ironically, popular educators have been slow to critically reflect on their own practices. Ricardo Zuniga in an article called 'La Gestion Amphibie' laments the lack of critical reflection on the part of popular educators and attributes it to an us/them mentality. For instance, if the funders (the state) are thought to be the 'bad guys,' emphasis is placed on the unity and internal solidarity of those who receive funding. It then becomes difficult to critically evaluate the project (other than in carefully constructed reports to the funding agency). Zuniga identifies the tendencies that exacerbate dichotomous thinking and make it difficult to deal with contradiction. (However, he is only objecting to the oppositional thinking and not to the view of language and voice as straightforwardly representational of reality. Consequently, he ends up arguing for more rationality and less emotion.) The popular educator, Zuniga argues, embodies contradiction: 'he [sic] is responsible for training in a context where only self-training is acknowledged; he does not want to control and he is conscious of the distance between him and his "clients," "collaborators" or "students."' The problems with appropriate terminology well illustrate the contradictions.[33] The only palliative, in Zuniga's opinion, that is available for this anguish is the reassurance of being on the right side, the alternative to the status quo.

If you are on the good side, then you define yourself not by reliance on *le savoir bourgeois*, scientific knowledge, but on *le savoir populaire*, popular knowledge – a firm rejection of empiricism, positivism, and science and a warm embrace of emotions, stories, narratives, nature, spontaneity.[34] Stories cannot really be critiqued within this dichotomy; they are unproblematically conceived of as suppressed therefore valued knowledge. There is an assumption that the living voices (and sometimes the written texts) of the oppressed express a truth that will win out. There is little room for questioning those voices or texts as the transmitters of authentic 'human' experiences.[35] Here, the authentic voices rest on a conception of the self as a coherent individual unit. Language is seen as simply representing reality rather than constructing it.

Feminists have long warned of the ultimate dangers of dichotomizing. With poetic eloquence, Gloria Anzaldúa writes:

But it is not enough to stand on the opposite river bank shouting questions, challenging patriarchal white conventions. A counterstance locks one into a duel of oppressor and oppressed; locked in mortal combat, like the cop and the criminal, both reduced to a common denominator of violence. The counterstance refutes the dominant culture's views and beliefs, and for this, it is proudly defiant. All reaction is limited by, and dependent on, what it is reacting against. Because the counterstance stems from a problem with authority – outer as well as inner – it's a step towards liberation from cultural domination. But it is not a way of life. At some point, on our way to new consciousness, we will have to leave the opposite bank, the split between the two mortal combatants somehow healed.[36]

To heal the split, we have to think about our way of life. 'The massive uprooting of dualistic thinking,'[37] which Anzaldúa and many other feminists have long called for, requires new ways of knowing. Yet, the narratives or stories, of which Zuniga complains, are frequently advanced by feminists as *the* way to challenge patriarchal dichotomies, in spite of the fact that they are primarily described as everything patriarchal knowledge is not. In other words, this use of stories is embedded in an oppositional approach. Thus, Bettina Aptheker concludes her book *Tapestries of Life* with this suggestion:

The point is that more than one thing is true for us at the same time. A masculinist process, however, at least as it has been institutionalized in Western society, accentuates the combative, the oppositional, the either/or dichotomies, the 'right' and 'wrong'. What I have been about throughout this book is showing that the dailiness of women's lives structures a different way of knowing and a different way of thinking. The process that comes from this way of knowing has to be at the centre of a women's politics, and it has to be at the centre of a women's scholarship. This is why I have been drawn to the poetry and to the stories: because they are layered, because more than one truth is represented, because there is ambiguity and paradox. When we work together in coalitions, or on the job, or in academic settings, or in the community, we have to allow for this ambiguity and paradox, respect each other, our cultures, our integrity, our dignity.[38]

In critical educational and feminist theory, what are being sought, then, are ways to come to terms with the contradictions of everyday life, contradictions that reveal themselves in the stories of the oppressed and in which are located the seeds for critical consciousness. How does this project take shape in the classroom?

'In the Field'

There is high demand for stories in the classroom – both the traditional academic classroom and the one in which I taught human rights activists at an annual summer college. There, Aptheker's 'respect for each other' (acceptance of tolerance and ambiguity, etc.), frustrated me in the same way that Elizabeth Ellsworth felt frustrated by the fine sounding phrases of critical pedagogy in her influential article 'Why Doesn't This Feel Empowering? Working Through the Repressive Myths of Critical Pedagogy.'[39] Stories intended to serve as an opposition to patriarchal discourse have *not* always felt empowering. This is due, in large part, to two tendencies: our failure to recognize the multiple nature of subjectivity and hence the complex ways we construct meaning, and our failure to develop an ethical vision[40] based on our differences. In the effort to untangle how we are constructed, we have sometimes failed to define what it is about the world that we want to change and why.

Ellsworth noted specifically that in a mixed-sex, mixed-race course on racism, students entered with 'investments of privilege and struggle already made in favour of some ethical and political positions concerning racism and against other positions.'[41] The strategies of empowerment, dialogue, and voice did not in fact work as neatly as they were supposed to because there was no unity among the oppressed and because our various histories were not left at the door when we entered a classroom to critically reflect. Her students were unable to 'hear' one another. The operative mode was rationality and the stories of various groups had to be justified and explicated using the very tools that held these stories to be inadmissible. (Here, the parallel to feminists working in law is striking. The rules of the legal game structure the telling of the tale in such a way that only some parts of it may be told or what is told is unrecognizably transformed by the fancy scientific dress.) Going beyond Aptheker's unproblematic call for a tolerance of ambiguity, Ellsworth suggests that we respect the diversity of voices, of stories as it were, and that we recognize that the voices are 'valid – but not without response.'[42] In other words, the stories must be *critiqued* and she has a number of concrete suggestions for doing so, which I would like to address in order to look for a way out of a return to rationality or to an uncritical reliance on stories.

Ellsworth recommends that we work hard at building trust, hence the importance of building in opportunities for social interaction (we did this at the summer college by making the program a residential program); that we stress the need to learn about the realities of others without relying on them to inform us; that we name the inequalities *in* the classroom and devise ground rules for communication (for this we used Uma Narayan's 'Working Together Across Differences: Some Considerations on Emotions and Political Practice');[43] that we consider strategies such as encouraging the formation of 'affinity groups,' made up of those who are most likely to share the same kinds of oppression; and that we consciously offer such groups the time to coalesce, so that individuals can speak from within groups. All of these recommended pedagogical practices come out of her central piece of advice, which is that we critically examine what we share and do not share, that we work from the basis that we all have only partial knowledge, and that we come from different subject positions. Most important of all, no one is off the hook since we can all claim to stand as oppressor and oppressed in relation to someone else. These suggestions, which I do practice, do not save me from some of the 'ethical dilemmas' that arose frequently at the summer college (although perhaps I could have minimized their impact had I paid closer attention to the ground rules above).

Two incidents from the summer college in human rights illustrate some of the difficulties with a critical use of storytelling. The summer college, held at the University of Ottawa but sponsored by the non-governmental Human Rights Research and Education Centre, brought together sixty human rights activists who work for social change within organized groups. Thus, there were members from women with disabilities groups, various anti-racist groups, the Assembly of First Nations, lawyers for human rights in South Africa, and so on. Although it frequently happened that individuals from dominant groups were working for organizations on behalf of the oppressed, the majority of students could, in one way or another, fit into the category of 'disadvantaged groups.' The first incident illustrates the unreasonably high demand for storytelling from those in dominant positions. Here I take some responsibility. The curriculum was designed to encourage storytelling and the pedagogical practices emphasized the need to make a space for different voices and, in fact, to forge a politics of alliances based on this sharing of daily experiences. One participant in my group, a white disabled woman, frustrated by the silence of a Black woman from South Africa during a discussion about South Africa, directly confronted her with a firm 'Why don't you tell us your experiences?' Realizing the harshness of what was said, another participant, also disabled but male, repeated the request more gently. The trust and sharing of the class, built over five days, instantly dissolved. The Black participant, confronted with a request to tell her story, defended her right to silence and then left the room in tears. In the chaos of what then ensued, it became clear that the sentence, so simply expressed by a white woman, innocently inviting a woman of colour to share her experiences of racism, recalled for every person of colour in the room (seven out of twenty and myself, the instructor) that this was not in fact a safe learning environment. As the instructor and a woman of colour, I tried hard to retain my composure. Later, distressed to the point of tears by the 'loss of control' in 'my' classroom, and not consoled by the learning value of the event, I wondered how it was that I could have been so powerfully affected in spite of many years' experience of just this type of situation. I recall trying clumsily to explain to a colleague that *we* (people of colour) are always being asked to tell our stories for *your* (white people's) edification, which you cannot *hear* because of the benefit you derive from hearing them. Suddenly, the world was still white after all and the pedagogy that insisted that the oppressed can come together to critically reflect and share stories seemed a sham. Other writers of colour have noted, of course, that few people of colour have ever considered learning in a mixed-race environment as safe. For example, Patricia Monture-Angus comments that in her many years as a student and as a professor, and often the only Aboriginal person in the room, she has never experienced the classroom as a safe space.[44] Yet the pedagogy of storytelling and the presence of a number of subordinate groups, including a number of people of colour, led many of us to throw caution to the winds. What we had failed to consider was how social hierarchies operated among subordinate groups.[45]

Let me leave this story for a while and tell another that occurred in the same context but among all three classes of the summer college. This story illustrates for me the sheer difficulty of understanding across differences and the need for some ethical guidelines for *listening* across hierarchies. The session in question took place in August 1990. At this time, during what would be later known as the Oka Crisis, the Government of Canada, at Quebec's request, decided to send in the army to try to end the stand-off between Mohawks and the Quebec provincial police (Sûreté Québec), and the students of the summer college decided to abandon the curriculum and take action. This, after all, was the basis of the education for social change they had come to get. In the very heated discussions that followed as to the most appropriate actions to be taken, the only two Native participants (not, however, of the Mohawk nation) assumed a leadership role, again in keeping with the principles of the college that struggles for social change must be led by the groups in question. Both Native participants endorsed a march on Parliament Hill to protest armed intervention and made a passionate plea (in the form of stories of their lives as Native women) that we all accept this as the only course of action. As in Elizabeth Ellsworth's class, we, the non-Natives in the room, then began to process the story we had heard. Some of us then required the two women to defend their position using the 'master's tools,'[46] since we felt that the army was in fact an improvement over the Sûreté Québec, a police force well known for its racism. In fact, we argued, members of the Assembly of First Nations, who represent Native groups, themselves agreed this was so although they deplored, as we did, armed intervention. The situation soon led to tears (from the Native women), recriminations (from some of the francophone participants who felt that sympathy for the Mohawks came easily for anglophones whose daily lives were not touched by the crisis as were the lives of francophone inhabitants of Quebec), sheer astonishment at the depth of emotion we had observed, and to our general confusion and failure to find a way out of this ethical dilemma. In a different way, the situation was repeated when a Native woman from an altogether different reserve (Akwasasne) came to speak against the Warrior societies of the Mohawks, while a Native leader later spoke in their defence. We had to employ the tools of rationality to choose between stories and to determine political action. The brilliant suggestion of Uma Narayan, that we grant epistemic privilege to the oppressed, falls apart when the subject positions are so confused. Unless we want to fall into the trap of demanding that the oppressed speak in a unified voice before we will believe them, we are still left with the difficult task of negotiating our way through our various ways of knowing and towards political action.

Both these incidents led me to reflect on classroom ethics, indeed on ethics in general, in mixed-sex and mixed-race groupings where there is a commitment to social change. First, I agree with Zuniga and Ellsworth: we do shy away from critically reflecting on the practices of those on the 'good' side. Ironically, our analytical and pedagogical tools seem to discourage internal critique by calling for respect for different voices with insufficient attention paid to the contexts of both the teller and the listener. Second, the risks taken in the course of critical reflection are never equally shared. This is almost a truism, yet we have not been careful to devise a pedagogy that would accommodate it or a political practice that would not sacrifice diversity, again I think because the game of good guy/ bad guy discourages it. What would a pedagogy that recognized the inequalities of risk-taking entail? We know more about what it would not entail, for instance Ellsworth's comments that acting as though the classroom is a safe place does not make it safe.

From feminists and practitioners of critical pedagogy alike has come the suggestion that caring is as important as critical pedagogy. For instance, Mechthild Hart warns of an overemphasis on cognitive processes.[47] We cannot absolutely know what is required in what instances. Are remaining open and caring the best we can do? There are, however, boundaries to our caring that have to be worked out when deciding how far we will commit ourselves to action. Furthermore, these boundaries are hard to discern across cultures and caring sometimes gets in the way. Lynet Uttal, writing about her experience of the differences between Anglo-feminist groups and those of women of colour, notes that in Anglo-feminist groups, the emphasis on providing care and support leads to white women's passive listening of diverse voices. There is seldom any heated discussion or disagreement; those who fail to fit in simply leave the group. She describes Anglo-feminists' 'blank looks of supportive listening' and their absence of critical engagement with the ideas proposed by diverse voices.[48] Making a related point, Monture-Angus notes that white conference participants who rejected her stories of subordination, did so covertly, that is, privately without the knowledge of the non-white participants, thereby avoiding open confrontation.[49]

Richard Brosio reminds us that, our professions notwithstanding, education is not the leading route to social change.[50] Perhaps we ought not to expect that a pedagogy can be devised that will help us transcend the dichotomies and the bind of partial knowledge. Iris Young wisely notes that 'too often people in groups working for social change take mutual friendship to be a goal of the group. Such a desire for community often channels energy away from the political goals of the group.'[51] I interpret this to mean that we frequently forget that community has to be struggled for, which I think Ellsworth very forcefully demonstrates by her critical analysis of her course on racism. What might assist us to promote the struggle for community?

If there is no automatic friendship, goodwill, or sense of community, where do we begin? The answer is of course already an axiom among us: we begin with critical thinking and critical pedagogy. But where critical pedagogy has traditionally begun is not far enough below the surface. We have to begin with how we know, giving this more attention than we have traditionally done. Epistemology, perhaps without using the word, has to enter into our pedagogy and our political categories. It is not an auspicious (or effective) beginning to build on the feminist insight that women appear to know differently to men because the universalizing tendency of the category 'woman' has been every bit as destructive as the universal category 'oppressed' has been in critical pedagogy.

Carolyn Steedman well illustrates the point that how we know what we know is central to our political practice because it helps us to locate the inconsistencies, the cracks we might then use to empower ourselves. Commenting on the fact that all women learn about patriarchy in the family, whether by the father's absence or presence, she remarks:

What is a distinction though, and one that offers some hope, is the difference between learning of this system from a father's display of its social basis, and learning of it from a relatively unimportant and powerless man (as in the case of her working-class father), who cannot present the case for patriarchy embodied in his own person.[52]

Our different subject positions, borne out in how we know, tell, and hear stories, are ignored at our peril. María Lugones describes the dilemmas that confront her as a Chicana woman in an intellectual context that is predominantly white, when invited to tell her stories. White/Anglo women, she writes, 'can see themselves as simply human or simply women. I can bring you to your senses *con el tono de mi voz*, with the sound of my – to you – alien voice.'[53] This, at any rate, is the assumption behind story-telling. For the woman of colour, the situation is altogether more difficult:

So the central and painful questions for *me* in this encounter become questions of speech: *¿ En qué voz* with which voice, *anclada en qué lugar* anchored in which place, *para qué y porqué* why and to what purpose, do I trust myself to you ... *o acaso juego un juego de* cat and mouse for your entertainment ... *o por el mio?* I ask these questions out loud because they need to be asked.[54]

If we are sensitive to this difference that Lugones brilliantly demonstrates, and we heed Ellsworth's practical advice on this score, that is that we problematize what the limits of our knowing are, based on our different subject positions, I think we end up realizing that storytelling serves various groups differently and that it should never be employed uncritically in mixed-race groups.

Trinh Minh-ha's work is a courageous attempt to delineate modes of story-telling, to explore the complex interplay between the subject positions of the tellers and the listeners. 'There is more than one way to relate the story of specialness,' she observes, and, furthermore, these stories can perpetuate domination. For instance, specialness can serve as entertainment for the dominant groups as 'that voice of difference likely to bring us what we can't have and to divert us from the monotony of sameness.'[55] Denied any other role but the role of exotic Other, the woman of colour is condemned to representing herself as she is seen by the dominant group:

Eager not to disappoint, I try my best to offer my benefactors and benefactresses what they most anxiously yearn for: the possibility of a difference, yet a difference or otherness that will not go so far as to question the foundations of their beings and makings.[56]

As a listener, one can be drawn into such a process very easily. I have seen students 'appropriating pain,' in the words of Monture-Angus,[57] and literally feeding off the tears of stories from the Third World, basking in the sense of having visited another country so easily and feeling no compulsion to explore their own complicity in the oppression of others.

The problems of voice and identity are packed with internal dilemmas not only for the listeners but also the tellers of the tale. Often women of colour are asked to tell their stories while others will do the theorizing and the writing up. Yet the chance to speak, to enter your reality on the record, as it were, is as irresistible as it is problematic. What kind of tale will I choose to tell, and in what voice? Trinh Minh-ha asks, '[H]ow do you inscribe difference without bursting into a series of euphoric narcissistic accounts of yourself and your own kind? Without indulging in a marketable romanticism or in a naive whining about your condition?'[58] There are penalties for choosing the wrong voice at the wrong time, for telling an inappropriate tale. Far better, one might conclude, as the Black woman from South Africa did, to keep silent. I found myself exploring, at the summer college, this right to silence and offer in this regard another of Trinh's observations: 'Silence as a will not to say or a will to unsay and as a language of its own has barely been explored.'[59] As an educator, however, I find the idea of silence extremely unsettling, reminding me of my own compelling interest in encouraging the telling of stories.

In storytelling, then, while asking ourselves what we can know and not know is important, particularly in terms of listening to others and then deciding how to act in a particular situation, I think there is a more basic task at hand. This is the task of calling into question the knowledge and being of both the teller and the listener, and struggling for ways to take this knowledge and being out of the realm of abstraction and into political action. 'What we do toward the texts of the oppressed is very much dependent upon where we are,' writes Gayatri Spivak,[60] echoing a Québecois proverb that *on pense ou on a les pieds* (we think from where we stand). Again I turn to Trinh Minh-ha who has illuminated for me most clearly why neither rationality nor emotional sharing will suffice. Trinh suggests we consider breaking the dichotomy mind/body, reason/emotion, as is done in Asian martial arts for instance, by adding a third category, 'instinctual immediacy,' by which I think is meant subject position or point of departure. Here, instinct does not stand opposed to reason; it requires us to relate to the world with immediacy, to allow 'each part of the body to become infused with consciousness.' Instinct requires us to reactivate the 'radical calling into question in every undertaking, of everything that one takes for granted.'[61] Give up, in other words, the quest for knowledge, that is to definitively know, either through the heart or the mind, and instead, question one's point of departure at every turn so that reversal strategies (such as replacing rationality with emotions) do not become end points in themselves.[62]

Trinh Minh-ha is optimistic about her proposal to engage in the ground clearing activity of radically calling into question:

The questions that arise continue to provoke answers, but none will dominate as long as the ground-clearing activity is at work. Can knowledge circulate without a position of mastery? Can it be conveyed without the exercise of power? No, because there is no end to understanding power relations which are rooted deep in the social nexus – not merely added to society nor easily locatable so that we can just radically do away with them. Yes, however, because in-between grounds always exist, and cracks and interstices are like gaps of fresh air that keep on being suppressed because they tend to render more visible the failures operating in every system. Perhaps mastery need not coincide with power.[63]

The *mestiza* consciousness described by Gloria Anzaldúa in her book *Border-lands/La Frontera* requires ground-clearing activity. The future belongs to the *mestizas*, Anzaldúa writes, 'because the future depends on the breaking down of paradigms, it depends on the straddling of two or more cultures. By creating a new mythos – that is a change in the way we perceive reality, the way we see ourselves, and the ways we behave – *la mestiza* creates a new consciousness.'[64] Anzaldúa makes concrete the tolerance for ambiguity called for by Bettina Aptheker when she situates it in the radical calling into question of all our subject positions. The first step of the *mestiza* is to take inventory: to ask critically, 'Just what did she inherit from her ancestors?'[65]

Pedagogically, then, ground-clearing activity is my suggestion for reshaping education for social change. In one way this is not any different from the axiom of continual critical reflection. What it refers to, however, is reflecting critically on how we hear and how we speak; on the choices we make about which voice to use and when to use it; and, most important of all, on developing pedagogical practices that enable us to pose these questions and use the various answers to guide those concrete moral choices we are constantly being called upon to make.

Concretely, I envision a more complex mapping of our differences than we have ever tried before. In the case of the summer college, for instance, it would mean that more time would be given in the curriculum for understanding the meaning of privilege from our various subject positions. Colonization from within and without will become a major theme and not only in terms of what colonization means for Third World peoples but also how it constitutes the colonizers themselves. The project at hand is Spivak's 'unlearning privilege,'[66] so that 'not only does one become able to listen to that other constituency, but one learns to speak in such a way that one will be taken seriously by that other constituency.'[67] In the past, it seemed such an enormous task to bring into the classroom some of the realities of various oppressed groups that it did not seem possible to concentrate on how we are 'processing' this information differently, based on our respective subject positions. In effect, were I to redesign my pedagogical approach in the summer college, I would want to pay more attention to how we know rather than primarily to what we know. It seems simple enough, but the complex ways of telling stories act as a reminder that the task is anything but simple.

In law, maintaining a similar vigilance about how we know what we know requires that we pay attention to 'the interpretive structures we use to reconstruct events.'[68] As feminists, for instance, we will need to devise alternatives for telling about the lives of women of colour that transcend the narrative about the white woman or the one about the Black man. Since the stories of women of colour fit into neither, telling them will require attention to multiplicities, contradictions, and relations of power embedded in interpretive structures.

To conclude, I endorse Trinh's passionate plea for a movement away from defining ourselves as and boxing ourselves into one subject identity:

You and I are close, we intertwine; you may stand on the other side of the hill once in a while, but you may also be me, while remaining what you are and what I am not. The differences made *between* entities comprehended as absolute presences – hence the notion of *pure origin* and *true* self – are an outgrowth of a dualistic system of thought peculiar to the Occident ...[69]

With no absolutes, no true self, no pure origin, it becomes all the more imperative to pay attention to how our multiple identities are constructed and played out at any one time in any one context. The white disabled student might then have not asked for the stories of the Black South African; she might have focused on critically examining her own need to hear those stories (to what end?). Similarly, we would not have been paralysed by guilt upon hearing Native women call for a particular form of action that did not meet our rational criteria. We might instead have asked what was affecting our comprehension of events (as indeed Native women might have asked themselves). In the same way, feminists who go to court might question their choice of narrative strategies *before* they go to court. More secure in our respective commitments to probing beneath the surface of what we know, to how we know, alliances might then be possible between women from dominant groups and women from subordinate groups. In the courtroom as in the classroom, ours 'is a responsibility to trace the other in self,'[70] a task that must become central to our practice.

3

What Is to Be Gained by Looking White People in the Eye? Race in Sexual Violence Cases

Was it just that old race thing that had thrown her off when her eyes met Grace's? Her neighbor Wilma's father said he'd never in his adult life looked a white person in the eye. He'd grown up in the days when such an act very often ended in a Black person's charred body swinging from a tree. For many years, Blanche worried that it was fear which sometimes made her reluctant to meet white people's eyes, particularly on days when she had the lonelies or the unspecified blues. She'd come to understand that her desire was to avoid pain, a pain so old, so deep, its memory was carried not in her mind, but in her bones. Some days she simply didn't want to look into the eyes of people raised to hate, disdain, or fear anyone who looked like her.

Barbara Neely, *Blanche on the Lam*

There is an older man with white hair & cowboy boots, whose blond, gum-chewing daughter sits bored beside him, who has been staring at me as I write this (YES AMAZIN' FACTS OF NATURE, there are Indians who read & write) I want to go up to him & say *Fuck you*   I'm 'not allowed' in the prison of racism to notice his attempts at intimidation or to respond in any way He's one of the guards of the system, a regulator This is a familiar stare, one quite common, the 'mildest' form of racism Usually if you pretend 'not to notice it,' nothing escalates We, People of Color, are stared at so much that we have high blood pressure, ulcers & alcoholism

Chrystos, *Dream On*

Conversations about Culture

'I had a Vietnamese doctor who wouldn't look me in the eye when we discussed the risks of amniocentesis,' a white woman says to me angrily at a Christmas party, and wonders whether or not the doctor ought to be compelled to put aside his cultural peculiarities in the interests of his white Western patients. Eye contact, a perennial favourite as a marker of the perils associated with cross-cultural encounters, is an ever popular topic. A Crown attorney's book on the cultural attributes of his Aboriginal[1] clients garners praise, particularly for his description of how Aboriginal men's failure to look judges in the eye is a mark of respect rather than an admission of guilt.[2] In academe, eye contact or culture talk goes on as professors are reportedly 'going for the judicial jugular,' subjecting judicial decisions on Aboriginal issues to scrutiny and itemizing the 'difficulties courts face as they are called to sit in judgment of another culture and, in the case of land claims, another time.'[3] The controversy over culture, and specifically over the cultural bias of the judiciary, has also emerged in the context of sexual violence against Aboriginal women and women of colour, although Aboriginal women more often have been at the centre of the debate. In the opening submission to the court in a sexual assault case involving a sixty-three-year-old Roman Catholic bishop and young Aboriginal girls under his charge at a residential school thirty years ago, a Crown prosecutor proposed to build the case of non-consent on a bedrock of culture.[4] Referring to the role of the expert witness the Crown intended to call to testify, an anthropologist specializing in Aboriginal culture, the Crown argued: 'the purpose of [Dr Van Dyke's] evidence is to put into context what these witnesses mean when they say, "I did it because he told me to do it." That is an indication of a reflection of their cultural background, the way they perceive this individual.'[5] Yet, culture used in service of proving the non-consent of young Aboriginal girls who have been sexually assaulted is highly unusual. Far more typical is culture used as a defence of the accused when the accused is of Aboriginal or non–Anglo-Saxon origin.

The cultural contexts of victims of violence and their attackers have also interested women of colour and Aboriginal feminist researchers and women's advocacy groups, but in this context there is likely to be more of an awareness of the risks of taking culture into account. For instance, feminist service providers of colour working with immigrant women have stressed the need to understand how culture shapes refugee and immigrant women's experiences of and responses to violence.[6] They also note, however, that in a racist society any discussion of culture and violence in immigrant communities can be interpreted by white society as 'another sign of backwardness.'[7] That is, violence in immigrant communities is viewed as a cultural attribute rather than a product of male domination that is inextricably bound up with racism. Patricia Monture-Angus, an Aboriginal scholar, makes the same point but adds that the racism that surrounds any discussion of Aboriginal men's violence is used to deny land claims and self-determination.[8] In the face of racism, it has sometimes not made sense for feminists working in the context of violence against women in immigrant and Aboriginal communities to talk about culture at all. When women from non-dominant groups talk about culture, we are often heard to be articulating a false dichotomy between culture and gender; in articulating our difference, we inadvertently also confirm our relegation to the margins. Culture talk is clearly a double-edged sword. It packages difference as inferiority and obscures both gender-based and racial domination, yet cultural considerations are important for contextualizing oppressed groups' claims for justice, for improving their access to services, and for requiring dominant groups to examine the invisible cultural advantages they enjoy.

This chapter is an attempt to examine how cultural conversations are heard and the uses to which they are put in courts of law when the issue is violence against Aboriginal women and women of colour. It is equally an attempt to explore the risks of talking culture for women of colour and Aboriginal women. We need to ask: Can we move the public discussion about culture from cultural modes of making eye contact to what is to be gained and lost by looking white people in the eye? As Barbara Neely, through her character Blanche, a Black woman, and the Aboriginal poet Chrystos both make clear, looking white people in the eye is historically an action full of peril. The consequences of looking white people in the eye must always be carefully calculated.

Both within our communities and outside of them, the risks Aboriginal women and women of colour encounter when we talk about culture in the context of sexual violence are manifested on several levels. First, many cultural communities understand culture and community in ways that reflect and leave unchallenged male privilege. Indeed, the notion of culture that has perhaps the widest currency among both dominant and subordinate groups is one whereby culture is taken to mean values, beliefs, knowledge, and customs that exist in a timeless and unchangeable vacuum outside of patriarchy, racism, imperialism, and colonialism. Viewed this way, culture maintains 'a superautonomy that reduces all facets of social experience to issues of culture.'[9] Second, when we bring sexual violence to the attention of white society we always risk exacerbating the racism directed at both the men and women in our communities. In this way, we risk being viewed by our own communities as traitors and by white society as women who have abandoned our communities because they are so patriarchal. Third, as communities of colour, we need to understand sexual violence as the outcome of both white supremacy and patriarchy; culture talk fragments sexual violence as what men do to women and takes the emphasis away from white complicity. When the terrain is sexual violence, racism and sexism interlock in particularly nasty ways. These two systems operate through each other so that sexual violence, as well as women's narratives of resistance to sexual violence, cannot be understood outside of colonialism and today's ongoing racism and genocide. When women from marginalized communities speak out about sexual violence, we are naming something infinitely broader than what men do to women within our communities, an interlocking analysis that has most often been articulated by Aboriginal women. These three risks of talking culture are particularly acute when, as so often happens, it is the dominant group that controls the interpretation of what it means to take culture into account.

In using the pronoun *we*, I do not want to claim, however, that as a woman of colour I incur the same risks in talking culture as do Aboriginal women in Canada. For each group (and neither group is homogeneous), the risks are different. Aboriginal women's need to talk about culture in spite of these risks emerges out of different histories and present-day realities. Aboriginal women often confront sexual violence in a context in which several generations have been victims of sexual violence, beginning in residential schools. Harsh socioeconomic realities have followed the uprooting and displacement of Aboriginal peoples. The continued denial of Aboriginal sovereignty and the Canadian government's consistent refusal to honour treaties and resolve land claims maintain these profound injustices. These historical specificities mark an important difference between Aboriginal women and women of colour. While the cultures of women of colour are inferiorized whenever male violence in their communities is discussed, for Aboriginal women, their claim to existence as a community is itself imperilled. These important differences notwithstanding, what I would suggest Aboriginal women and women of colour share is the fact that we are both required to talk about culture and violence within the context of white supremacy, a context in which racism and sexism and their intersections are denied. Both groups of women, therefore, in talking about our cultural specificities, run the risk, in significantly different ways, of winning an acknowledgment of some cultural differences, but at the cost of having our experience of sexual and

racial violence and genocide rendered invisible. Culture becomes the framework used by white society to pre-empt both racism and sexism in a process that I refer to as culturalization. The risks of talking culture require
us to exercise great caution whenever cultural considerations enter legal
discourse or discussions about access to services. In working through
the risks and in identifying how cultural considerations often work in
the service of dominant groups, I hope to explore how Aboriginal women
and women of colour might talk about the specificities of our cultural
experiences without risking a denial of the realities of violence, racism,
and sexism in our lives.

The Culturalization of Racism

Contemporary discussion about culture and violence takes place within
the context of modern racism, a racism distinguished from its nineteenth-
century counterpart by the vigour with which it is consistently denied.
In its modern form, overt racism, which rests on the notion of biologically based inferiority, coexists with a more covert practice of domination encoded in the assumption of cultural or acquired inferiority. This
'culturalization of racism,' whereby Black inferiority is attributed to 'cultural deficiency, social inadequacy, and technological underdevelopment,' thrives in a social climate that is officially pluralist.[10] We speak
more of cultural and ethnic differences and less of race and class exploitation and oppression. The concept of culturalized racism is important, it
seems to me, for three reasons. First, it highlights a major feature of how
modern racism works: its covert operations. Second, it explains why
denial is so central to how racism works. To quote Philomena Essed, 'There
are two levels at which racism as ideology operates: at the level of daily
actions and their interpretations and at another level in the refusal to
take responsibility for it.'[11] If we live in a tolerant and pluralistic society
in which the fiction of equality within ethnic diversity is maintained,
then we need not accept responsibility for racism. We can conveniently
forget our racist past and feel secure in the knowledge that at least the
residential schools are closed. Like the Dutch Essed writes about, whose
newspapers put the word *racism* in quotation marks, Canadians are outraged when racism, particularly indirect racism, is named, as it is not
supposed to exist. What is really denied is that 'whites regularly ideal-
ize and favour themselves as a group.'[12] Thus, there can sometimes be a
more or less general rejection of overt racism and, at the same time, 'an

increasing reluctance to see race as a fundamental determinant of white privilege and Black poverty.'[13] Third, a 'declaration of faith in a plural, diverse society,' comments Homi Bhabha, serves as an effective defence 'against the real, subversive demands that the articulation of cultural difference – the empowering of minorities – makes upon democratic pluralism.'[14] Cultural differences are used to explain oppression; if these differences could somehow be taken into account, oppression would disappear. According to this logic, as Arthur Brittan and Mary Maynard note in *Sexism, Racism and Oppression*, power is subsumed under culture and oppression is reduced to a symbolic construction in which there are no real live oppressors who benefit materially and no real oppressed people to liberate.[15] In effect, minorities are invited to keep their culture but enjoy no greater access to power and resources.

In the context of law, because democratic pluralism means, to borrow Bhabha's aphorism, that 'multiculturalism must be seen to be done, as noisily and publicly as possible,' white judges are being urged to be culturally sensitive.[16] Judges begin to practice what Dwight Greene has described for the American context as a kind of 'pluralistic ignorance': 'Mostly affluent white males talking among themselves about what are the reasonable choices for poor people of colour to be making in situations virtually none of the judges have ever been in.'[17]

The culturalization of racism operates differently for Aboriginal peoples than it does for people of colour, as I noted above. When racism and genocide are denied and cultural difference replaces it, the net effect for Aboriginal peoples is a denial of their right to exist as sovereign nations and viable communities. Nowhere is this more clearly demonstrated than in the final outcome of the land claim of the Gitksan and Wet'suwet'en nations of British Columbia. Rejecting the land claim, Mr Justice Allan MacEachern concluded that the Gitksan and Wet'suwet'en could hardly be described as having culture and that 'the Indians' lack of cultural preparation for the new regime was indeed the probable cause of the debilitating dependence from which few Indians in North America have yet escaped.' Culturally inferior, the Gitksan and Wet'suwet'en have only themselves to blame for the current land distribution where all of their previous lands are now owned by whites.[18] As the chiefs of these nations commented upon reading Mr Justice MacEachern's decision:

This judge concludes, more or less, that prior to contact, native people in British Columbia led a life that was nasty, brutish and short and that it took European contact to make them culturally self-aware and to give them any sense of territoriality. In short, prior to contact, this judge thinks native people were little more than fairly bright animals.[19]

It is within the material context of land claims and the contemporary reality of Aboriginal communities subsisting on the very edges of survival that white judges discuss Aboriginal culture and its relevance to the sentencing of Aboriginal males convicted of sexual assault, among other offenses. At least three judicial education programs have been undertaken to 'sensitize' judges to issues of cultural diversity among immigrant as well as Aboriginal communities (projects conceived of as entirely separate from gender sensitivity training, thereby rendering racialized women invisible). Sensitivity in this context means learning how to read culturally specific behaviour in the courtroom setting. When it is the behaviour of generic women (read white) that must be translated, sensitivity includes such things as understanding that a victim of a sexual assault may giggle on the witness stand, not to express her agreement with the sexual assault but rather to convey her discomfort.[20] For Aboriginal women who are sexually assaulted, cultural sensitivity, as I shall show below, can be about both victims and offenders unable to make eye contact. In the context of the latter, sensitivity is often about the culturalization of rape: how cultural and historical specificities explain and excuse the violence men direct at women. Culture, working in tandem with judicial tendencies to minimize the harm of rape, then becomes a mitigating factor in the sentencing of Aboriginal and minority men convicted of sexual assault. At the same time, it reinforces decisions such as Mr Justice MacEachern's above. No culture, no land, no survival. In this way, an argument about what men do to women masks what white people have done and continue to do to Aboriginal peoples and the role that sexual violence has played in these colonial encounters. Uncovering the crucial links between these two systems is, therefore, necessarily the first challenge that Aboriginal women confront when they talk about sexual violence.

Between a Rock and a Hard Place: Aboriginal Women's Responses to Sexual Violence

Community has not been a safe place for women, and Aboriginal women have not failed to note this in spite of the risks they take when they do so. For example, the Ontario Native Women's Association (ONWA) confirmed in a study on violence what many earlier studies had noted: the level of violence directed against women and children in Aboriginal communities and families was much higher than for non-Aboriginal populations. Eighty-four percent of the respondents to their survey thought that family violence occurs in their communities and 24 per cent personally knew of cases of family violence that had led to death, most frequently of women.[21] Indeed, male violence was one reason the Native Women's Association of Canada (NWAC) went to court in 1991 to demand the right to sit at the table during the constitutional talks on Aboriginal self-government. Arguing that their exclusion from the table posed a grave threat to Aboriginal women, NWAC members explained to the court the basis for their fears:

Why are we so worried as women? ... We have a disproportionately high rate of child sexual abuse and incest. We have wife battering, gang rapes, drug and alcohol abuse and every kind of pervasion imaginable has been imported into our lives. The development of programs, services, and policies for handling domestic violence has been placed in the hands of men. Has it resulted in a reduction of this kind of violence? Is a woman or a child safe in their own home in an Aboriginal community? The statistics show this is not the case.[22]

Disallowing NWAC's claim on the grounds that the constitutional discussion had now moved to the legislature and was thus beyond the court's jurisdiction, the Federal Court of Appeal's Mr Justice Mahoney nonetheless agreed that the 'record suggests that some "nations" ... will continue to opt for male domination.' When NWAC later applied to the court to have the result of the constitutional talks invalidated as a continuing violation of their rights, the same argument – that the Charter of Rights and Freedoms does not apply to constitutional talks – prevailed.[23]

Both the statistics on violence gathered by ONWA's and NWAC's arguments concerning the right to sit at the constitutional table reveal the perils for Aboriginal women of raising issues of violence within their communities while under the gaze of white society – a society engaged in drafting a constitution *without* recognition of Aboriginal self-determination. How these conversations about violence are heard in the context of a denial of Aboriginal sovereignty, as well as a wider context in which sexual violence is understood within a Western feminist framework as an issue of what men do to women, are concerns that have led many Aboriginal women to urge a deeper contextualizing of sexual violence.

Patricia Monture-Angus, for example, questioned ONWA's study on sexual violence (as did the chiefs of many nations) with the argument that 'focusing on a moment in time, or incidents of violence, abuse, or racism – counting them – disguises the utter totality of the experience of violence in Aboriginal women's lives.'[24] While Monture-Angus notes that the chiefs were wrong to dismiss ONWA's study as they did, she suggests that their silence on issues of sexual violence and abuse cannot be interpreted as merely being about patriarchy. Describing what it means to acknowledge sexual abuse in small, isolated communities where each individual disclosure reveals a web of other disclosures, Monture-Angus makes clear the multiple systems of domination and levels of abuse:

Indian communities do not experience the process of disclosure as incidental anymore than the experience of abuse is lived as a single episode. Where to place your anger is difficult to determine. Residential schools are behind us. Who will carry that anger? Apparatus and individuals of the state are far away and inaccessible. How do you deposit that anger? The perpetrator is victim too (and may be someone you love). How do you trust in a criminal justice system that is foreign (colonial) and based on values that you do not share? The anger and frustration of Aboriginal communities swirls and swirls and all too often there is no channel for release. It is a cyclone of pain. It is a cyclone of pain that has no parallel in urban communities. I am able to understand why some people, faced with that cyclone of pain, may prefer to choose silence.[25]

The cycle to which Monture-Angus refers is often a central theme whenever Aboriginal women describe the sexual violence in their communities. Beverly Sellars, past chief of the Soda Creek Indian Band of British Columbia, describes the same cycle when she examines her own band's attempt to name and confront sexual violence. Sexual violence, Sellars recounts, 'seemed to be something like an ulcer inside our community and we just couldn't put our finger on it ... We started saying, well, that's a symptom, that's not the cause; that's a symptom, that's not the cause, and it got so that it came down to one thing: residential schools.' This analysis, Sellars reminds us, is not simply a story about herself, but one about her mother, grandmother, and ultimately the people in her community.[26] Along with Sellars and Monture-Angus, many other Aboriginal women have suggested that the tremendous violence directed at Aboriginal women cannot be understood except through the lens of the devastation that colonization has wrought on Aboriginal peoples, and particularly the breakdown of traditional social systems which has destroyed a sense of self in community.

Madeleine Dion Stout, a Cree scholar, is one such writer for whom the argument that violence against women arises simply because society is misogynist is 'too superficial.' Considering both Aboriginal men who abuse women and white men who kill women, such as Marc Lépine, who murdered fourteen women in Montreal, Dion Stout comments: 'From my perspective, Marc Lépine and indeed Aboriginal men commit violence against women because their "spiritual compact" with themselves, their communities and their heritage have not been fostered.'[27] Such men have all lost community, although in different ways. Understanding their violence begins with understanding the factors that minimize a sense of self, family, and community. In the Aboriginal context, this story has to begin with the violence of colonization.

The multilayered stories that Monture-Angus and Sellars and others must tell about sexual violence are not easily heard amidst the bald statistics of the ONWA's report on sexual violence, nor do they appear fully in the story that NWAC told in the courtroom when pressing their claim for a seat at the constitutional table. One wonders if there are in fact any narratives upon which to draw to explain both sexual violence and colonial violence as they occur simultaneously on the same bodies. The difficulties of presenting the story of sexual violence in its fullest complexities leave Aboriginal women between a rock and a hard place when they consider how and where to name sexual violence. Aboriginal communities are male dominated, as are all other communities, and women's stories of oppression are not often heard. As the Royal Commission on Aboriginal Peoples reported, many Aboriginal women appearing before the Commission felt that they were isolated and accused of disloyalty to their nation whenever they spoke out about violence.[28]

Confronting male domination within Aboriginal communities has required an understanding of how white domination has contributed to the causes and extent of male violence as well as how to formulate strategic decisions on how and where to name the violence. The Ontario Native Women's Association stressed in their report on violence that Aboriginal peoples do not have self-government and are regulated in much of their everyday affairs through the federal government. This continuing colonization and the devastating impact of past domination are the contexts in which Aboriginal family violence must be examined.[29] Aware of racism but equally concerned about the violence inflicted on women and children, respondents to the Ontario Native Women's Association's province-wide study on Aboriginal family violence were emphatic that they did not condone violence and wanted it stopped: 82 per cent of respondents wanted their abusers charged even though they also expressed a fear of the wider implications of involving Canadian police in Aboriginal family disputes. The Association's report emphasizes healing of all members of the family but solidly maintains 'Of course, the needs and safety of the abused woman and children are more urgent at first.'[30] Their recommendations reflect this priority, referring first of all to the need to provide services and healing lodges for women and children who are victims of violence, and secondly to treatment programs for batterers.

In other reports by Aboriginal women on family violence, it is clear that the twin realities of racism and violence inform the analysis of strategies. In Alberta, the author of a report on abused Aboriginal women notes that for 'too many Aboriginal women the inability of Aboriginal communities to protect her [sic] and her children from abuse means the only option is to relocate outside the community.'[31] Victimized inside their own communities and victimized outside of it, even in shelters, such Aboriginal women do indeed find themselves between a rock and a hard place: between either continued violence or double victimization and the harsh reality of being without community and family. Their insistence that culture is an issue when dealing with violence springs from an acknowledgment of this predicament. In the Northwest Territories, the Status of Women Council has also been clear that women's relationship to community is fraught with contradictions. The Council's report on violence identifies as problematic community denial of abuse, alcohol used as an excuse for violent behaviour, and the fact that 'some of our worst abusers may be community leaders.'[32] Finally, in *Voices of Aboriginal Women: Aboriginal Women Speak Out About Violence*, a booklet published by the Canadian Council on Social Development and the Native Women's Association of Canada, Aboriginal women once again make clear why they prefer an approach to violence that is community-centred and focused on healing:

Most of the Aboriginal victims of family violence are women and children and the offenders are men. The Aboriginal victims must deal with the offender or be subject to exile outside the community, from their home, far from close relatives. It is important to realize that the victims and members of the family are victimized again by the system because they must leave their home and community. Aboriginal women feel that it is the offender that is most in need of help to break the cycle of violence, but is the most ignored. But the women do not want to give up their right to safety. So the logical approach is to intervene and take the offender away from home.[33]

The dilemma that Aboriginal women face in being forced to choose between their personal safety and community was also expressly acknowledged in the *Report of the Aboriginal Justice Inquiry of Manitoba*. Acknowledging the submission of Professor Emma Laroque on the issue of violence against Aboriginal women, Mr Justices Hamilton and Sinclair succinctly commented: 'What they [Aboriginal women] are forced to run to is often as bad as what they had to run from. Why they feel they have to leave is a matter worthy of comment.'[34] Drawing on submissions made to the *Inquiry* by Aboriginal women, the two Justices describe in considerable detail the specific strategies necessary for the protection of Aboriginal women and close their *Report* with a discussion that emphasizes healing for Aboriginal women:

As the victims of childhood sexual abuse and adult domestic violence, they have borne the brunt of the breakdown of social controls within Aboriginal societies. There was substantial support for an entirely new system, to break the cycle of abuse and to restore Aboriginal methods of healing designed to return balance to the community, rather than punish the offender ... We recommend that women be involved in the implementation of our recommendations, and that they be represented on the various administrative bodies that will become necessary. While the role of Aboriginal women in Aboriginal society is not well understood in non-Aboriginal circles, we have been told, and accept, that a resumption of their traditional roles is the key to putting an end to Aboriginal female mistreatment. The immediate need is for Aboriginal women to begin to heal from the decades of denigration they have experienced. But the ultimate objective is to encourage and assist Aboriginal women to regain and occupy their rightful place as equal partners in Aboriginal society.[35]

Responses such as these speak of healing and community but also speak of the safety of women and of women's equality. Because the Justices attempt to come to terms with women's realities at the intersection of racism and sexism, their responses are significantly different from the forgiveness approach promoted by most white judges and lawyers, as we see below.

Although forums such as the Aboriginal Justice Inquiry of Manitoba and the Royal Commission on Aboriginal Peoples demonstrate some of the complexities for Aboriginal women of confronting violence within their communities, the discussion of strategies for change, while sensitive to some of these complexities, nonetheless reveals the ways in which women's lives continue to be fragmented – that is, understood as an out-come either of sexism or racism but not of both. For example, the discussion of healing in the Manitoba Inquiry is placed alongside of, but never integrated with, another central issue: Aboriginal women as offend-ers. Aboriginal women are vastly overrepresented in prisons (more so than Aboriginal men relative to other men). Status Indian women are 131 times more likely to be incarcerated than white women. Maintaining that Aboriginal women are the largest over-sentenced group in Manitoba's prisons, and that their crimes have a great deal to do with their responses to being abused, the Inquiry recommends that alternatives to incarceration be developed for Aboriginal women. However, when alternatives to incarceration are discussed in a separate chapter of the *Report*, the Justices do not then consider women offenders. Healing and culturally appropriate sentencing are nearly always in reference to the healing of male offenders.[36] This focus on men, which I refer to below as the culturalization of sexism, enables judges to keep the colonial relation intact. As benevolent patriarchs, they consider the special circumstances of the Aboriginal male offender, and sometimes his tragic history, but their gaze remains a colonial one in which the colonizers never consider the continuing effects of colonization and their own complicity in it. Unlike Aboriginal women who consider colonization as it operates through gender,[37] these judges and lawyers separate the systems of patriarchy and colonization, considering the former to be active and the latter to be over.

The Culturalization of Sexism

Culture as a Defence: Aboriginal Offenders

In cases of sexual assault when victims and their attackers are of the same race, it is often assumed that it is gender and not race that is the meaningful factor at work in influencing how rape is 'scripted' in court.[38] Yet, as Kristin Bumiller has pointed out, rape trials are most often about fallen angels who must prove their innocence in contributing to their fall from grace. The emphasis in a rape trial on the victim's purity 'reinforces the presumption that punishing violent men is justified to the extent that women are worthy of trust and protection.'[39] Aboriginal women and women of colour, however, are considered inherently less innocent and less worthy than white women, and the classic rape in legal discourse is the rape of a white woman. The rape script is thus inevitably raced whether it involves intraracial or interracial rape. The criminal justice system, Jennifer

Wriggins argues, takes less seriously the rape of Black women either by Black men or white men.[40]

Rape trials involving Aboriginal offenders and victims are propelled by two dominant narratives: the savage and the squaw. The stereotype of Black men as bestial, violent, and criminal has an Aboriginal counterpart in the bloodthirsty Indian.[41] The gendered version of the violent Indian is the squaw on whose body violence may occur with impunity. As Aboriginal scholar Emma Laroque explained to the Aboriginal Justice Inquiry of Manitoba,

the portrayal of the squaw is one of the most degraded, most despised and most dehumanized anywhere in the world. The 'squaw' is the female counterpart to the Indian male 'savage' and as such she has no human face; she is lustful, immoral, unfeeling and dirty. Such grotesque dehumanization has rendered all Native women and girls vulnerable to gross physical, psychological and sexual violence ... I believe that there is a direct relationship between these horrible racist/sexist stereotypes and violence against Native women and girls. I believe, for example, that Helen Betty Osborne was murdered in 1972 by four young men from The Pas because these youths grew up with twisted notions of 'Indian girls' as 'squaws.'[42]

Other Aboriginal writers suggest that the squaw stereotype and the violence that sustains and is sustained by it, deeply alters how Aboriginal men can think of Aboriginal women.[43] How then does this show up in the courtroom?

Examples from the Canadian context of Aboriginal offenders, while they show that male judges continue to minimize the harm of sexual assault, also confirm that race never absents itself from the rape script, and that the savage and the squaw continue to regulate what is seen and acknowledged. The recognition that colonization has had a devastating impact on Aboriginal men does little to rupture these scripts. Viewing Aboriginal men as dysfunctional (and not, for example, as oppressed), and Aboriginal women as inherently rapeable confirms the superiority of white men in the cases discussed below.

In Teressa Nahanee's study of sentencing decisions in cases involving Inuit men and women,[44] in Margo Nightingale's study of Aboriginal women in sixty-seven cases of sexual assault,[45] and in my own work on the cases discussed here, Canada's history of colonization pervades the legal environment just as extensively as do historical and social attitudes towards women, and it becomes impossible to untangle which factor is contributing most to lenient sentencing of Aboriginal males accused of sexual assault. For instance, Nahanee and Nightingale both note that the stereo-type of the drunken Indian still operates to ensure that alcohol abuse is viewed as more significant for Aboriginal than for white offenders. What is interesting, however, is the gendered response to this stereotype. For an Aboriginal man accused of rape, alcohol abuse can be seen as a miti-gating factor, sometimes a root cause of the violence against women. For an Aboriginal woman who is raped, however, intoxication becomes a form of victim-blaming. A woman who has passed out, Nightingale notes, is often considered to have suffered less of a violation, and the number of victims who have passed out is greatly exaggerated.[46] Similarly, the ostracism that might be suffered by a woman who complains of rape in an isolated northern community is not noticed, while the suffering a male offender might experience in a jail far from home where no one speaks his language has occasionally been taken into account.

Just what are the statements that flag the coming together of race and gender under the banner of culture in ways that diminish the reality of sexual assault and its impact on Aboriginal women? Nahanee identifies perhaps the most notorious Canadian case to date to illustrate the com-bination of gender and cultural bias in sexual assault sentencing. In *R. v. Curley, Nagmalik and Issigaitok*, a sentence of seven days was meted out to three Inuit men found guilty of having intercourse with an Inuk fe-male under the age of fourteen. Relying on his experience in the Eastern Arctic, Judge Bourassa considered the culture of the accused men and was especially lenient on the basis that, according to his information, in Inuit culture, a young woman is deemed ready for intercourse upon menstruation. An assumed cultural difference was also used to bolster the defence's argument that the accused men were ignorant of Canadian law on sexual assault. On appeal, cultural considerations continued to shape the rape script by eclipsing the realities of the violence done to the young girl. Although the sentence was increased to reflect the view that ignorance of the law was no excuse, there was no effort made to deter-mine if the victim had in fact suffered great harm.[47]

Similar cultural considerations have arisen in cases where the defence has argued for a community-based treatment program as an alternative to prison. In *R. v. Naqitarvik*, the same Judge Bourassa accepted the community-based solution on the basis that the community's unique cultural methods of dealing with sexual assault (in this instance a healing circle) had a sig-nificant role to play in healing the offender. On appeal, the issues once again revolved around culture as the court elected to impose a stiffer sen-tence on the basis that the community-based program was no more than a counselling program and that further, 'the witnesses in this case do not describe a culture markedly different than that in the rest of Canada. Rather, the incident itself arose as the victim and her sister played music on a modern player for which there was an electric cord,' an indication in the court's eyes that Inuit culture was sufficiently modern that it could not be characterized as different from the mainstream.[48] The gender considerations and clumsy cultural arguments that equate difference with inferiority do not seem to have intruded on the consciousness of the Aboriginal Justice Inquiry of Manitoba. The Justices consider that *R. v. Naqitarvik* is an example of how appeal courts can 'thwart judges who search for culturally appropriate sanctions.'[49]

Judges, and the lawyers who argue the cases before them, can work with a notion of cultural difference as inferiority but recognize, at the same time, the damaging impact of colonization (at least in sexual assault cases if not in land claims where such recognition would have a bearing on the restitution of land); that is, they sometimes display a willingness to consider the history of colonization and its present-day effects as mitigating factors in the sentencing of Aboriginal males.[50] One reads in decisions, for instance, some empathy for sexual offenders who come from 'the worst Indian reserve in the province.'[51] In *R. v. Whitecap & Whitecap*, the very difficult social and economic conditions on the Red Earth Indian reserve in Saskatchewan are noted;[52] in *R. v. Okkuatsiak*, the offender is described as a victim of the economic conditions in Nain, Labrador.[53] Judges also note in their decisions the vicious cycle of sexual abuse that began with residential schools.[54] What is absent here is any acknowledgment of how the history and present-day legacy of colonization has affected Aboriginal women, rendering them as the victims of sexual assault. This is how gender and race conflate to produce an absence of the realities of Aboriginal women.

Pauktuutit, the Inuit Women's Association of Canada, as Nahanee reports, launched a constitutional challenge of sentencing decisions on the basis that lenient sentencing of Inuit males in sexual assault cases interferes with the right to security of the person and the right of equal protection and benefit of the law of Inuit women.[55] Nahanee emphasizes Pauktuutit's position that 'sexual exploitation of the young must stop because it is not "culturally" acceptable, and it is not part of Inuit sexual mores and practices.'[56] Cultural defence in this context, both Nahanee and Pauktuutit stress, minimizes the impact of sexual assault on Inuit girls and women, a minimizing made possible by the view that Inuit women are sexually promiscuous. The cultural defence thus depends upon the squaw stereotype, but its usage in the court enables white judges to feel as though they have taken culture and colonization into account, a position of superiority that also indirectly confirms the Aboriginal man as savage.

Both Nightingale and Nahanee focus on cases in which cultural sensitivity rested on a highly gendered, unsophisticated view of culture and, I would add, on a gendered view of the impact of colonization. My own research into cases of sexual assault confirmed their conclusions.[57] Recently, however, some judges have been more careful of the gendered consequences of viewing rape through the lens of race or culture or both, as well as history. For example, in *R. v. M. (G.O.)*, the Court noted: 'The seriousness of the offence does not vary in accordance with the color of the skin of the victim, her cultural background or the place of her residence,'[58] and in *R. v. Ritchie*, the Court noted that sexual assault 'is not acceptable in society whether it be within the Indian society or the general society.'[59] There is an emerging awareness of the dangers of relying on culture as a mitigating circumstance. In *R. v. J. (H.)*, this use of culture is specifically refuted:

There have been instances when Canadian judges were persuaded to bend the rules too far in favour of offenders from Native communities or disadvantaged backgrounds. When that happens a form of injustice results; specific victims and members of the public generally are given cause to believe that the justice system has failed to protect them ... H.J. cannot properly be portrayed as a naive young man who should only be pitied and not condemned. He is not a 'child of the forest.'[60]

If Aboriginal offenders are no longer 'children of the forest,' the dangers for Aboriginal women of deficient and clumsy attempts on the part of legal players in the justice system to interpret culture and history remain none the less. It continues to be primarily white male judges and lawyers with little or no knowledge of history or anthropology who interpret Aboriginal culture and its relevance to the court. Wrapped in a cloak of sensitivity to cultural differences and recognition of the consequences of colonization, the anthropologizing of sexual assault continues to have gendered overtones and to maintain white supremacy as securely as in days of more overt racism and sexism.

Eye Contact and the Cultural Differences Approach

In 1989, a Crown attorney with extensive experience prosecuting Native offenders in the North wrote an article on how cultural bias affects the sentencing of Native accused men. Two years later, the article became a book. In *Dancing with a Ghost*, Rupert Ross begins from the standpoint of cultural sensitivity, urging lawyers and judges to critically examine their own cultural assumptions and advising them do their best to discover Aboriginal realities and truths.[61] Ross explains with an example: 'I have learned, to my chagrin, that in some northern reserve communities looking another straight in the eye is taken as a deliberate sign of disrespect for their rule is that you look inferiors straight in the eye.'[62] He then goes on to elaborate how such cultural differences affect sentencing. Significantly, Ross is responding to his perception that sentencing of Native offenders has been too harsh and at variance with the wishes of Aboriginal communities themselves. His identification of cultural differences, then, is intended to avoid this outcome. Largely anecdotal, Ross's commentary serves to highlight where cultural interpretation through white male eyes can take us in the area of sexual assault.

Ross intends to make an argument for community-based justice and for lenient or non-existent jail terms, an outcome he considers justifiable if it can be shown that Aboriginal communities both desire it and can offer protection to the community. The first part of this argument, that Aboriginal communities desire this outcome, relies on anecdotes of the victims themselves. A teenage rape victim refuses to testify, Ross reports, because she believes that her assailant has paid enough of a penalty while waiting for the case to come to trial.[63] Another victim of abuse by an assailant described as dangerous also refuses to testify, and Ross opines that, in such cases,

it is more than fear or embarrassment at work: I suspect instead that it is perceived as ethically wrong to say hostile, critical, implicitly angry things about someone in their presence ... In our ignorance, we have failed to admit the possibility that there might be rules other than ours to which they regularly display allegiance, an allegiance all the more striking because it is exercised in defiance of our insistent pressures to the contrary.[64]

Ross feels certain that Aboriginal communities do not want violent, abusive men punished but instead healed and forgiven. In describing the sentencing of a young man who had beaten his wife in an alcoholic rage, Ross compares his own position that such an offence required a jail term as a deterrent with that of the men and women of the community. Aware perhaps that he might well be criticized for this gendered account of community, Ross notes that while the community leaders asking that the young man remain in the community were all male, the courtroom was jammed with women. As he speculates:

Each of those ladies knew that when his jail term was over he would come back. If he came back feeling reviled by the women of the village, his problems with women would only grow worse. If, in contrast, they demonstrated their forgiveness, their support and their waiting welcome, the opposite result might occur. In their view, while jail sentences might on occasion be necessary for the protection of all, the person who has to pay that price should not be cut off from community affection and support. To do so would only put the community further at risk.[65]

Finally, to support his speculation that Aboriginal women endorse community sanctions as an alternative to jail, Ross cites a recommendation in the 1989 report by the Ontario Native Women's Association (which he mistakenly dates as 1990) for the establishment of healing houses for women, children, and abusers.[66]

While it would be wrong to overdramatize the impact of Ross's cultural interpretations, or to fail to note that he himself warned that his comments were restricted to isolated Aboriginal communities of his experience in Northern Ontario, his comments have been taken up by the chief justice of the Yukon Territory, Heino Lilles, and reflect the approach of the court in some recent sexual assault cases in the North. Chief Justice Lilles's own theorizing about cultural bias is noteworthy not only because of his position in the justice system and his involvement in various judicial education programs but also because, like Ross's, his statements are accompanied by an acknowledgment that Aboriginal communities are highly disadvantaged communities. These interpretations are not, in other words, overtly racist; rather, they are presented as culturally sensitive, even antiracist, initiatives.[67]

Like Rupert Ross, Chief Justice Lilles has spent some of his professional life within the context of Northern justice, hence has had ample opportunity to see how harshly the criminal justice system has dealt with Native offenders, a situation he attributes to two principal factors: 'The social and economic poverty in which many Natives live, and a subtle, unintentional but persistent discrimination by the decision makers in the criminal justice system.'[68] If players in the judicial system can do little about poverty, they can certainly address discrimination, and it is to this end that Chief Justice Lilles writes about culture and cultural bias. Decision makers in the justice system in the North, including police, lawyers, and judges, come from a cultural, social, and economic background different from that of the majority of persons in the communities where they serve, notes the judge. Such individuals are unintentionally biased; that it is to say, they may possess 'an inclination, bent, or predisposition to make decisions a certain way, based on the sum total of the individual's own cultural and social experiences.'[69] Put this way, the problems of Northern justice originate in poverty as well as in a 'misinterpretation' of cultural differences.[70] Admitting that it is difficult to generalize about Aboriginal values (but apparently not so difficult to do so about white culture), Chief Justice Lilles nevertheless proceeds to rely on a chart comparing the value systems of Aboriginal peoples and non-Aboriginal peoples and to suggest how these differing values enter into judicial proceedings.[71] The question of eye contact surfaces once again, and Chief Justice Lilles, relying on Ross, notes that the justice system often unnecessarily criminalizes and labels young Aboriginal people because of the assumption (based on their alleged tendency not to make eye contact) that they are unreliable, remorseless, and uncooperative.[72]

It is important to note that under the umbrella of cross-cultural sensitivity, Chief Justice Lilles includes a number of practices that do not originate in culture but rather in the material practices of Northern justice: Crown prosecutors prosecute more readily because they are unwilling to overrule the police; police charge more readily – the level of policing is 200 to 300 per cent greater than in other jurisdictions; and jail sentences rather than alternative community sentences are given out. These practices contribute to a scenario that is explained away by poverty and misunderstandings of cross-cultural encounters. Significantly, the word *racism* does not occur throughout his article. If cultural differences and poverty are the source of the problems of Northern justice, then Aboriginal community-based justice in which, presumably, cross-cultural concerns disappear, is at least one important strategy towards greater justice.[73] It is precisely this option that is now being considered in the disposition of some sexual assault cases, and it appeared in two recent cases in which Chief Justice Lilles presided, although, significantly, in both cases it was a white judge who was in the position of deciding what a community-based disposition should be.

Healing the Offenders

Culture as a defence and the pursuit of a 'culturally relevant disposition' in the case of *R. v. P. (J.A.)* revolved around the Aboriginal concept of healing, an approach to justice described in the *Report of the Aboriginal Justice Inquiry of Manitoba* as follows:

The underlying philosophy in Aboriginal societies in dealing with crime was the resolution of disputes, the healing of wounds and the restoration of social harmony. It might mean an expression of regret for the injury done by the offender or by members of the offender's clan. It might mean the presentation of gifts or payment of some kind. It might even mean the forfeiture of the offender's life. But the matter was considered finished once the offence was recognized and dealt with by both the offender and the offended. Atonement and the restoration of harmony were the goals – not punishment.[74]

P pleaded guilty to sexually assaulting his two daughters and a foster child over the course of several years. The assaults began when each of the girls reached the age of thirteen years. The defence urged the court to adopt a community-based disposition in lieu of a period of incarceration (normally a two-year minimum and a maximum of life imprisonment for sexual intercourse with a minor). Notwithstanding the serious breach of trust involved, Chief Justice Lilles agreed to the community-based disposition on the basis of three factors, each of which bears examination for how culture, community, and colonization can be used to compete with and ultimately prevail over gender-based harm. First, the chief (on behalf of the five clan elders) supported P's bid for a community-based disposition. As described by Chief Justice Lilles in his decision and later in an article, the chief spoke in some detail about the community's efforts to recover from the devastating effects of colonization and, in particular, from the construction of the Alaskan Highway, which was built through the community in 1942. Alcohol, sexual abuse at residential schools and in homes, and the breakdown of the traditional community structure resulted, in the chief's words, in a 'time of great cultural downfall.'[75] The community's response was to break the cycle of abuse through a healing circle in which both victims and offenders would come forward for treatment and rehabilitation. Also testifying on P's behalf were a number of witnesses, including one of his daughters and his wife, who both supported the call for a community solution already in place in the form of a weekly collective counselling session. A third factor in P's favour was the fact that he had been a leader in bringing Native culture back to the community and possessed, in the eyes of the judge, 'the potential to be a future leader in the Teslin community.'[76] Aware that his decision was likely to attract censure, Chief Justice Lilles accepted the community alternative, as does Rupert Ross, on the basis that a community disposition can be 'hard time' and even more difficult for the offender than a term of imprisonment. As he elaborates:

In this case I heard evidence about the humiliation which accompanies disclosure of an offence like this in a community the size of Teslin. 'First one must deal with the shock and then the dismay on your neighbor's faces. One must live with the daily humiliation, and at the same time seek forgiveness not just from the victims, but from the community as a whole.' For in a Native culture, a real harm has been done to everyone. A community disposition continues that humiliation, at least until full forgiveness has been achieved.[77]

Culture and community remain in this decision unexamined and ungendered while the subtext of colonialism (never named as racism and thus maintained as a legacy of the past and not part of the present) informs white judicial cultural sensitivities. It is never explored whether the young girls who have been harmed are equal stakeholders in the community-based healing. How do their own gender- and age-specific positions in the community enable their concerns in the collective healing to be addressed? Will their speaking out about the violence (a speaking out that occurred in a white court) be bitterly resented precisely because sexual violence is, as Patricia Monture-Angus and Beverly Sellars describe, so deeply connected to the histories of abuse of others?

It is mainly in the context of remote Northern communities that culturally relevant sentencing has occurred. In the Yukon and Northwest Territories, there is, as Chief Justice Lilles is concerned to note, 'an exceptionally harsh system of justice' with an imprisonment rate of 790 per 100,000 population as compared with 112.7 for the rest of Canada, and 426 per 100,000 for the United States.[78] Arguably, such an environment demands that alternatives to incarceration be explored. At the very least, they demand that we examine the root causes of the problems apparent in the judicial system. In this context, it seems sensible to explore, as the judge has advised, the potential of probation reviews as a means of monitoring whether or not community-based dispositions are working. What is worrying, however, are the male-offender-centred features of this approach, the almost entirely male cast of spokespersons for the community, the denial of racism as a key factor affecting the treatment of all Aboriginal peoples, and sexism in Aboriginal women's lives. Of concern, too, is the failure to question whether what may be appropriate for a small Aboriginal community of 300 is appropriate in and may be transposed to altogether different contexts.

Chief Justice Lilles's decision in R. v. P. (J.A.) has not, to my knowledge, drawn public criticism but another decision of his, also involving sexual assault and healing, has. The connections between R. v. P (J.A.) and R. v. Hoyt are instructive in that cultural considerations in the former appear in the latter despite significant differences in context. Between 1965 and 1971, John Hoyt, a white probation officer in Whitehorse (the capital of the Northwest Territories, population 60,000) who also served as a volunteer assisting Native youth, molested three underage boys of Aboriginal origin whom he supervised on a camping trip and whom he counselled and befriended. In view of Hoyt's early guilty plea, the over forty letters of reference sent on his behalf, the devastating impact on Hoyt's family, and his own remorse as an offender who would like to assist his victims in their 'healing,' the judge imposed a fine of $2,000 per victim. While he did not ultimately accept the defence's suggestions that Hoyt contribute to the community by 'researching alternatives in sentencing for sexual abuse cases, assist the authorities in developing badly needed programming for sexual offenders, assist the Native community, while allowing him to facilitate the healing process for himself and his victims,' Chief Justice Lilles did concede that such suggestions were 'very attractive.'[79] The Court of Appeal in January 1992 dismissed an appeal by the Crown that the sentence was too light.[80]

The Lilles decision in Hoyt did draw criticism from the Yukon Association for the Prevention of Community and Family Violence. As the authors of the response argued, Chief Justice Lilles gave no weight to the one victim who testified about the harm done to him and presumed on the weakest of evidence that there was no risk of recidivism, notwithstanding the testimony by Hoyt's psychologist that the accused's understanding of the consequences of his behaviour for his victims was limited. Finally, on the judge's attraction to the defence's proposal of community work, the authors state their association's response bluntly: 'To be crass, one wonders if the criminal offence of arson qualifies one for the position of fire marshall.'[81]

Chief Justice Lilles's decisions may simply be illustrative of a more generalized tendency to dispense male-offender-centred rather than victim-centred justice in cases of sexual assault, but what is interesting about the P. (J.A.) and Hoyt decisions is the extent to which they reflect the judge's acceptance of community-based dispositions and of healing in particular, concepts that are intended to reflect his sensitivity to the social and economic conditions of Aboriginal communities in the North, to their history of colonialism, and to specific cultural differences. That Chief Justice Lilles is himself a white man and that Hoyt, a white probation officer, is one of those players in the justice system whom the judge earlier identified in his article as likely to possess cultural biases, seem not to have altered the strategy or to have encouraged a cautious interpretation of cultural considerations. One wonders if the historical context of a white man who works with Aboriginal men is not somehow conflated with the context of Aboriginal men themselves. The victims, in this case Aboriginal boys, also are not considered in the eager acceptance of community-based justice.

Judges dispensing justice in Canada's North are confronted with the vulnerability of the North's Aboriginal children. Children are at risk, as many cases show, because they are in close relationship with pedophiles who are also authority figures, because a heritage of colonialism forces the rape of a sister by a brother who was himself raped as a child by a white authority figure, and because they experience high suicide rates and extensive alcohol abuse.[82] Judges must thread their way through culture and history in order to determine, in legal terms, who is offender and who is victim. In the context of violence in Aboriginal families, there are only victims, but they are certainly not all equally placed. While a few decisions do not constitute a trend, *Hoyt* and *P. (J.A.)* and others nevertheless suggest that judging in this context demands more careful attention to the meaning of community, history, and culture. As the Association for the Prevention of Community and Family Violence noted in the case of Hoyt, his standing in the community might look very different if one took the perspectives of the victims into account.[83]

White judges and lawyers seeking neat, culturally sensitive, ungendered solutions to justice have not often stopped to question their authority to interpret Aboriginal culture, history, and contemporary reality. Self-reflexivity has been entirely absent from discussions of culture and the courts. Talal Asad's point that '"cultural translation" is inevitably enmeshed in conditions of power – professional, national, international' would suggest that Canadian courts must begin with the *contemporary* fact of white supremacy in and out of the courtroom and not simply get by with a passing reference to its history and hazy references to contemporary cultural biases and social conditions.[84] There are, however, perils in calling for an interrogation of notions of culture in a legal context. Clearly, women and children who are victims of violence do not stand in relation to culture as do their assailants. The question remains, as Leila Abu-Lughod asks in respect to the Bedouin communities she studied, how cultural practices work to sustain the power differences within groups, such as the difference in status between men and women.[85] This does not then become a dichotomy between culture and gender but an interrogation into how culture is gendered and gender is culturalized. Madeleine Dion Stout suggests that an Aboriginal conception of human relations, one which stresses the 'multi-generational and "transdirectional" nature of human development,' still has room in it for critical thought and thus for asking such questions as 'is the new class of young, educated, male leaders hostile to the Aboriginal women's cause?' and 'are traditionalists true protagonists' for Aboriginal women?[86]

A second, equally compelling issue is that a discussion about culture may well displace an inquiry into domination:

Culture is the essential tool for making other. As a professional discourse that elaborates on the meaning of culture in order to account for, explain, and understand cultural difference, anthropology also helps construct, produce and maintain it. Anthropological discourse gives cultural difference (and the separation between groups of people it implies) the air of the self-evident.[87]

A knowledge of cultural difference of the Other helps those in dominant groups to classify and manage subordinate groups. The eagerness with which theories of cultural difference are taken up in the justice system, while racism and sexism remain unnamed, is a reminder that culture is treacherous ground to travel in a white supremacist and patriarchal society. The two cases that follow illustrate this danger.

Culture or Racism?

Kitty Nowdlok-Reynolds and Donald Marshall

The case of Kitty Nowdlok-Reynolds, an Inuk woman brutally raped by an Inuk man, provides one example of how little culture can have to do with the way Aboriginal women who are victims of violence are treated in the justice system.[88] Following the arrest of her attacker, Kitty Nowdlok-Reynolds moved from the Northwest Territories to Vancouver, British Columbia, as she had arranged to do before her attack. The police failed to get a statement prior to her leaving and, after a series of inept police bureaucratic manoeuvres, Crown counsel sought and obtained a warrant for her arrest in order to compel her attendance in court in the Northwest Territories, two thousand miles away. The warrant was executed and Nowdlok-Reynolds was arrested and handcuffed, jailed for five days, and escorted by the police from Vancouver to Edmonton, Alberta, to Yellowknife, NWT, back to Edmonton, then to Toronto and to Ottawa, in Ontario; and finally to Iqaluit in the Northwest Territories. Uninformed of her rights, kept in five different jails, denied showers, and ultimately transported to the Iqaluit courtroom in the same vehicle as her attacker, Nowdlok-Reynolds was eventually released and arrangements were made for her to fly unescorted back to Vancouver, whereupon she was left to find her way home at one in the morning.

Kitty Nowdlok-Reynolds filed a complaint against the Royal Canadian Mounted Police and an RCMP Public Complaints Commission was established to hear her grievance. As the commissioners appointed to hear her complaint concluded, Kitty Nowdlok-Reynolds was the victim of a brutal rape and the victim of the criminal justice system: We 'may be pardoned,' they opined, 'for wondering which victimizing incident had the greater effect, the sexual attack on June 7, 1990 or the treatment accorded to her by the criminal justice system.'[89] The commissioners noted the practices and policies of the criminal justice system that focus on the accused and fail to respond to the needs and rights of the victims. They also identified bureaucratic and individual incompetence. As at no time could it be clearly established that the police were overtly racist or sexist, the commissioners did not acknowledge that racism was an important factor in how Kitty Nowdlok-Reynolds was treated.[90] In response to Nowdlok-Reynolds's assessment that at least one constable exhibited a prejudicial attitude to her because she was Inuk, the commissioners suggested that all new police recruits receive cross-cultural training. The report does not consider what it was that enable police officers to exhibit the callousness they did to an Aboriginal victim of a brutal rape. Such a question would have required the commissioners to delve deeper into the social context of Aboriginal-white relations in order to reveal how racism produced responses to Kitty Nowdlok-Reynolds. Yet, even if the question of what causes such callousness cannot be answered, we must at least ask what sustains it. Either we conclude that police are generally insensitive to this degree (for the commissioners clearly established police insensitivity) or we face the fact that together Kitty Nowdlok-Reynolds's race and gender produced specific police responses. A knowledge of Inuit culture, even knowledge that took into account gender, would hardly have altered these responses to her. What would have dislodged the squaw stereotype that must have surely influenced how Nowdlok-Reynolds was treated?

In an altogether different region of Canada, the East Coast, when it was established that Donald Marshall, a Mi'kmaq, was imprisoned for eleven years for a murder he did not commit, an inquiry into the Nova Scotia justice system forced a naming of what remained unnamed in the case of Kitty Nowdlok-Reynolds: racism. Here, too, as Aboriginal and white commentators noted, the difficulties around naming and describing racism were manifest throughout the inquiry. For example, as James Youngblood 'Sakej' Henderson pointed out, 'race was perceived as an essential quality that marks a person's identity.'[91] Racism could only consist of overt, intentional acts (of which there were ample examples); systemic racism and 'the hazy line between racism and incompetence and negligence' remained unexamined as they did in the Nowdlok-Reynolds inquiry.[92] The end result, as Joy Mannette argues, was that notwithstanding testimony of an overtly racist nature from police, judges, and lawyers, Donald Marshall was deemed to have lost eleven years of his life in jail due to 'human fallibility, in the guise of individual incompetence, which caused the apparent systemic breakdown.'[93]

In the face of such a widespread denial of racism in the justice system, culture had an interesting role to play in the Marshall inquiry. Minority voices were included in the Inquiry through Aboriginal witnesses and in the form of testimony from a white psychiatrist as to what happens when Mi'kmaq people encounter the judicial process, testimony that resembled the kind of cultural information with which Ross and Chief Justice Lilles were working, namely the tendency of Aboriginal witnesses to remain aloof and uncommunicative when testifying in court.[94] Instead of helping to contextualize the responses of Aboriginal witnesses in the court. Mannette suggests that such testimony psychologized what might be better characterized as an institutional problem: Donald Marshall's cultural unease with the entire judicial process. She maintains that the distinct and non-Western configuration of Mi'kmaq society remained unacknowledged and its distinctiveness disappeared under the banner of cultural diversity: 'Mi'kmaq world view emerges in the Marshall Inquiry, then, as an excluded, not preferred interpretive framework within a dominant ethnic hegemonic order.'[95] Mannette has identified, in this argument, a major risk that is taken whenever culture and not racism becomes the focal point: the answer to the 'problem' becomes one of inclusion, most often through the device of cultural sensitivity and, by extension, cross-cultural training. At no time is the justice system examined for the ways in which it is organized to the cultural advantage of the dominant group. At no time does white domination enter the picture.

Immigrant Women

As in the case of Donald Marshall, when immigrant women plead for cultural considerations to be taken into account, they can very quickly find themselves backed into a multicultural corner. As Homi Bhabha commented (in reference to the exoneration of Clarence Thomas from the charge of sexual harassment of Anita Hill):

Suddenly, lip service is paid to the representation of the marginalized. A traditional rhetoric of cultural authenticity is produced on behalf of the 'common culture' from the very mouths of minorities. A centralizing, homogeneous mode of social authority is derived from an ever-ready reference to cultural 'otherness.'[96]

The culturalization of racism, whereby minorities are seen as culturally inferior, makes any foray into cultural difference risky. Attempts by women of colour to draw the connections between racism, sexism, and violence have sometimes floundered in the wake of these powerful currents of racism. How will the story of rape from within one's own cultural group be heard by the dominant group when, as Yasmin Jiwani concluded from her study of South Asians in the media, South Asian women, 'whether Muslim, Hindu or Sikh,' are portrayed 'as victims trapped in the patriarchal mould of the east?'[97] Muslim, Hindu, and Sikh men confirm handily the superiority of Western men (and not incidentally, the right of Western men to eradicate them in the Gulf War) in this scenario. Indeed, as Jiwani recounts, white women's responses to articles on Muslim women and the veil included the sentiment that in comparison to Eastern women, Western women should consider their own men 'as gems of enlightenment and kindness.'[98]

Culture as a defence used by men of colour has been rejected by Canadian courts, for example in *R. v. Betancur*, when the offender, of Columbian origin, attempted to argue that his cultural background explained how he might have misinterpreted the behaviour of the victim. However, Canadian judges have also accepted a cultural defence from men of a non–Anglo-Saxon background, relying in some instances on testimony from psychiatrists about the connection between rape and a 'cultural and perverse lifestyle.'[99] Judicial comments include, in *R. v. S. (D.D.)*, that a culturally based 'absolute patriarchy' explained the offender's character and tendency to dominate his wife, and, in *R. v. L. (K)*, that the accused's and the victim's South Vietnamese cultural backgrounds sanctioned 'a pathological relationship' of physical abuse by the male and acquiescence of the women.[100] Culture, when it is taken into account, usually reinforces Anglo-Saxon superiority, as when a male of Polish origin who is found guilty of sexual assault is described sympathetically by the court as being a new immigrant 'perhaps unfamiliar with Canadian social mores or the rules of social interaction.'[101]

Although women of colour, like Aboriginal women, have consistently named patriarchal violence within the context of racism and the histories of colonialism and imperialism, the second part of the message is unlikely to be heard as strongly as the first. Women of colour have often found it necessary, for instance, to distance themselves from the culturalization of violence – where violence is viewed as a cultural practice – while arguing at the same time for culturally sensitive services for women who have been victims of violence. Thus, the Coalition of Immigrant and Visible Minority Women of British Columbia states in its report to the British Columbia Task Force on Family Violence that 'no culture condones violence.'[102] African women in Toronto observe in their study that culture is a 'cocoon in which people, especially men, hide and which is used to oppress others.'[103] And, an Ontario study of the needs of culturally diverse assaulted women makes equally clear that 'contrary to the prevalent stereotypes about the cultural acceptance of violence against women in non-Western countries, there is no tolerance for violence anywhere.' This study also affirms unequivocally that

[t]he contexts in which women experience abuse by their partners must be taken into account if abuse is to be understood and adequate services provided. Women's experiences in their home countries, their approach to community, their encounter with racism, sexism, and classism in the dominant culture, are part of these contexts.[104]

Immigrant women have described two key problems around their recovery from violence: inequality of access to services that assist survivors of violence and provision of services that are suitable for only meeting the needs of Anglo-Saxon or French-Canadian women.[105] From this point of departure, cross-cultural service delivery becomes the goal for service providers of the dominant groups. Yet rarely is it noted that majority group members usually know very little about the impact of racism on the lives of the racialized women they serve. For instance, one handbook for service providers working with immigrant women includes a chapter on culture that begins with the notion that 'it is just a gap in aware-ness that we need to fill in order to improve the quality of our service.'[106] Although racism is mentioned and the author cautions that ethnocultural factors should not be confused with broader societal factors, the practical steps she suggests to improve cross-cultural service delivery emphasize learning about behavioural differences such as eye contact and a variety of 'cultural cues' that identify a person's cultural identity. Culture is once again taken to encompass a specific set of readily identifiable values, practices, and responses that characterize all the members of a particu-lar group. More important, broad generalizations about various cultures (non-rational, stress on spiritual grace rather than material comfort, etc.) reveal an enormous potential to stereotype and rank cultures according to racist assumptions. The popularity of cross-cultural awareness sessions, in which service providers of the dominant group learn about cultural cues from charts that categorize the values of various cultures, indicate that little has shifted in terms of who provides service. Immigrant women's demands for equality of access are being reduced to a smattering of stereo-types acquired by white service providers and legal professionals in the name of cross-cultural sensitivity.

Culture as an Oppositional Weapon

The risks of talking culture are immense. What is too easily denied and suppressed in this discussion is power. Reflecting on the problems of anthropologists in doing cross-cultural representation, Thomas McCarthy comments:

Good intentions and literary inventions alone cannot compensate for massive inequalities in the conditions of communications. The crisis of cross-cultural rep-resentation could be resolved in the end only through cross-cultural communi-cations that were actually, rather than virtually, decentered and multivocal, that is, only through the actual empowerment of 'others' to participate as equal part-ners in the conversation of humankind.[107]

Massive inequalities in the conditions of communications require us to pay attention, in McCarthy's words, to text consumption – that is, how texts and stories are received – as well as text production. While cultural con-siderations may be intended to promote sensitivity, dominant groups too readily adopt the cultural differences approach, relieved not to have to confront the realities of racism and sexism. The challenge is, therefore, how to reduce these massive inequalities in communication so that Aboriginal women and women of colour can speak as well as be heard as they intended, without risking further marginalization.

Cross-cultural sensitivity training will be of little use unless it is pursued in the context of the greater empowerment of the subordinate group. The project of working across cultures must, for a start, include an acknowledgment of contemporary relations of domination and how they are lived. For example, the cross-cultural training endorsed by the Aboriginal Justice Inquiry of Manitoba includes not only matters relating to Aboriginal culture but also issues of discrimination and profiles of the enormous socioeconomic injustice that is contemporary Aboriginal reality. More important, this cross-cultural training is pursued alongside of self-determination and the creation of a separate Aboriginal justice system. For our part, immigrant women such as myself, who are not faced with the issues of land claims and sovereignty, must watch out instead for the ethnicization of our concerns. Legal professionals and service providers must come from our own communities. While it may be worthwhile to communicate cultural differences to members of the dominant group, we also ought never to forget how rooted such differences are in our histories of racial oppression. In exploring what Euro-American nurses need to know about their African-American clients, Evelyn L. Barbee suggests that a priority has to be understanding 'the consequences of Euro-American patriarchy' and the role that racism plays in supporting the abuse. Specifically, she cites Jo-Ellen Asbury's six factors that influence a battered African-American woman seeking help: (1) the number of shelters available in African-American communities; (2) the amount and nature of friend and family support systems; (3) social isolation experienced in a society dominated by Euro-Americans; (4) reluctance to expose an African-American man as a batterer because he is more vulnerable than a white man; (5) internalized media-stereotypes of African-American women; and (6) concern for endangering her relationship when there are so few African-American men available.[108]

Cultural considerations might be effectively deployed if they remain grounded in the realities of domination. In the courtroom, the cultural background of Aboriginal women and women of colour can be used to explain the structural constraints of our lives. For example, in seeking to have the court admit an anthropologist as an expert on Aboriginal culture in the rape trial of Bishop Hubert Patrick O'Connor (accused of raping several of his female Aboriginal pupils, four of whom appeared at the trial), the Crown prosecutor argued as follows:

Dr. Van Dyke is simply going to tell us, tell the court, something about general widely applicable attributes of, we call it not necessarily Native culture, but traditional culture. The witnesses are going to say, they're not going to say, 'I came from a traditional culture'; they're going to tell the court, 'When I came to school I didn't speak English, and this is what happened to me and this is how I dressed differently and I ate different food … ' Dr. Van Dyke is going to say that that creates a certain relationship between the dominant culture and the subordinate culture, and whether that's of any value to the court or not is for the court, my lord.[109]

It will not be easy, however, to talk about culture and domination in the same breath. In the trial above, the judge raised a host of objections to such testimony, which we might expect. Displaying some irritation that the expert would in fact be telling the court what to think and how to assess the evidence, Mr Justice Thackray wondered how he could be expected to move from generalizations about Aboriginal communities to the specific complainant.[110] He also complained about the impending prospect of being given a seminar on social issues in a forum in which one was not appropriate.[111] Finally, the charges against Bishop O'Connor were stayed after the Crown failed to comply with earlier orders to disclose to the defence the notes and tapes of interviews with the four complainants and the files of therapists and other medical personnel. The Crown's appeal of the decision to stay charges brought to the fore the issue of access to women's confidential medical records, residential school records, and a wide range of other records. Groups representing Aboriginal women and women with disabilities, the Women's Legal Education and Action Fund, and the Canadian Mental Health Association were granted intervenor status in the case and argued that mandatory disclosure of private communications with medical professionals would have the effect of deterring victims of sexual assault from pressing criminal charges, seeking treatment, finding treatment from providers who are reluctant to have their records subpoenaed, and so on.[112]

To fully contextualize the lives of women and children who are sexually assaulted, feminists working in law take a risk that information is likely to be used against women and children as much as for them. In talking about culture and domination, therefore, while we will have to stand on firm ground and stay away from broad unsubstantiated generalizations about cultural values and practices, we will also have to be careful in how we choose to describe specific practices of domination against Aboriginal women and women of colour. There can be no casual, unreflective use of culture in the courts.

4

Policing the Borders of Nation: The Imperial Gaze in Gender Persecution Cases

My project is an effort to avert the critical gaze from the racial object to the racial subject; from the described and imagined to the describers and imaginers; from the serving to the served.

Toni Morrison, *Playing in the Dark*

Immigration cases, Deborah Cheney suggests, ought to be 'valued as accounts of how people are seen and families conceptualized.' Cheney advises us 'to see those party to the cases less as mere ciphers of legal watersheds than as individuals; to regard the tenor of reports less as objective accounts of two sides within a legally boundaried reasoned debate than as emotionally complex human beings trapped and manipulated within the pressures of a wider sociopolitical framework.'[1] Applying Cheney's perspective to refugee cases, I would begin by noting that in the First World, the refugee hearing is a profoundly racialized[2] event. That is, implicitly or explicitly, race is central to how decisions are made. Border control is, in the wider sociopolitical framework Cheney alludes to, an encounter between the powerful and the powerless, and the powerful are always from the First World and mostly white, while the powerless are from the Third World[3] and nearly always racialized or ethnicized.

In this chapter, my exploration of border control is largely focused on racial subjects, rather than racial objects, on the decision makers in immigration hearings, on lawyers, on legislators, on journalists – in short, those elites who are, to use Morrison's words, the describers and the imaginers whose gazes construct asylum seekers from the Third World either as unworthy claimants or as supplicants begging to be saved from the tyranny of their own cultures, communities, and men. Related in central ways to the previous chapter's imperialist, who as a knowledgeable patriarch felt able to thread his or her way through the maze of cultural differences, the imperialist as saviour, in various gendered forms, is further discussed in this chapter.

In the Canadian context, the imperialist as saviour of Third World peoples is an important construct in nation building. Canadians define themselves as unimplicated in the genocide of Native peoples or the enslavement of African peoples, a position of innocence that is especially appealing because it enables Canadians to imagine themselves as distinct from Americans.[4] Canadians also mark themselves as the peacekeepers of the world, as living in a country that welcomes immigrants and as having few imperialist pretensions. As the American Aboriginal writer Elizabeth Cook-Lynn comments on this position of innocence:

A broader look at history might suggest that the idea that Indian hating was non-existent and empire building less violent in Canada than in the United States is simply a delusion of the imagination. Racism and its relationship to colonization and nation building on the North American continent seems fairly pervasive and consistent. For Stegner [the writer Wallace Stegner] to exempt his beloved Canada is a combination of compelling fantasy and bad history.[5]

The fantasy of the imperialist as saviour is, as Gayatri Spivak reminds us, a 'long-term toxic effect' of imperialism.[6]

The racial text of border control notwithstanding, the geography of race, as Michael Omi and Howard Winant note, is becoming more complex. If, as they suggest, 'the territorial reach of racial hegemony is now global,' and 'it is now possible to perpetuate racial domination without making any explicit reference to race at all,' the racial subtext of immigration and asylum laws may not be obvious at first glance.[7] This is even more the case when immigration involves women seeking refuge from the violence of patriarchal states, communities, and families. The issue of patriarchal violence seems to eclipse racial domination so that we see the former but not the latter. How is a petition for refugee status in Canada *inevitably* an encounter between the white First World and the racialized Third World, and what are the consequences of these power relations for women seeking asylum from domestic violence or oppressive social mores? These are the underlying questions in this exploration of gender persecution as the basis for women's claims for asylum.

That women can now seek asylum from gender-related persecution is perhaps one of the most remarkable achievements in Canadian legal history in this century. For the first time, it has been acknowledged that woman can be persecuted simply because they are women. In March 1993, the Canadian Immigration and Refugee Board (hereafter IRB) released the *Guidelines Issued by the Chairperson Pursuant to Section 65(3) of the Immigration Act (1993)* (hereafter *Guidelines*), reputedly the first guidelines in the world to address gender-related persecution.[8] The *Guidelines* are the culmination of intensive lobbying by women's groups and various Canadian and international efforts to address the issue of domestic violence as a form of persecution. Women fleeing severely abusive spouses, who can show that their countries of origin are unwilling or unable to protect them, can now argue that domestic violence is a form of persecution as understood in Canadian refugee law. Similarly, women living in countries where they encounter severe state-sanctioned discrimination can also make the case for persecution.[9] Canadian recognition of gender persecution represents an important moment for women worldwide. For the first time in international law, private violence against women, and the state's complicity in failing to protect them, is recognized as an injustice for which the law can offer redress. Potentially, the concept of gender persecution can be the most significant legal gain for women in this century, opening the door to the recognition that women can be persecuted as women, and that this is a violation of their human rights. There can be no doubt of the significance of such legal protection, as many legal scholars have ably analysed.[10]

Precisely because of the overall significance of recognizing gender-based persecution, it is important to track how gender-based harm becomes visible within the racial text of the refugee hearing. I want to explore in this chapter how gender persecution, as it is deployed in refugee discourse, can function as a deeply racialized concept in that it requires that Third World women speak of their realities of sexual violence outside of, and at the expense of, their realities as colonized peoples. The concept of gender persecution as it is currently understood can therefore further First World interests by obscuring Western hegemony and its destructive impact on the Third World. More important, when the histories of imperialism, colonialism, and racism are left out of sexual violence, we are unable to see how these systems of domination produce and maintain violence against women. It becomes difficult to evaluate an individual woman's chances for survival within her community when she flees from domestic violence. Emphatically I state at the outset that in recognizing the limits of how gender persecution is utilized in law, I do not suggest that we abandon it. Instead, I want to explore ways in which we might talk about women and the violence they experience in their states, families, and communities, about interlocking systems of oppression, and specifically, about the ways in which there is First World complicity in both the sexual and racial persecution of Third World women.

We must talk about First World complicity if the lives of refugees are to make any sense to us as Western feminists; that is, if we are to make any sense of the interlocking systems of patriarchy, white supremacy and capitalism that produce refugees. By complicity, I mean the West's implication in the contemporary patterns of global economic exploitation and the political contexts that produce the world's refugees. From imperialism and colonialism to neocolonial dominance, the West is thoroughly implicated in the production of the world's refugees. A. Sivanandan partially describes this circle when he comments:

The governments of the Third World are not self-governing any more, if they ever were. Their regimes are not regimes chosen by the people. And yet they stay in power, because they open up their countries to western investments, provide markets for western goods and services, a dumping place for western waste, a venue for western charity. And what this means for Third World countries is ecological devastation, population displacement and poverty. Poverty creates political strife and political repression and political repression creates political refugees.[11]

Behind the economic patterns Sivanandan describes, the West is also implicated in the production of a discursive apparatus that entrenches notions of Western superiority and Third World inferiority. Edward Said, perhaps more than any other scholar, describes the cultural and knowledge production that accompanies imperialism, colonialism, and racism. Over the course of several centuries, the West has represented itself as a civilized, rational, scientific, culturally and morally superior entity in relation to the East, while the East has been depicted as uncivilized, irrational, unscientific, culturally inferior, and immoral. Said describes this discursive production as orientalism, and he traces its endurance in Western cultural and scholarly production.[12] It is through such images that, in the refugee context, when people of the Third World come knocking on our doors, we are able to view them as supplicants asking to be relieved of the disorder of their world and to be admitted to the rational calm of ours. In this way racialized distinctions underpin the deceptively ordinary and outwardly compassionate process of granting asylum.

Racialized knowledge production, that is, the plethora of images and texts establishing First World superiority, is integral to what constitutes knowledge in refugee discourse. As Goldberg has argued, 'racialized power is primarily conceived through conceptual orders like the Primitive, the Third World, and the Underclass ... [P]ower is here expressed, managed, and extended in and through representing racial Others to themselves and the world.'[13] From anthropologists who produced the knowledge about 'primitive' cultures that enabled colonizers to justify their colonial projects in the nineteenth century, to present-day social scientists who prescribe Western models of state formation and economic development for the Third World, the West has produced, under apparently neutral scientific categories, the mechanisms for domination. Goldberg writes that 'social science of the Other establishes the limits of knowledge about the Other, for the Other is just what racialized social science knows. It knows what is best for the Other – existentially, politically, economically, culturally.'[14] The West knows the Third World as underdeveloped states that require Western expertise and aide, the more so when, unable to manage its own affairs, the Third World erupts and produces the displacement of large numbers of peoples. Refugees, the outcome of Third World barbarity and underdevelopment, are known to the West only in terms of how they might be contained, policed, and regulated. In a familiar inversion of reality, refugees are understood as the products of a mess that the Third World has made and that the West must clean up.

Acknowledging Western hegemony and the enduring regulatory power of racist discourse, I begin with an interrogation into the Eurocentrism of Western feminist interventions in refugee discourse. Part one is a discussion of the subject of gender persecution: 'Who is the subject in Western feminist theory?' and, subsequently, 'Who is the subject in the burgeoning legal scholarship on gender persecution?' I suggest that the binary of the civilized West/the uncivilized East characterizes most feminist and legal discourse about gender persecution. I then turn to examples of the operation of the concept of gender persecution in cases brought before the IRB. The cases I will discuss involve survivors of domestic violence and women who have transgressed the social mores or laws of their country and who find themselves at risk of having their human rights violated, in particular women whose security of the person is under attack or has been attacked. I suggest that women's claims are most likely to succeed when they present themselves as victims of dysfunctional, exceptionally patriarchal cultures and states. The successful asylum seeker must cast herself as a cultural Other, that is, as someone fleeing from a more primitive culture. That is to say, it is through various orientalist and imperialist lenses that women's gender-based persecution becomes visible in the

West. Without the imperial or colonial component, claims of gender persecution are less likely to succeed and asylum is denied. I consider how we might move towards First World accountability when we consider refugee women's experiences, and how we may avoid requiring women to separate their gender from all other aspects of their being. I refer in this chapter to imperial[15] stories and gender stories, tracing how the two combine to result in the erasure of the experiences of many racialized women seeking asylum.

Gender Persecution: Who Is the Subject?

In a trenchant critique of testimonial literature, Robert Carr persuasively argues that First World–Third World relations infuse and structure the texts of women of the South whose narratives are marketed for consumption in the North.[16] Carr selects as an example of the commodification of the experience of Third World women, the construction and presentation of the story of Guatemalan Aboriginal activist and Nobel Peace Prize winner Rigoberta Menchú. The book *I, Rigoberta Menchú* is Menchú's testimonial as introduced and framed by the anthropologist Elizabeth Burgos-Debray. Carr shows how Menchú is constructed in Burgos-Debray's text as 'the symbol of all indigenous people, dead and alive, throughout the Americas.'[17] As a universal symbol, Menchú is invoked to express the idea of a universal sisterhood. For example, at one point in the book, Burgos-Debray describes Menchú cooking in the Paris apartment where her testimonial is being recorded by Burgos-Debray. The meal of tortillas and black beans, which they both like, is a symbol of their common humanity and sisterhood to Burgos-Debray. Carr notes that labour exploitation, guerrilla warfare, and genocide, the very conditions that gave birth to the activist that is Rigoberta Menchú, neatly disappear in this image of global sisterhood and solidarity. Finally, Carr makes the important point that sisterhood and solidarity expressed in the trope 'they are like us' can easily slide into 'they want what we have.' Sisterhood and solidarity can backfire as a device for attracting political support because the recognition of commonness makes it easier to imagine that individuals are not fleeing persecution, genocide, and war as much as they are simply seeking a better material life.

The analytical move in Western feminism that ultimately produced the concept of gender persecution utilizes a universal woman, and a similar erasure of histories of genocide and exploitation has sometimes ensued. For the most part, this erasure has been accomplished by the narrative of violence against women. When Western feminists speak about prostitution, pornography, mass rapes, domestic violence, dowry burnings, and genital mutilation, they have often done so using the universal 'we.' In doing so, differences between women of the North and South have almost entirely disappeared. The multiple sources of sexualized violence remain uninterrogated as do the many ways in which women are complicitous in oppressing other women.

'Women's rights as human rights' represents the apotheosis of what has been called dehistoricized and deterritorialized 'mappings of Otherized communities and their worlds.'[18] As a formula, it can be simplistic or complex, but in either case, what is difficult to introduce into 'women's rights as human rights' is the notion of First World domination. At its simplest, women's rights as human rights begins with the logic of Joanna Kerr's introduction to the collection *Ours by Right: Women's Rights as Human Rights*:

Violence against women is the most pervasive abuse of human rights. It exists in various forms in everyday life in all societies. In Mexico, a woman is raped every nine minutes. An estimated 1000 women are burned alive each year in dowry-related incidents in the state of Gujarat alone, in India. One in ten Canadian women is abused or battered by their husbands or partners. The world must recognize that the protection of women's bodies and identities in not a privilege, but a right.[19]

A more nuanced analysis emerges when Charlotte Bunch argues for women's rights as human rights. Anticipating the criticism that a focus on what men do to women will eclipse what the United States does to the South, Bunch is emphatic that a concern about violence against women not be used as an excuse for the United States to avoid its obligations around socioeconomic rights.[20] Nonetheless, Bunch pursues an understanding of violence that is itself likely to lead to a de-emphasis on socioeconomic factors when she stresses that when 'you look at women's lives, what is very clear is that the private sphere is where much of the violation of women's rights occurs.' Although this is followed by the conclusion that the 'separation of the private from the public is simply not viable,'[21] like Burgos-Debray's analysis of Rigoberta Menchú's life, this analysis can easily mask the difference that genocide, the repressive regulations of the International Monetary Fund (IMF), or an American embargo (all public sphere activities) make in the lives of Third World women, thus begging the question, 'When and for whom is it advantageous to stress the private sphere over the public?' which isolates women from the politics of nations.

When advocates of women's rights as human rights mention structural economic conditions, the strategy proposed is often to pursue
equality between men and women. Thus Rebecca Cook reports that the
participants to a human rights consultation on women concluded that

the first step to rethinking human rights with reference to structural adjustment
is to recognize the double injury it causes women. Once recognized, this injury
can be addressed in a number of fora in the international system. An additional
approach is to confront the financial institutions themselves. As international
actors, the World Bank and the IMF are bound by international law, including
human rights norms, and therefore are legally obligated to ensure that women
share equally with men in the benefits of their loans.[22]

Gender inequality replaces First World–Third World relations in this
approach, if not by design then by impact. It is not the conditions of the
loans themselves, but how they affect men and women differently that
becomes the focus. It is important to note, however, that it is possible to
utilize the idea of gender inequality to launch a full-scale protest of debt
repayment. Indeed, many Caribbean feminists have done just that by referring to the double burden imposed on women *and* to the destructive impact of Western economic domination on their societies.[23]

For scholars taking on the issue of violence against women as a priority,
most notably Catharine MacKinnon, there has also been a de-emphasis
on First World and white complicity. MacKinnon is more explicit than
Bunch about how women's subordination is accomplished in both the
public and the private sphere. And her most remarkable contribution is
to stress, with considerable clarity and passion, the complicity of the state
in failing to protect women from violations that occur in both the private
and the public sphere. But for MacKinnon, as Martha Mahoney, Erin
Edmonds, and others have noted,[24] gender is what is done to women,
and the list of what is done centres on sexual exploitation. Thus 'women's
situation combines unequal pay with allocation to discredited work, sexual targeting for rape, domestic battering, sexual abuse as children, and
systematic sexual harassment; depersonalization, demeaned physical characteristics, use in denigrating entertainment, deprivation of reproductive
control, and forced prostitution.'[25] Pornography and rape play central roles
in this constellation of wrongs, enabling MacKinnon to suggest elsewhere
that 'pornography emerges as a tool of genocide' in Bosnia.[26] What remains undertheorized is how many of these wrongs work in concert with
other systems of oppression, systems that benefit some women at the ex-

pense of others. For example, how do multinationals, all based in the Third World, rely on a racial and gendered division of the labour market and how is this wrong inextricably linked to the standard of living enjoyed by elite men and women in North America and Europe?

Given their emphasis on sexual violence, MacKinnon and Bunch have advocated that rape, domestic battering, and pornography be considered torture and hence a violation of human rights.[27] By redefining sexual violence as torture, domestic violence against women becomes public, which applies pressure on states to prosecute perpetrators. Arguing as I have above that Western feminists such as MacKinnon and Bunch pay little attention to transnational power relations, Vasuki Nesiah has suggested that the universal woman of Western feminism needs the Third World woman as a necessary backdrop. This symbiotic relationship is evident in MacKinnon's discussion of violence against women as a form of torture. As Nesiah argues,

By invoking the international community of women, MacKinnon is able to juxtapose highly detailed examples of violence against women in the 'First World' against examples of torture from the 'Third World.' She thereby highlights the brutality of 'First World' against examples of torture from the 'Third World' ... 'Third World' women are pulled into the transnational community of women only so they can provide the harsh backdrop of torture for someone else's agenda.[28]

If private violence against women becomes the paramount international human rights issue, then we might expect that the Third World woman continues to play the same role in legal scholarship as she does in Western feminist theory – that is, she remains the necessary backdrop that makes the case *simultaneously* for a universal woman and a superior West. The Third World woman, now defined as a woman who encounters sexual violence, can then be saved by the West. Asylum claims on the basis of gender persecution is the terrain on which we see these imperial relations shaped through Western feminism.

Not surprisingly, then, those legal scholars and activists who pursue the path of gender persecution direct their attention to non-Western societies, expressing great concern for those women who are caught in the barbaric hold of their cultures and religions. In his early article on sex-based persecution as a ground for asylum, David Neal articulated this concern succinctly: 'While the third world is not alone in failing to accord women sufficient protection, the social relations of many third world nations are still dominated by religious, tribal, or societal customs which accommodate, if not sanction, the persecution of women.'[29] The duality of backward Third World nations, and by relation civilized First World ones, is, in fact, so conspicuously present in legal scholarship supporting gender persecution that it is difficult to think of many scholars working on immigration and refugee issues whose work escapes this hierarchy of nations and cultures. For example, Neal, Karen Bower, and Linda Cipriani make central the 'problem' of oppressive Islamic states.[30] Neal calls abuses within Islam 'the most conspicuous in contemporary time,' a statement he later qualifies in a footnote where he mentions that 'the identification with Islam in this note is in no way intended to isolate it.' Acknowledging that nearly every religious tradition oppresses women, that Islam is not a monolithic faith, and that it has other progressive laws, Neal suggests that Islam none the less provides 'the most graphic and current example for the Western reader.'[31] Cipriani is equally clear that institutionalized misogyny is most severe in Islamic countries, but notes 'similar conditions exist in India under the Hindu religion, in Africa under tribal laws, and in Latin America under the tradition of *machismo*.'[32] Bower relies on examples of gender persecution from Latin America, Africa, India, Pakistan, and the Arab world, pausing in particular, as many other North American scholars have done, to offer explicit details about the practice of genital mutilation.

Seen as an outstanding example of Third World barbarity, female genital mutilation (FGM) has attracted disproportionate attention from North American scholars.[33] Few of these scholars have heeded Isabelle Gunning's advice for achieving a respectful First World–Third World dialogue. Gunning suggests that any feminist analysis in the area of international human rights begin with: '1) seeing oneself in historical context; 2) seeing oneself as the "other" might see you; and 3) seeing the "other" within her own cultural context.'[34] Instead, as Karen Engle concludes in reviewing how women's human rights advocates have taken up the issue of FGM, what most feminist positions share on this issue is a failure to engage Third World women as subjects. Western feminists have imagined Exotic Other Females in need of their benevolent protection.[35]

In seeking to protect African women from FGM, Western scholars have contributed to the policing of immigrants and refugees in North America and in Europe and to the representation of these groups as invading or polluting the North. While early articles unabashedly depicted African women as superstitious, childlike, and victimized by their cultures, later articles have displayed more subtlety and the attention has shifted to African women seeking sanctuary in the North. The concern has become how to prevent the importation of customs and rituals from the South that might 'take root'[36] or 'spread'[37] when people of the South migrate to the North. This language bears an uncomfortable similarity to the language around AIDS. As Simon Watney has written in his analysis of newspaper coverage of AIDS, the 'situation in "Africa" is offered as a premonitory image of "our" future in Europe and the United States, as planes fly out carrying away "the seeds of infection to be planted on foreign soil."'[38] Scholarly descriptions of FGM are usually offered in graphic detail accompanied by documentation that FGM is culturally sanctioned. In comparison, African women's own efforts to eradicate the practice are seldom reported in detail. In this respect, the analysis in a brief prepared by African, Middle Eastern, and Asian Canadians working to prevent FGM in Canada differs considerably from white feminist interventions of the same kind in that these Canadian feminists of colour make repeated comparisons between FGM and practices in the West such as voluntary vagino-plasty, surgery advocated in some Western women's magazines to improve the sexual pleasure of men. When advocating the legal proscription of FGM in the West, Canadian feminists of colour have taken pains to stress the vulnerability of immigrant families and to find ways to penalize the surgeons who perform FGM without penalizing the families who procure it for their daughters.[39]

The concept of gender-based persecution has thrived, and continues to do so, in the fertile environment of imperialism, colonialism, and neocolonialism. While there are scholars who warn of the danger of decontextualizing women's lives, for example Annie Bunting who notes that the gender story is a 'partial and skewed story' when it is divorced from history and culture,[40] most do not question the grounding of the concept in a process of othering and ahistoricism. The near unanimity of legal scholarship in this respect begs the question of whether or not a focus on sexual exploitation can in fact have substance without its accompanying imperial tropes. As Mahoney has pointed out with respect to MacKinnon's work, when women are defined by what is done to them, rather than what they do as social actors, it becomes difficult to see the social construction of race and the more complex realities of who is doing what to whom.[41] In the case of gender persecution, what is difficult to see is the totality of relations in women's lives and particularly the complicity of First World men and women in sustaining these conditions. To return to Rigoberta Menchú, if her story is limited to a story of gender persecution, we need not ask questions about sustained American support of the Guatemalan military. It is difficult, however, to infuse the concept of gender persecution with a stronger historical and socioeconomic analysis, given its birth in a feminist context that has paid too little attention to Western hegemonic practices. When the concept meets up with the deeply racist discourse of border control, Western complicity in violence against women is buried even deeper. A focus on violence against women outside specific social contexts, I argue below, enabled public support for the *Guidelines*, since by giving them support, Canadians were able to feel morally superior and more civilized as the saviours of battered Third World women. In this instance, a universal definition of gender as sexual violence enables and is enabled by a racist notion of the First World helping the Third World out of barbarism and social chaos.

Gendered Imperial Stories in the Canadian Context

Refugee Discourse

On 9 March 1993, when Canada issued the *Guidelines* to assist women refugee claimants fearing gender-related persecution, public response was largely positive. As IRB Chairperson Nurjehan Mawani noted, the two aspects of the *Guidelines* that aroused the greatest public interest were the 'claims involving women who have transgressed religious laws or social mores and domestic violence.'[42] Two cases in particular caught the media's attention well before the *Guidelines* were adopted and became central to the lobbying efforts that secured legislative commitment to recognizing gender-based persecution. In the first case, an Indo-Trinidadian woman, Dularie Boodlal, who had fled from a severely abusive husband in Trinidad, claimed refugee status. Her husband had followed her to Canada, continued his abuse, and was ultimately charged and convicted in Canada of assault and uttering death threats. He was eventually returned to Trinidad from where he continued to threaten his wife by mail and telephone. Although she was found to be credible, Dularie Boodlal's claim for refugee status was initially rejected because she did not fit the definition of a Convention refugee. Her claim was subsequently rejected when she was found inadmissible under humanitarian and compassionate grounds.[43] Dularie's story was first publicized by the community newspaper *Indo Caribbean World*,[44] but she ultimately became a *cause célèbre* on the national news media. The Minister of Immigration received hundreds of faxes from individuals and women's groups, and a telephone poll conducted by the *Toronto Star* revealed that 78 per cent of callers voted for Dularie to be granted refugee status.[45] Following the media furore, the Minister lifted Dularie Boodlal's deportation order. Other similar cases involving Indo-Trinidadian women were widely discussed in the media.[46] The second case, which I discuss later, to symbolize gender persecution for Canadians was the case of Nada, a Saudi-Arabian woman harassed by Saudi authorities because she refused to wear a veil.

Oppressed Third World women, particularly the passive, downtrodden Indian woman and the veiled Muslim one, are recurring and familiar images in Canadian public discourse,[47] and it is in this context that the *Guidelines* for gender persecution were publicly understood. The *Toronto Star*, for instance, ran a typical series on 'The Third World Woman' one month before the *Guidelines* were announced. In this series, replete with large photographs of veiled Muslim women and poor South Asian women and girls shown reaching for handouts, the headlines proclaimed that Third World women were 'doomed to a life of misery';[48] were 'phantoms of the census forms' (since five Asian countries have approximately 77 million fewer females than they should have demographically);[49] and were 'sold as prostitutes each year.'[50] Although it was once mentioned that 'poverty is the great oppressor,'[51] the real culprits according to the *Toronto Star* were clearly Third World men. Thus, the headline 'Mutilation and Rape "Normal" for Girls' introduced an article on the 'deep-seated tolerance' for violence against women in African societies,[52] and the article 'The Start of a Social Revolution' profiled Indian village women who were fed up with their drunken husbands and had begun to destroy liquor shops.[53] 'Slowly, Islamic Women Trade the Veil for White Collars' described 'a small but significant minority in Arab countries' who have overcome 'male biases, societal pressures, religious taboos and legal impediments' to attain professional success.[54] These formulas, Yasmin Jiwani notes, serve to remind Western women that they are better off than their sisters in the East,[55] generally, serving to promote Western superiority. More important, within this framework, it is not possible to discuss the ravages of colonialism and neocolonialism on the economies of the South without disrupting the powerful simplicity of the colonial subtext.

The oppressed Third World woman thus easily came to mind when the *Guidelines* were proclaimed and helped secure public support. Canadian newspapers were, for the most part, in favour of the *Guidelines* and made much of the narrative that Canadians were a civilized, tolerant, and fair-minded people who extended a generous welcome to those in need. For example, Heather Bird of the *Ottawa Sun* reminded critics of the *Guidelines* that it would be 'un-Canadian' to turn back battered women, who were mainly women of colour, from Canadian shores.[56] Ironically,

the few media opponents of the new *Guidelines*, newspapers and magazines known for their right-wing views, pointed to an imperialist subtext but they did so in order to make their point about the need to restrict
entry into Canada. The *Financial Post* wrote scathingly of the white woman's
burden, which would now enable Canadians to impose their values on
other nations. The *Financial Post* argued, as did most critics of the *Guidelines*,
that half the world's women would now be let in as refugees.[57] Barbara
Amiel followed suit with her denunciation of 'Canadian-Fem cultural
imperialism.'[58] When the *Toronto Sun* rejected the *Guidelines* as yet another
loosening of the rules of entry, it heaped scorn on the suggestion of a
woman activist that the West was in fact responsible for Third World
chaos and so should accept more refugee applicants. (The *Toronto Sun* quoted
her, however, as saying that Canada should accept all refugee claimants.)[59]

If the new *Guidelines* captured the public's imagination because they
activated enduring racial stereotypes, those same imperial relations under-
pinned refugee discourse in general. The media most dramatically illustrate this with stories about the importation of Third World chaos into
the First World. Canadian politicians, in their discussions of amendments
to the *Immigration Act*, also demonstrate how deeply embedded in refugee discourse is the racist construct of the benevolent, generous First World
once again extending a helping hand to a hopelessly backward Third
World. As Teun van Dijk has shown in his examination of parliamentary
discourse on immigrants and refugees, debates in this milieu are essentially focused on control: 'how to limit influx, or who can or will be sent
back under what conditions.'[60] However, since most politicians define
themselves as tolerant and fair-minded, and as opponents of colonialism
and racism, the language of control is masked by the language of humanitarian values and economic rationalism. In an analysis of 'text and talk,'
van Dijk charts the linguistic devices, the semantic moves, and rhetorical
ploys that several European Parliaments used when they were discussing
refugees and immigrants to present the West as tolerant, humanitarian,
and civilized. Politicians often presented themselves and their countries
positively immediately prior to a negative, often subtle presentation of
the Other. The phrase 'firm but fair' was used to legitimize controls as
was the justification 'for their own good.' Politicians also justified their
restrictions by noting that relaxed controls would provoke the racist
Right and would not reflect the wishes of the people. Finally, the numbers of refugees were manipulated to convey that strong measures were
needed to keep out the hoards.

Most of van Dijk's observations of European Parliaments hold true for

Canada. In one short address to Parliament on the opening of the debates on amending the *Immigration Act*, the Minister of Employment and Immigration employed several of these rhetorical devices to introduce his speech: 'We are not going to turn away genuine refugees who are seeking asylum in this country. We are not going to do that. We are not a people who will do that. What we are trying to stop are the bogus claims that are made.' He then continued: 'Canadians have a right to know whom we are welcoming to this country on their behalf. They have a right to know who is entering their home.' The fake refugee problem then, and not Canada's inhumanity, became the justification for greater controls. As the Minister reminded his colleagues in the House of Commons, Canada 'has earned a special position in the world for our work on behalf of refugees.' Having engaged in a positive self-presentation to justify controls, the Minister then added that it was really for the refugees' own good since real refugees would be processed faster. Canadians were then described as a people able to understand the pragmatism of these controls, understanding as they do 'the integrity of an immigration program that has contributed to our sense of identity and served as a source of prosperity for more than 125 years.'[61] In this particular debate, opposition members would occasionally speak of the racist impact of the proposed immigration bill, pointing out that it did not enable Canada to claim that it was tolerant and fair, but the discussion would quickly return to talk of humanitarian ideals. This is perhaps an illustration of van Dijk's observation that a strategic appeal to shared values and principles is often how speakers secure racist effects.[62] The *Guidelines* emerged in this context, a context van Dijk describes as elite racism, a process through which political and financial elites prefigure racist constructs that later find more popular expression in sentiments such as 'immigrants are stealing jobs.'

The Guidelines

According to the United Nations *Convention and Protocol*[63] relating to refugees, a refugee is defined as a person seeking sanctuary from persecution based on race, religion, nationality, membership in a particular social group, or political opinion. Gender is not one of these five enumerated grounds, the only conditions under which claims for asylum can be made. Canada's *Immigration Act* relies on the U.N. *Convention and Protocol*. Rather than explicitly adding gender to the list of enumerated grounds (reasons for persecution), the Canadian government chose to develop a series of *Guidelines* to the *Immigration Act* which would enable the Immigration and Refugee Board to take gender into account when hearing refugee claims on the basis of the five grounds.

The *Guidelines* are based on the idea that women refugees often have difficulty linking their gender-based persecution to one of the five enumerated grounds. For example, violence against women was seldom understood as persecution based on one of the five grounds. The *Guidelines* sought to remedy this difficulty by spelling out how the link could be made by the IRB between gender-based persecution and one or more of the five grounds. They make explicit that women who fear persecution because of the status, activities, or views of their spouses, parents, siblings or family members must be considered to have suffered persecution. Likewise, women who endure severe discrimination and acts of violence based on gender, either from the state or private citizens, and women who fear persecution as a consequence of such discriminatory laws and social practices are also considered refugees.

In sum, the *Guidelines* spell out that the persecution women endure because they are women must be considered at each stage of adjudication of their claims for asylum. The adjudication process normally includes the assessment of the particular circumstances of the claim, the general conditions of the claimant's country of origin, the seriousness of the treatment the claimant fears, the relationship between a claimant's fear and one of the five grounds, the degree of state protection available, and the possibility of an internal flight alternative.

Feminist activists and legal practitioners in the field of refugee issues have expressed concern primarily around three areas: the hearing itself; the research available on gender-specific country conditions; and the issues surrounding disclosure of sexual violence. For example, a consultation on refugee women claimants organized by the Table de Concertation de Montréal pour les Réfugiés[64] shortly after the *Guidelines* were proclaimed concluded, as did James Hathaway in his official review of information gathering at the IRB of Canada[65] several months later, that IRB panels were not always respectful towards claimants, Refugee Hearing Officers who assisted members were often adversarial by cross-examining the claimant, and most parties operated with skeletal information about country conditions. Better research gathering and educational sessions were proposed as solutions for panel members (for example, about issues of gender and culture).[66] As I suggest below, it is not primarily cultural information of which panels are most in need, but analytical tools and information about a country's socioeconomic conditions that would enable a more thorough evaluation of the potential of an individual claimant to protect herself from her abuser.

In November 1996, the *Guidelines* were revised to clarify and strengthen the principle that adjudicating gender-persecution claims requires making the links between a woman's gender, the feared persecution, and one or more of the enumerated grounds for persecution.[67] The amended *Guidelines* also clarify that sexual violence in the context of civil war must be recognized and that women in these situations as well as in others where there is state-sanctioned discrimination against women, may encounter special evidentiary problems that must be taken into account when assessing their claims. Perhaps in response to the floodgates argument, that is, the fear that there will be too many gender persecution claims, the new *Guidelines* note that a claim cannot be accepted simply because a woman objects to the laws discriminating against women, nor, however, can it be automatically rejected because all women in a country undergo the same discrimination. As we see below, the problem in distinguishing between when women are simply having a very hard life and when they are being persecuted can often only be solved with recourse to cultural othering. We know a woman is persecuted if the context is one in which we can see ourselves as saving her from a dysfunctional, overly patriarchal state.

Exploring the Tension between Race and Gender

Indisputably, the *Guidelines* have enabled acknowledgment of sexual violence and abuse as persecution.[68] Claimants such as V, an Indigenous woman from Ecuador whose claim was dismissed in November 1992, succeeded under the *Guidelines* when her case was referred back for rehearing in 1993. In V's case, the pre-*Guidelines* IRB panel accepted that V was the victim of her husband's severe violence and that she had sought police protection that failed to stop the violence. V was persecuted, in the panel's view, but not on the basis of her gender or on any of the five enumerated grounds. Rather, she was persecuted because her husband felt he owned her and could do what he liked with her. V therefore could not establish a connection between her persecution and her gender; she could only establish a difficult personal situation.[69] In marked contrast, in January 1994, a second panel ruled that V could stay in Canada and that no internal flight alternative existed for her due to her husband's extensive networks and connections. The fact that V is an Indigenous woman is noted in this second decision as further evidence that, as a member of a group whose social origins place her at risk, she would find it difficult to survive economically in Ecuador if she had to flee to a region in which she had few familial connections.[70] Similarly, in June 1994, a panel concluded that an Ecuadorean woman who had endured several years of domestic abuse and who had repeatedly sought police protection was a Convention refugee.[71] Describing the absence of social and legal condemnation of domestic violence, the panel noted at length, in an argument reminiscent of MacKinnon and Bunch, that documentary evidence

makes it abundantly clear that the government of Ecuador is unwilling to protect the rights of women who are subject to domestic abuse. They have to endure the trauma of violence in silence while the enforcing authority of the state does nothing in their defence, and regards such abuses as domestic issues. This culture of tolerance has been built up over the years and forms part of the ethic of Ecuadorean society. The question is whether the violence endured by these women in appropriate cases should be regarded as persecution. There is a vast difference between a matrimonial home and a torture chamber. If a wife is subjected to violence repeatedly then in our assessment, she stands in no different situation than a person who has been arrested, detained and beaten on a number of occasions because of his political opinion ... Until penal measures are effectively implemented to punish those guilty of wife abuse, the situation of abused women will continue. Social organizations and womens' [sic] committees merely provide solace to those who suffer. They do not mete out sanction to wife abusers for their inhumanity towards their spouses.[72]

These two decisions exemplify the most straightforward route to granting asylum for women who are victims of domestic violence. State, community, and family protection are each assessed and found inadequate to protect these specific claimants. For example, after V had divorced her husband, her brother who tried to help her was also beaten up by V's husband, and the police ignored his complaints. There is no attempt to demonize the Ecuadorean state or culture except to trace the difficulties encountered by the claimant and to note a general tolerance for violence against women. To critics who anticipate that thousands of abused women will now beset Canada's borders, the *Guidelines* reinforce, as David Neal and many other scholars have argued, that asylum is deliberately an individual remedy.[73] Political conditions prevailing in the country play an evidentiary role but are not intended to be determinative in and of themselves. Thus, the task of the hearing is to determine the vulnerability of the particular woman who, as in the above cases, is well able to show the state's indifference, the absence of an internal flight alternative, and the absence of any other effective help.

The severity of the abuse, the power of the abuser, and the difficulty of internal flight enabled another claimant from Barbados to obtain asylum in January 1994.[74] In this case panel members further illustrated the strength of an individualized approach to gender persecution when they noted:

As the evidence shows, the claimant's ex-husband is an extremely abusive man who may not let the threat of legal sanctions prevent him from harming her. Moreover, the claimant, is in a specific vulnerable position, in that, [she] is a mother of four young children. This would undoubtedly restrict her mobility and hence she would not be in a position to remove herself quickly from the harm feared. The panel also considered whether the filing for divorce would remove her fear. After a careful consideration of the claimant's testimony the panel concludes that given the ex-husband's violent behaviour in the past, there is a reasonable chance that he will pursue and harm her. The only refuge the claimant has, is to remove herself from Barbados, to another country where her husband will have no physical access. It is this panel's opinion that *this claimant in her particular circumstances, because of her specific vulnerability* [panel's emphasis], cannot receive timely and adequate protection from the state from her abusive husband. This is in spite of the fact that Barbados is not a country in which domestic violence is condoned or that there is no recourse for victims of domestic violence, generally.[75]

When the specific persecution of domestic violence is taken into account in this way, that is when a woman's capacity to flee her specific abuser is assessed in light of her country's conditions, gender persecution as a construct is extremely valuable. Women whose partners possess more than usual power, for example, men who are politicians, prominent members of their communities, or have well-developed police connections, all limit the capacity of individual women to access the state's protection. This has been recognized in the cases of several women, including a Bulgarian woman whose husband held a high position in the police,[76] a Kenyan woman whose husband was influential in the government,[77] and an ethnic Somali woman living in Kenya whose husband was a powerful politician supporting the president of Kenya.[78] In these last three cases, one wonders if it is more possible to believe in a husband's unchecked political or social power when the country in question is thought to be more chaotic and sexist than countries of the West. In the case of Kenya, the panel noted the corruption of Kenyan authorities, the conflict between customary law and British-based law, and the alleged indifference of Kenyans to the brutal rape of schoolgirls in a Kenyan school.

The recognition of domestic violence as the basis of a claim for asylum, however, has not been categoric in Canada, nor has it been as straightforward as the decisions above might suggest. As the *Guidelines* indicate, domestic violence must still be tied to persecution and to an enumerated ground. Reports about a country's state and community responses to violence against women remain quite crucial in this respect. Some refugee panels have tended to view very skeletal country conditions reports as determinative and have failed to sufficiently explore the claimant's specific context. Country reports on the status of women, where such reports exist, are equivocal and seldom amount to more than a paragraph to convey how the socioeconomic conditions of the country affect women's capacity to resist violence. For example, the reports for both Jamaica and St Vincent note that while legal avenues of redress exist, and there is community activism on domestic violence, there has yet been little change – the police are reluctant to intervene and the courts are slow to prosecute.

As I show in the next section, on the whole, it has been easier for panel members and counsel to rely on these reports to deny women asylum rather than to interrogate how country conditions affect a claimant's ability to seek protection. When a claimant cannot successfully present herself as a Third World supplicant or Exotic Female Other, it is more likely that panels will accept the skeletal country reports and reach negative decisions. Making an argument around cultural dysfunction, however, requires the use of well-known stereotypes. In this respect, I suggest that, in the Canadian context, Indian and continental African women are more easily perceived as exotic victims of exceptionally patriarchal cultures than are African-Caribbean women, who are viewed as mammies and matriarchs as well as criminals and, hence, more able to survive the violence of their cultures and families. It may also be that African-Caribbean claimants are overwhelmingly from the poorer classes, while Continental African claimants are more often from the middle classes, and that it is class that accounts for a difference in how the two groups' claims are heard; but I have no statistical support for this contention. Without a better statistical profile and access to the transcripts of hearings, I can only suggest the racial narratives that shape how decision makers respond differently to various groups of asylum seekers.[79]

Indo-Caribbean Women

Prior to the *Guidelines*, some women claiming refugee status on the basis

of domestic violence were Indo-Trinidadian women who were confronted with two legal obstacles. The first was how to show membership in a
social group defined as Trinidadian-women-subject-to-abuse; the second
was to prove persecution, that is, that the abuse was sustained and life
threatening, and that the Trinidadian and Tobagonian state had failed to
protect them. Prior to the revised *Immigration Act*, claimants first had to
be found credible by an IRB tribunal before they could proceed to a full
IRB hearing.[80] When Leela Mahabir, an Indo-Trinidadian woman, made
her refugee claim in 1987, an adjudicator for the IRB tribunal found that
her story of domestic violence in rural Trinidad was credible. He accepted
her testimony that the Trinidadian police, composed largely of men of
African origin, failed to protect her, a single Indo-Trinidadian woman, primarily because of her race. The population of Trinidad is largely made
up of equal numbers of peoples of African and Asian descent. However,
until 1995 when an Indian prime minister and an Indian-dominated party
was elected, the government and much of the civil sector were African.[81]
The adjudicator ruled in her favour in spite of the *Country Reports on
Human Rights Practices* that concluded that Trinidad and Tobago did not
officially have systemic discrimination based on race.

Marcel Mayers, also a Trinidadian woman, but not identified in her
testimony as an Indo-Trinidadian woman, also claimed refugee status
on the basis of domestic violence and she, too, submitted extensive testimony of ineffective police response. As she noted in her Personal Information Form, she was largely ignored by the police who even asked her
on one occasion whether she was going to put her husband in jail for a
little slap. Mayers and her children suffered extreme domestic violence
and she went to considerable lengths to flee from her husband.[82] The events
she described all took place before Trinidad and Tobago had begun to
officially acknowledge domestic violence as a social problem, and before
its Domestic Violence Bill was proclaimed in 1991. By the time the *Guidelines* were announced, women claiming that they belonged to the group
Trinidadian-women-subject-to-abuse were on firmer ground with respect
to the definition of social group (as a result of the Federal Court decision
in *Mayers*), but, by this time, the state of Trinidad and Tobago had its
new Domestic Violence Bill and the IRB had begun to collect gender-
specific human rights country reports for Trinidad and Tobago. In the cases
below, the *Guidelines* and new 'knowledge' about the state of Trinidad and
Tobago in terms of ethnic tensions and state responses to family violence
affected how a case of gender persecution could be made. It became even

more necessary to focus on the claimant's cultural context in order to explain why she did not have access to the state's protection.

Indra's Case

At the centre of a woman's claim for refugee status on the basis of domestic violence is the story of the violence itself. In Indra's case (a pseudonym), the violence was extreme and unrelenting. As her counsel submitted:

The claimant was a victim of very severe abuse by her own family as a child and adolescent. This abuse included physical abuse (beatings, burning with hot oil, deprivation of food), psychological abuse, and sexual abuse. She ran away from home at the age of 16 and was taken in by the family of X [her husband's family] whom she married when she turned 18. When she was pregnant with their first child, her husband began to beat her and this abuse continued with increasing severity throughout her marriage.[83]

When Indra's husband left Trinidad in 1987, she found herself facing continuing abuse from his family. She fled to join him, hoping that in Canada the beatings would stop. However, they continued until neighbours called the police and the husband was charged and sentenced to fifteen days in jail. Upon his release, he beat her severely and she, fearing another reprisal if she were to call the police, fled, returning on occasion to visit their three children. More beatings followed whenever she visited until her husband indicated that he was returning to Trinidad and would leave the children with her. Before leaving, he made clear that he would 'finish' her in Trinidad. He was officially deported from Canada, although he failed to report for deportation. At the time of her hearing, Indra did not know if her husband was in Trinidad.

When Indra's claim was prepared for the IRB hearing, her counsel submitted that she was 'an unsophisticated witness with only primary education' who was considerably traumatized by the experiences she had lived through.[84] Indra was also described as 'visibly emotional whenever she was attempting to describe her fear of her ex-husband or her painful past.'[85] Linda Alcoff and Laura Gray have convincingly argued that survivors of sexual abuse are obliged to be 'intensely and explicitly emotional' in order to be believed. They note: 'If the survivor does not cry when she tells her story, she will not be believed; this is true in places as disparate as police stations and TV talk shows.'[86] Emotional disclosure serves in this way to 'establish the hierarchy between expert and survivor and to discredit survivors in a variety of ways.'[87] In the refugee hearing, I would suggest, a hierarchy is established although it is not only between expert and survivor. In Indra's case, her story had to function to establish her as a pitiable victim from the South who must be rescued by her compassionate Northern saviours.

Racial and cultural othering, as an important part of how her claim is presented, arise initially from the need for a refugee claimant to establish that she has a well-founded fear of persecution from which her own state will not or cannot protect her. The simplest and most effective means of doing so is for the claimant to present an image that recalls the old imperial notion of the barbaric and chaotic Third World and, by implication, the more civilized First World. Thus, alongside the evidence that Indra exhibited 'the classic profile of the victim of spousal abuse'[88] as documented in the First World, there had to be evidence that her situation as an Indo-Trinidadian woman was clearly due to a cultural and social context in which women of East Indian origin are, as the *Toronto Star* article so graphically put it, 'doomed to a life of misery.'

The evidence that Indra was indeed in the classic Third World woman's situation was presented with more care than one usually sees in refugee cases (owing to the extremely low legal-aid payments to counsel). Her lawyer diligently collected and carefully utilized gender-specific country information as to the situation of Indo-Trinidadian women. A senator of Indo-Trinidadian origin, for example, submitted in a letter considerable details about the status of women in East Indian families of lower economic status in rural Trinidad. The senator noted that 'women are treated like property or livestock ... incest is not uncommon – girls are property and are used as such by less principled men, particularly in poor rural areas ... Many such victims "escape" from their male relatives by running away and getting married. Their female relatives are unable to help them. Their male relatives often won't.'[89] The senator's statements were then confirmed in the IRB's own study 'Women in the Republic of Trinidad and Tobago,' in which a Caribbean scholar, Rhoda Reddock, and a senator both comment that the East Indian woman in Trinidad often finds her efforts at autonomy undermined by Indian men on whom she is often financially dependent. Hindu women in particular are identified as a group at great risk of domestic violence,[90] as are Indian women without family protection.

Ultimately, this portrait of the oppressed Hindu woman has to be connected to the state's unwillingness or inability to protect her. In Trinidad

and Tobago, the *Domestic Violence Act* was passed in July 1991 to facili-
tate the processing of protection orders in cases of spousal abuse. Indra's
counsel, relying primarily on articles in the country's tabloid newspaper,
argued that social attitudes have in fact not shifted. Trinidadian lawyers
and activists provided additional evidence that the Act resulted in the
imprisonment of only a small minority of violators of protection orders.[91]
Indra's counsel, Geraldine Sadoway, made an unusual attempt to connect Indra's situation not simply to a dysfunctional culture, but also to
the breakdown in services for battered women. However, even this less
culture-bound argument relies on the relation between the civilized First
World and the chaotic Third World, and there is little room in the schema
for acknowledging that some efforts are being made to deal with violence against women in Trinidad:

It is respectfully submitted that although the claimant continued to suffer abuse
from her husband while in Canada, she was gradually able to extricate herself from
the abusive situation *with the help of authorities and support services in Canada. It
was in Canada that she learned that men had no right to beat their wives, whereas in
Trinidad she knew that they could do so with complete impunity* [emphasis added].
Her husband's uncle was a police officer [who] used to beat his wife.[92]

To the extent that it is possible to do so, Indra's counsel attempted to situate the problem in the state as well as in the culture. In Sadoway's view,
this approach enables a woman to obtain protection at the same time that
it embarrasses the Government of Trinidad and Tobago and potentially
contributes to a reformed system.[93] The task of demonstrating the inadequacy of state services for battered women in Trinidad and Tobago is,
ironically, made considerably easier because there is an active women's
movement and activists are available to comment on the inefficacy of services.

In what other way would it be possible to speak about violence against
women in Trinidad and Tobago without invoking an imperial relation?
Trinidadian feminist activist and lawyer Roberta Clarke suggests that
while no activist would say that the situation in Trinidad and Tobago
was a good one for battered women, she is equally certain that it is no
worse than Canada's. For the individual woman confronted with an
excessively violent man, however, the law in either country is often of
little help. Indeed it often makes things worse, as Indra discovered in
Canada. Clarke suggests that feminists reframe the issue, moving from
women as victims (violence against women) to men as aggressors (vio-

lence by men). States then have to take responsibility for the many ways in which they support the production of violent men. A bill which enables women to obtain protection orders would not then be seen as the panacea, but as one element of a multipronged strategy in which the goal would be to change social structures that propel men to be violent and that condone their excesses.[94] Clarke's suggestion is a useful one for the refugee context. Individual women fleeing domestic violence still need to be able to protect their bodily integrity, but the focus can be on the patterns of violence of the man (and, of course, the state's failure to implement measures against him or for her) rather than the pathology of the woman as victim. With such a strategy, and in the absence of sufficient Third World information, we will then be able to rely on research in the North American context to discuss what we know thus far about the tendencies of abusive men. Moreover, we might also discuss how the realities of sexism combine with the realities of neocolonialism to worsen the life conditions of such women. Thus it is not simply that the debt crisis is worse for women, but that the debt crisis itself, combined with patriarchal perspectives, leaves Third World women in a no-win situation.

Pathologizing the victim is, however, a short-hand means of communicating gender-based harm and racism is a handy tool in this endeavour. Discussing the battered women's defence in North America, Elizabeth Schneider notes that when lawyers use the victimized aspects of battered women's experience, it reconfirms female incapacity.[95] In refugee hearings, both female incapacity and Third World dysfunction are reconfirmed and the cycle of imperialism continues uninterrupted. What Schneider calls 'the short-hand way to solve the problem of sex-bias,' the use of victimization, is evidently in use in the case of a young Indo-Trinidadian woman, Savi (a pseudonym), whose claim for refugee status was made on the basis that her alcoholic father severely abused her, her sisters, and her mother. In its decision, the IRB panel described the claimant as 'a diminutive 19 year old woman, an ethnic East Indian' from Trinidad who belonged to the social group 'dependent female members of an abusive father's family.' The claimant's nationality, the panel concluded, was an important factor in her claim since 'the cultural tradition of the claimant's nationality, namely East Indian, produced the dependency described in the first reason.' Thus, while the violence created 'a paralysing dependency,' her 'cultural tradition' prevented her from striking out and seeking help, which appeared to be available.[96]

If a story of cultural othering is required to save a woman from violence, there would be little cause to complain of what one scholar has described as 'fighting sexism with racism.'[97] The problem with this approach, however, is its built-in limitations. First, it will only work when the victims can access readily understood racial tropes, a difficulty I explore in regard to African-Caribbean women.[98] Second, if gender-specific country information is forthcoming at all, it is likely because the issues *are* being debated and there will thus be a fine line to draw between countries that protect and those that try and often fail. Third, there need not be any interrogation into the larger context that contributes to the breakdown in services or exacerbates the economic vulnerability of an abused woman. The light need never be shone on First World complicity. Finally, racist constructs operate on the logic that women of the Third World are to be pitied, and pity is unlikely to emerge when the women in question demonstrate that they are also strong individuals who can make decisions to flee and survive. I shall discuss these possibilities in greater detail when I turn to decisions that have denied asylum to African-Caribbean women.

African-Caribbean Women

Ingrid Harper is an African-Caribbean woman whose progress through the twin systems of asylum and landing on humanitarian and compassionate grounds reflects the difficulties women have when they cannot easily fit their gender-based realities into an imperial frame. Harper's claim for refugee status was denied at the first stage of the process when she was found not credible in 1991, prior to the introduction of the *Guidelines*. She had fled the Caribbean island of Dominica two years earlier, claiming that she suffered spousal abuse from her Rastafarian husband who had also raped her eldest daughter and burnt down her family's banana plantation. It is possible, as her counsel later speculated, that her claim would have succeeded had it been heard after the *Guidelines*. However, when the Federal Court of Canada heard her application to stay a deportation order (issued after a humanitarian and compassionate grounds review had also failed), the judge relied primarily on Dominica's country reports on violence against women. He then concluded that while mindful of the problem of domestic violence, 'I am not satisfied that Dominica is a country in which domestic violence is condoned or where there is no recourse for victims of domestic violence.'[99] The cross-country information for Dominica is essentially the same as it is for most Caribbean countries: violence against women is acknowledged as a social problem but the police are slow to charge and public attitudes have not shifted. That her situation was complicated by the alleged informal power of Rastafarians in Dominica was not taken seriously in her story since there was skeletal evidence for this, most of which was only available in newspaper clippings. These clippings allude to Rastafarian violence and lawlessness but mention in passing the government's interest in and active efforts to suppress news of the violence in the interests of tourism.[100]

Furthermore, Ingrid Harper herself was less likely than the so-called passive Indo-Caribbean claimants were to activate stereotypes of the oppressed Third World woman. Her story is one of extraordinary survival. At the time of her first claim in 1991, she had succeeded in bringing five of her six children to Canada and had taken on parental responsibilities for two grandchildren born to her oldest daughters (one of whom was raped by her father). When her children were still in Dominica, Harper supported them by sending them half the salary she earned as a babysitter ($60 per week) and, once they were in Canada, she supported all of them through a number of sales and service jobs, while also attending night school. Immediately prior to her court hearing to stay deportation, Ingrid Harper was detained and charged with simple possession of a narcotic, having been one of the passengers in a car in which the narcotic was found during a 'routine' stop by the police. It is of course speculative on my part to suggest that Harper did not succeed with her claims due to her race and her difficulties with what I have been calling the gendered imperial story. Certainly, the paucity of information about Dominica, the problems associated with Harper's claim being processed by counsel who was only familiar with her circumstances through the office files, and the pending criminal charge would not have been favourable factors. None the less, she had few attributes of the stereotypical Third World woman but some attributes associated with the stereotype of the Black woman that depicted her as a mammy and as a criminal. When her daughter later tried to claim asylum in Canada, the fact that she had been arrested in Canada for possession of a small amount of cocaine, and that she was now an adult with no formal ties to her abusive stepfather, both weighed heavily against her.[101]

In 1993, another African-Caribbean woman's claim for asylum on the basis of domestic violence failed. Irene (a pseudonym) had fled her Caribbean island home Grenada to escape her husband's repeated beatings and threats, and claimed refugee status on this basis. She obtained a divorce while in Canada in exchange for paying her husband $500. He concluded the exchange with a threat to 'get her' if she ever returned,

and he continued to make threatening calls to her in Canada. Her opening statement to the panel made clear the central part of her claim:

claimant: (cry) nobody helped me before, my people they are very chronic in
reacting to situations like these. They have been raised to ignore violence against
women. It's prevalent, prevalent all around us in my country it happens everyday, it's a fact of life. They never do anything about it, they never did, I can't rely
on them. Everybody knew about it, you can't not go in my district and not hear
about my abuse. Everybody knew about it and nobody helped me. I am afraid
to go back I really am, I really am (big cry).[102]

Apart from this early statement, the IRB panel decided that it need not
hear any more from Irene because it accepted the information she gave
in her Personal Information Form. Perhaps knowing the value of emotional disclosure, her counsel sought to have her testimony heard and
although this was accepted, the transcript revealed that the panel was
ill-disposed to hear her story. The panel focused on the issue of her seeking police protection for a criminal matter and her failure to secure the
services of a lawyer. In Irene's case, as the decision made clear, two important elements that were present in the previous cases were missing.
First, her claim could not be linked to an enumerated ground in the Convention definition. In the Trinidadian cases, all claimants were of East
Indian ethnicity (with the possible exception of Marcel Mayers) and all
stressed the implications of this ethnicity either in terms of getting state
aid or in terms of their capacity to resist the abuser. Second, very little
gender-specific country information existed for Grenada, and the Refugee Hearing Officer advised the panel that the testimony of the expert
witness, Dr Johnson, about country conditions in Grenada might not be
based on expertise. Not surprisingly, the panel concluded that 'the claimant
stands on the same footing as any other citizen of Grenada with respect
to seeking police protection from her former spouse.'[103] Although Irene's
counsel argued that the mere fact that a woman needs private counsel
before she stands a chance of having an abuser charged by the police in
Grenada is evidence of the state's failure to protect, the panel judged the
claim 'extraordinarily weak on the merits.'[104]

    Given the suppression of stories about the socioeconomic context of
an abused woman and the operation of specific stereotypes of African-
Caribbean women, it is not surprising that N's case for asylum based on
spousal abuse also failed. N filed her claim for refugee status shortly after
the *Guidelines* were announced. She was a twenty-two-year-old Grenadian

woman whose claim closely resembled Savi's (the young Indo-Trinidadian woman described above) in that both were victims of a severely abusive alcoholic father. N's father routinely beat his children, often with a machete. His last attack on N resulted in her seeking hospital treatment. N claimed that she did not call the police because her father was a policeman and furthermore the Grenadian police did not take domestic violence seriously. Whenever she could, she stayed with her sisters and when they could no longer support her, she came to Canada as a domestic worker, filing for refugee status two years later when she learned that she could do so. In the intervening time, N had a baby. The essence of N's claim was that if she were to return to Grenada, she would be obliged to live with her father for economic reasons, since jobs were very scarce and even her brother who was a qualified mechanic could not find work.

There were several facts to N's story which the panel noted strained her credibility. For example, in one incident, when she was living at home, her father demanded that she get off the phone. Since the phone was installed by N and she paid the phone bills herself, N declared to her father that she would not get off the phone. He then went off and returned with a machete with which he struck her. The panel questioned N about the fact that she had the financial resources to own a phone. N responded that she never said she owned a phone and didn't realize that she had included this detail in her Personal Information Form. Another fact was that her father was certainly not a respected policeman since he was demoted for his drinking. The panel wondered, then, whether or not the police would in fact shield him in the event that N complained. These facts notwithstanding, the official reasons that N's claim was denied relate to the Grenadian state's response to domestic violence and to the issue of N's economic vulnerability. With respect to the first, the panel cites Ingrid Harper's case and repeats it verbatim with respect to Grenada. That is, while Grenada, like Dominica, is not perfect, it 'does not turn a blind eye to violence against women.'[105] What is more significant in the panel's decision, in my view, is its conclusion that N could avail herself of an internal flight alternative and that 'employment opportunities may not be abundant [but] there is no persuasive evidence in the documentary material considered at this hearing to suggest that Grenadian women such as the claimant cannot maintain themselves in that country.'[106] This conclusion stands in marked contrast to the outcome in Savi's case where her cultural dependency was assumed to preclude internal flight. Savi asserted that without a father or husband to protect her, she would be unsafe on her own since she had no other support in her country.

N's case is similar to other African-Caribbean women's cases in which panels also relied on the court's assessment in Harper's case that Dominica is doing something about domestic violence. For example, in *A. (I.E.)*, the IRB determined that the spousal abuse of A by her husband in Jamaica did not constitute persecution because, although she reported her husband to the police on numerous occasions, she did not file a complaint because she was reluctant to send him to jail.[107] Further, there was evidence that domestic violence is not state-condoned in Jamaica. This evidence came from the U.S. Department of State's *Country Reports on Human Rights Practices*, in which Jamaica is described as a country of increasing violence against women, but also a country in which women are reluctant to bring assault charges against their partner when jail is the likely result. The report does not explore this tendency. Had it done so, it would have become clear that one important reason for not sending an abuser to jail is the loss of his income. As community worker Daphne Binns reported to researcher James Ferguson in his exploration of the impact of IMF policies on Jamaica, many women, in particular single mothers, often don't work at all in urban Jamaica and are completely dependent on men. Under the economic conditions of the debt crisis most of the poorer classes, urban or rural, do not have enough to eat.[108] Such socio-economic conditions obviously affect a woman's ability to cope with violence as they affect her community's and state's capacities. In a report on Jamaica's position on domestic violence, Women's Mediawatch[109] pointed out that while Jamaica has signalled its intention to adopt legislation on domestic violence, the country's constitution does not contain a provision on the ground of sex and, further, there is as yet no law that separates domestic violence from common assault. More important, while married women can seek an injunction, unmarried women (the majority in Jamaica) can only do so in conjunction with a claim for damages or other remedy for trespass. Such injunctions are expensive and take a very long time to process. Under these legal conditions, even middle-class women are forced to flee the country. There is only one shelter for battered women, which can only accommodate eight women at a time, and no state resources sustain it.[110] If we relentlessly rule this information out of the refugee hearing, we artificially separate the violence from its context and we are required to rely on imperial sub-texts to give the woman's case credibility. That is, we insist that a woman make the link between the violence she suffers and her cultural incapacities or those of her state. While the individual claimant's credibility obviously affects the final decision, and while women like A may not have been entirely credible, how are we to assess persecution without examining the claimant's chances for economic survival given domestic violence or her real chances of getting state help? A, for example, was a sixty-four-year-old woman with significantly reduced earning power and who had endured almost two decades of severe beatings before she fled to Canada. Her husband was a violent man who had assaulted others. The imperial subtext of the strong Black woman erased the evidence that A was a Black woman in need of asylum from a violent man.

Between October and December 1993, three more African-Caribbean women from St Vincent, Grenada, and Jamaica respectively were turned down.[111] Each case must be evaluated on its merits and it is certainly true that each one had its own specific weakness. For example, a woman abused since childhood by her father, his friends, and an unknown assailant, had a generalized fear that if she were to return to St Vincent, she would encounter the random sexual violence so common in her history.[112] The claimant had sought police assistance after one of these assaults in St Vincent and they responded by informing her that her assailant was already wanted for similar charges. She noted that when she saw her assailant three weeks later and reported it to the police, they suggested that she be more patient. The panel concluded that since the claimant was now a mature woman of thirty, and the police had previously responded, she could reasonably expect to get help in St Vincent were she to be assaulted again. Quoting *Harper* once more, the panel noted that the *Country Reports on Human Rights Practices* for St Vincent indicated that women did have some state protection when they encountered sexual violence. This logic is analogous to the decision in *K. (L.M.)*, in which a Jamaican claimant who suffered severe beatings and rape from her husband, both in public and private, and whose husband was allegedly a henchman for a major political party, was judged to have access to state services.[113] Even claimants whose abusers show unusual tenacity cannot successfully demonstrate that flight is their only option. This was the case for the Grenadian woman whose abuser was detained by police, and on release continued abusing her. She could not convince the panel that, due to the size of Grenada, her only option was to flee the country.[114]

Economic and social conditions are seldom part of the contextualizing that ought to be done in order to fully assess an individual woman's vulnerability. In its place, as I have been suggesting, a stereotypical view of the claimant's culture is often the only factor considered and where this is less easily invoked, claims for asylum are not recognized. In the next section, I explore more deeply this argument by examining cases involving Muslim women, as well as those involving women from tribal cultures little known in the West. These show once again the cultural othering that characterizes the evidence in such claims. Further, I speculate on the limits of this approach of arguing gender-based persecution.

The Role of Culture and Religion

Muslim Refugee Women

The case of Nada, the Saudi-Arabian woman whose story of harassment at the hands of Saudi authorities for her refusal to wear a veil captured the Canadian public and feminist imaginations in 1992, achieved a kind of prominence that few other cases have enjoyed, then or since. Although a few Iranian Muslim women fleeing from somewhat similar conditions gained admission to Canada in 1990 and 1991, most Muslim women's claims have been rejected on the basis that dress requirements for women are considered 'inconveniences' at best, discriminatory at worst, but do not amount to persecution.[115] IRB panels have found laws requiring women to wear veils, banning the use of make-up, or otherwise limiting women's freedom and movements 'lamentable' but not a violation of women's human rights. Indeed, in one instance, a claimant charged with violating the Islamic dress code of Iran, who received thirty-five lashes resulting in her hospitalization, received little sympathy either from the IRB or the Federal Court. This was because she was considered not to have been deprived of an inalienable human right.[116] Why this changed with Nada probably has more to do with an intense and timely feminist lobby coupled with readily accessible orientalist frames than it does with any permanent recognition of gender-based persecution in this context.

From the beginning, Nada told a story succinctly captured in the following excerpt from her hearing:

BY REFUGEE HEARING OFFICER (to person concerned)
   Q. Why didn't you wear the veil?
   A. Because I'm a feminist.

BY PRESIDING MEMBER (to interpreter)
   Q. Because?
   A. I'm a feminist.

BY PERSON CONCERNED
    I don't believe in a woman having to wear their veil. The reason has nothing to
do with Islam. All they want is ... they don't want the women to have their thought,
her own thought. Because for them this is, they would consider this like a beginning for her gaining her freedom.[117]

Nada's account of persecution described her harassment on the streets
from individual men as well as from members of the Morality Commission, who on one occasion, threatened her with a medical examination
in order to check her virginity. She also noted that as a Shiite Muslim, a
minority in Saudi Arabia, she was denied easy access to education. The
panel initially rejected her case, following precedent, on the basis that
there had been no evidence of state persecution. The decision ended
with a particularly paternalistic comment that 'the claimant, like all her
compatriots, would do well to comply with the laws of general application she criticizes.'[118] By the time Nada had launched an appeal on humanitarian and compassionate grounds to the Federal Court, the panel's
closing remarks were featured in numerous articles in the media. The
press reports headlined 'the feminist refugee' and ran pictures of veiled
women alongside articles on the status of women in Saudi Arabia.[119]
Although Nada insisted that her experience had nothing to do with Islam,
and continued to insist on this in her public interviews and in a private
communication with the author, she was mostly ignored on this point.
Ultimately, her case generated support from a wide variety of women's
and community groups, unions, and American organizations such as Middle East Watch, Equality Now, and the Association of the Bar of the City
of New York. All of these organizations championed Nada 'for her commitment to independence and equality.' Finally, the then leader of the
opposition New Democratic Party, Ed Broadbent championed her cause
in a lengthy article published in several newspapers.[120] A number of edi-
torials supported him.[121] The Minister of Citizenship and Immigration
responded to Mr Broadbent with the announcement at the end of January 1993 that Nada was granted status by ministerial discretion.
    The veil, as Homa Hoodfar notes in her research on the experiences of
Muslim women in Canadian universities, is a powerful symbol for both
the West and for Muslim societies. For Muslim societies, the veil's significance and functions have varied historically whereas for the West, the
veil has remained a static colonial image that symbolizes Western superiority over Eastern backwardness.[122] It is likely that colonial images of
Muslim women played a part in how Nada's story was heard.[123] The femi-

nist argument that severe gender discrimination such as Nada's amounted to persecution based on gender appeared to have been adopted in the new *Guidelines*. Yet, the success was provisional as the following case suggests, and serves as a reminder that relying on colonial images to prove gender-based persecution is problematic. When Muslim women attempt to contextualize their claims of persecution for Westerners, they encounter a monolithic understanding of Muslim culture and must negotiate between the dominant group's perceptions of sexism in their own cultures and the imperialist lens through which Muslim culture is viewed in the West. Since the analytical tools employed in refugee hearings seldom include a fully contextualized approach to the meaning of gender, Muslim women are likely to find that unless their story is a stereotypical one that matches prevailing conceptions of the East, they will not be given asylum.

In the 1992 case of a young Muslim woman from Yemen whose arranged marriage to a Yemeni man in Canada ended in domestic violence and divorce, orientalist responses to Islam did not suffice to make the case for asylum. Aisha (a pseudonym) was a twenty-five-year-old citizen of Yemen who spent the 1980s with her family in the United Arab Emirates, where her father held a work permit. Aisha argued that, as a divorced woman who left her husband, she was likely to be persecuted in North Yemen, the only country in which she had citizenship rights. As she put it in her Personal Information Form:

I am seeking the help of the Canadian authorities because the only country I have the definite right to return to will not protect me from our cruel social and religious culture. I am a woman, my marriage has failed, and despite the harsh treatment of my husband no one will believe that I am not at fault. My own family is likely to refuse to help me and I may be left at the mercy of Yemeni society, where I have no home, no work, and no hope of receiving any state assistance to help me resettle my life. I know that Canadian culture does its best to prevent this kind of cruelty to women and that here I could be given a safe, fresh start. I will still have to deal with virtual exclusion from my family, but I will be in a better position to heal my emotional pain if I am given shelter.[124]

In her statement, Aisha, like the many women discussed earlier who based their claim for asylum on domestic violence, begins with an old imperial trope, namely the civilized, compassionate West and the barbaric East, a trope that is sometimes successful, particularly when the context is Islam. The conditions for entry appear to require this starting point, as most lawyers realize, and this trope quickly takes us into the realm of culture and gender.

Aisha's counsel began her written submission with the argument that country conditions in North Yemen, as described in the *Country Reports on Human Rights Practices* for 1991, show that North Yemen favours a very traditional approach to the status of women. Again, the information was skeletal. For example, it was noted that North Yemen's family laws are oppressive to women and that women do not participate in the work force in the same proportions as they do in South Yemen. Since the *Country Reports* offered few details, Aisha's counsel supplemented this portrait of North Yemen with interviews by the Western journalist Laurence Deonna. Deonna published an account of her travels in Yemen in 1991 in her book *Le Yemen que j'ai vu*, in which she describes how women's activities are tightly controlled (they cannot, for instance take a taxi alone, walk easily without a male relative or eat in public with men), and especially how difficult life is for a single woman earning a living.[125] Thus far, the kind of information offered resembles most other documentation in refugee claims. Gender-specific country information is more often than not skeletal and thus routinely supplemented by Western media accounts. In Nada's case, for instance, articles from *Time* magazine and *National Geographic* on women in Saudi Arabia were introduced as evidence, sources which, as Goldberg reminds us, reinscribe the Primitive in the guise of critique.[126]

Taking exceptional care, Aisha's counsel, Constance Nakatsu, also submitted the expert evidence of a professor of Middle-Eastern studies who described generally how religion intersects with culture and how the Arab-Muslim concept of family honour refers to a tightly controlled family structure in which women's behaviour and activities are closely regulated. A second expert on culture and gender offered further contributions on how culture can be gendered in that the state reinforces those cultural norms that reflect male privilege. Counsel attempted to inform the IRB panel about 'intersection theory' in law, that is, how a woman's realities at the intersection of gender, religion, and culture combine to create a specific vulnerability. Although there was, in this case, an unusual attempt to explore the complexities of culture, tradition, and gender as they intersect, a competing orientalist analysis offered an opportunity for a much simpler argument: that the claimant's country was inherently (and irrevocably?) oppressive to women. Such a claim succeeds if it can tap into imperialist sensibilities, but fails if the imperial story is not vivid enough to enable the panel to see how a divorced woman from North Yemeni would encounter severe discrimination amounting to persecution. In this case, I would speculate, there was simply not enough of an imperial story to suffice. As it is, we have fewer images of Yemen then of other Islamic countries. Additionally, at the time Aisha's case was heard, the political winds had shifted with respect to Iran and friendlier relations ensued.

Aisha's case failed for a number of reasons. The panel member who wrote the decision is the same one who, prior to the *Guidelines*, rejected the notion of abused women as belonging to a social group (see V's case above). Using exactly the same argument as before, and simply rejecting the *Guidelines* and 'politically correct' talk about gender persecution, he rejected the counsel's argument that Aisha belongs to the social group of divorced Muslim women in North Yemen. More significant, in my view, was his underlying opinion on the severity of the discrimination, an opinion not unconnected to his expressed hostility to gender-based claims. In reasoning exactly corresponding to how women claimants from Iran were evaluated prior to Nada, he simply concluded that Aisha's life was probably going to be unpleasant in North Yemen. She might even be homeless and out on the streets, as her counsel suggested, but a gloomy future and homelessness did not amount to persecution.[127] Moreover, she could simply relocate to South Yemen.

It is speculative on my part to attribute some women's success in gaining asylum to the fact that their cultural contexts are understood by the IRB panel to be one of excessive barbarity towards women. I venture to argue along these lines because there are successful examples of cases in which arguments that turned on culture could have just as easily focused on violence perpetrated by an individual man, and on the social and economic constraints on the claimant's specific capacity to resist. For example, in the widely reported case of Khadra Farah, a Somali woman whose husband was extremely violent towards her and the children, female genital mutilation (FGM) became the focus of the case, and effectively eclipsed spousal violence.[128] Farah testified that her husband was a powerful man who was supported by a Somali law that gives fathers custody of the children in the event of divorce. Her husband had already successfully abducted her son. Farah claimed that if she and her daughter were to be returned to Somalia, her daughter would be subjected to FGM, as she herself had been at the age of eight. FGM helped, I would suggest, to transform the situation of a man oppressing a woman to the point of persecution from an ordinary case into an extraordinary one. Khadra Farah's case resembles many others in which abusive, domineering men get their way using children as a weapon, threatening, for instance, to abduct them and successfully doing so. Typically, the state was on his side; for example, the police chief was a relative. How the concept of gender persecution works is to enable us to understand this situation as one of persecution. My concerns have to do with how persecution becomes visible to us.

The decision of the IRB panel in Khadra Farah's case is respectful in that it does not capitalize entirely on FGM and the panel members do stress the other dimensions of Khadra's life, including her husband's abduction of one of the children. Yet a very long description of mutilation is quoted from the claimant's Personal Information Form and it is this, rather than her husband's violence to her, the violence of the state's laws, or even the threat to take away the children, that determines the case. The effects of this decision, as was clear from the media responses to it, was to enable the West to feel once again as the civilized, appointed saviours of more barbaric peoples. When we consider that the all-news television network CNN recently showed an FGM in progress,[129] and did so throughout an entire day, we can grasp the place that FGM has come to play in the Western psyche. Thus, the decision helps to reinforce the strong tendency within refugee law to require exotically persecuted women. It will not be of help to those women whose cases are less cinematic but who face no less severe domestic violence. It also reinforces the view that refugee law is about First World saviours and Third World supplicants. Within this framework, we cannot have an understanding of an expanded notion of gender persecution: the many sources and levels of violence in women's lives, and the layers of violence that implicate us in the West. The violence Farah suffered resembles domestic violence in Canada, and the constraints she faces, among them a Conservative Islamic government, are political rather than cultural. The extent of the violence, the abductions, the inaction of the police, and the power of Khadra Farah's husband should have sufficed to make the case of gender persecution.

The case of gender-based persecution appears to go more smoothly when the cultural context can be 'anthropologized' – that is, presented as non-Western, inferior, and unusually barbaric towards women. A Ghanaian woman who is a student in Canada and who endured the beatings of her husband, can make the case that she cannot return to Ghana when she argues that were she to do so, as her husband has demanded, she would be subject to rituals and sacrifices, including 'the searing of the body with a hot instrument.'[130] Her husband can successfully practice polygamy and so is likely not to be inclined to grant her a divorce. As the panel noted, 'it was the claimant's exposure to Canada which made her aware of her own plight.'[131] Because the Ghanaian government is on record as opposing domestic violence and severe discrimination against women, the claimant's case must also include the component of her tribal affiliation which, the panel concludes, 'expresses itself in family control' including the mutilation of the claimant's sister.[132] Similarly, W. (Z.D.), a Zimbabwean woman, argued successfully that she had been forced into a polygamous marriage with a wealthy, physically abusive contractor.[133] In a third case, W. (Y.J.), married to a highly influential and abusive man, found herself forced to wear the veil and to endure numerous beatings. Divorced by her husband, W. (Y.J.) argued that were she to return to Morocco she could be forced to remarry her husband and would in addition have her passport and her permit to work removed. The decision to grant asylum in this case was accompanied by a long elaboration on the impact of the Muslim fundamentalist movement on Moroccan women's status in law.[134] W. (Y.J.) married while she lived in Canada; therefore the marriage would be considered null and void in Morocco. The panel speculates that W. (Y.J.) would then be liable to an accusation of adultery and the 'severe penalties that such an accusation would entail.'[135]

Images of mutilation, barbaric customary rites, severe penalties for adultery, forced veiling, and polygamy are all highly powerful symbols of the barbaric East or South and, correspondingly, the civilized West or North. The cases I have examined show it is hard to imagine that a case for gender-based persecution can be sustained without some component of this form of cultural othering and inferiorizing. Ordinary cases of intolerable domestic violence in states that are as male as our own, but infinitely poorer, and where there are no readily accessible orientalist tropes, for example the Caribbean nations, tend to fail.

Tentative New Beginnings

Is there another way to justify who gets in and who does not, who is worth saving and who is not? Is there a way, as I have asked elsewhere, to work from the basis of respect rather than pity?[136] Like many others, Aisha began with an approach that was fundamentally grounded in cultural othering. This framework is a risky one for Third World women. Without sufficient evidence of the dysfunction of their cultures and states, women cannot successfully claim asylum from domestic violence or oppressive social mores. Either it is blithely assumed that their states will protect them, or that the consequences of sex discrimination do not amount to persecution. The unspoken subtext of this value judgment is that we need not grant asylum to a woman who is simply having a hard life. Moreover, the country reports that are usually available are skeletal and most will report that conditions are mixed. Refugee discourse, as I have been arguing, is one of pity and compassion. It is not one of justice and responsibility.

If we were to begin from the vantage point that Canada is a First World country, and one that is certainly not innocent in its perpetuation of Northern hegemony, our responsibility in refugee cases would be to ascertain how restricted a woman's options have become due to an infringement of her human rights. Women who encounter spousal violence often need to put considerable distance between themselves and their abusers, and even very strong legal support has often failed to stop men who are out of control. Where the social infrastructure is strained, both social and state supports will be less effective. For Indra, as her lawyer pointed out in an interview, the most that awaits her is a maximum of four months in a shelter, no employment opportunities, and no easy access to the police to enforce a protection order.[137] Indra's choices are severely constrained in a small Caribbean island in ways in which they would not be in Canada because of the difference in the geopolitics of both areas. This is also true for Ingrid and Irene, N and A.

Similarly, when women transgress the social mores (which are sometimes legally entrenched) of their countries, their transgression can be judged severely enough to deny them their human rights. In the case of Aisha, the employment situation of single women without family connections or social approval should have sufficed to make the case that her choices had become intolerably constrained as a result of her failed marriage. Here culture and the Yemeni state's complicity played a role in making her case, but successful cases ought not to require demonization of the claimant's culture and her country's political climate. It is frequently argued that more information, for example on the employment situation of single women in Yemen, would have yielded a more just result. Yet this is unlikely if the current framework prevails whereby we demand as a price of entry evidence of the most pitiable of victims. Aisha's situation was unlikely to give us the proof we desired, that she didn't simply want what we have.

My suggestion that we move away from pity and towards responsibility will be met by the floodgates argument. Opponents may argue that just about everybody will get in on these relaxed terms, and that Aisha, Ingrid, and Irene are merely queue-jumpers in the line of immigration and not *genuine* refugees. Feminist refugee lawyers have been responding to the floodgates argument by arguing that the focus in refugee cases has to remain on the individual woman and that the *Guidelines* strongly support this approach. As Sadoway puts it:

I feel very strongly that you have to continue to focus on whether or not that person is going to be protected in that situation, and will have the rights of a citizen not to be victimized by another citizen in the country, and will have the sense that she has protection in her country ... [I]f there is not very effective protection, then my argument is that her fear is well-founded of serious persecution.[138]

Effective protection, however, has to be judged in a context of responsibility and not pity. And our responsibility has to stretch wide. At the very least, we in the West cannot begin by dispensing with historical specificities and the contemporary realities of colonialism and neocolonialism. We have to push for greater acknowledgment of this context in the same breath that we push for an acknowledgment of the violence men do to women. Unless we do, we repeat the imperial story and we do not save many women in the bargain. How might this begin?

In her discussion of Chinese novelist Xiao Hong, Lydia Liu discusses the critical role that rape plays in nationalist discourse. In Chinese nationalist novels, for example, rape is used 'to represent, or more precisely, to eroticize China's own plight. Thus a raped woman comes to signify not what is done to woman but what is done to nation.'[139] Liu discusses how Hong radically subverts this trope in her own novel using women's bodily experiences of childbirth, death, disease, aging, and sexuality to provide 'the critical angle for viewing the rise and fall of the nation rather than the other way around.'[140] Liu's work suggests to me that there *is* a story of gender to tell, but it is not simply or exclusively a story of sexual violation. We are compelled to explore this broader story, tracing women's status across all dimensions if we are to subvert relations of domination, specifically imperial relations, as they play themselves out in refugee discourse.

In Aisha's case, her counsel, Constance Nakatsu, attempted to introduce intersectionality as a theory of oppression in the hope that Aisha might be assessed in a wider context. While this is a promising approach, it cannot proceed utilizing imperial tropes, however seductive these are as a shorthand means of communicating vulnerability. We can begin by acknowledging that the private violence of patriarchy is universally condoned by community and state, but it is also resisted in a variety of ways.

The task of a refugee hearing, when the issue is a claim for asylum based on domestic violence or oppressive social mores, is to determine the likelihood for the specific claimant to resist. The paths we take to evaluate this would differ. For example, in the Caribbean cases, rather than pathologizing the claimant or her culture, we would first look to the abuser and then to the possibility that neither state nor community supports would suffice to offer her protection at this specific time. If the abuser appears from the evidence to be out of control, or if community and family support are not available, then the claim should be accepted. We will need to evaluate a woman's chances of survival in her country not only in terms of fleeing from her abuser but also in terms of economic and emotional survival. If she is unlikely to find work, or if she has to relocate to an area of the country where there are limited chances for social support, then this should be a part of the assessment of persecution. In assessing economic and emotional chances for survival in a situation of abuse, we will need to turn to how race, religion, sexuality, age, and mental or physical capacity affect a specific woman's situation in her home country *given her situation of abuse*. In making this assessment, we need not freeze her into a pathological frame, but recognize instead that a full life for a woman or a man includes a life lived in community and a life lived in stages. Our inquiry should concern what her community is likely to be like for her at a specific historical moment. Expanding the boundaries of who a woman is also means expanding the boundaries of how she can be persecuted.

It will, of course, be difficult to abandon simple cultural frames and move to a broader and more generous contextualizing, given the imperial agendas of refugee hearings. At the very least we know, however, that indulging in a process of cultural othering to make the claim of gender persecution does not serve most women refugees well. Deborah Cheney, wrestling with the dilemma of having to choose in immigration cases a framework that ignores culture (for example, the assumption that the norms of mothering in the West are the same in all societies) versus one in which each society has its own culturally specific norms (but these are considered inferior in comparison with Western traditions), suggests that we work with the manner in which immigration decisions are made rather than the matter of the law, that is, with each case's specific content and process.[141] In the case of the Canadian *Guidelines* on gender persecution, the matter of the law has changed, at least at the level of guidelines, but this change does not appear to have greatly interrupted the traditional lens through which refugees are viewed. They continue to be viewed as cultural Others who, for the most part, want what we have.[142] The institutional culture of the IRB, what counts as relevant knowledge, and many structural aspects of the process sustain this perspective. To change this requires, I would suggest, an unmasking of the trope of pity and compassion and a move towards a more political understanding of why women flee and what our responsibilities are to them. They flee from domestic violence, but they also flee from the conditions that inhibit their regular means of resistance. Would this make them too obviously like us to be accepted? The real task is to critically examine our own stake in keeping them out. Can we attempt educational initiatives around this rather than around the intricacies of sharia law, customary rites, or FGM, or would the whole structure of policing borders collapse?

5

From Pity to Respect: The Ableist Gaze and the Politics of Rescue

The biggest problem that we, the disabled have is that you, the able bodied, are only comfortable when you see us as icons of pity.

Nabil Shaban, disability rights activist

I heard recently of a nine year old sterilized. It's happening mainly in institutions. I know of a mentally disabled man who was put in jail or an institution because he was accused of purse snatching. In fact, he just sideswiped the person. Things like that I'm interested in: *how the judge gets the answer* [emphasis added].

Barb Goode, activist with a developmental disability

Disability rights activist Shirley Masuda, who co-authored with Jillian Riddington the manual *Meeting Our Needs* for the DisAbled Women's Network, makes the following impassioned plea:

We are women. We are women with disabilities. We are women who are abused. We are your sisters. We are just like you. We have the same thoughts, the same feelings and the same passions as you have. Your issues are our issues, and each of our issues is also your issue. We are who you are. *We are women*.[1]

Masuda's comment can be heard as a plea to consider the interlocking systems of gender and disability as they might come together in law and in feminist politics. For a number of reasons, non-disabled feminists working in law, among whom I would count myself, have found it difficult to respond to such a plea. In the area of sexual violence, feminist law reformers have become increasingly attentive to differences among women, yet,

I would contend, we have been less than successful in interrogating just what such differences mean beyond an apparently increased vulnerability to violence. As non-disabled feminists, we do not ask often enough about those differences that confer privileges, opting instead to list those that produce disadvantage. Women from dominant groups thus fail to interrogate how our own advantages in law are produced on the backs of other women. Mary Louise Fellows and I refer to this failing as the difference impasse, an inability to confront how we are implicated in other women's lives.[2] As we wrote in an article reporting on an attempt to hold a roundtable discussion of issues in feminism and law, when feminist law reformers travel down an analytical path of compound oppression – double and triple oppression – the relations between women, and the ways in which the advantages some women enjoy come at the expense of other women, are masked.

I have found it hard to consider my own complicity with respect to women with disabilities. In this chapter, I am the imperial gazer rather than the gazed upon, the one who engages in a politics of saving other women. I am aware that I do not feel the passion that I do when what I am describing is my own daily life. The writing, as some early readers noted, has a clinical detachment to it that other chapters do not. I also do not feel *watched* and made to be accountable here, as I did in chapter 3 when I discussed the realities of Aboriginal women, another group in relation to whom I stand in a dominant position. Scholars with disabilities are, for the most part, not in the academy and I will not often run into women with disabilities when I go about the business of teaching and research. The disability rights movement has hardly entered the consciousness of non-disabled feminists. This is a material exclusion that enables the ableist gaze at the same time that the ableist gaze enables it. How do we break the cycle?

The compelling question underlying this chapter is thus: How might feminist law reform serve all women? I shall argue that feminist law reform cannot meet the needs of women with disabilities unless we, non-disabled feminists, critically examine the ableist gaze so succinctly described by Nabil Shaban. This gaze has informed feminist politics as well as the law, influencing, as activist Barbara Goode hints, how the judge gets the answer. In the previous chapter, I suggested that women asylum seekers from the Third World were often seen as deserving asylum only when they could present themselves as victims of unusually patriarchal, hence culturally inferior, states and communities. Only then could their Western adjudicators make themselves into imperial saviours. Here I want to suggest that a similar politics of rescue prevails when women with disabilities are seen as doubly or triply vulnerable, as 'icons of pity.' Pity is the emotional response to vulnerability and being saved, the only outcome. How do we move from pity to respect, where we acknowledge our complicity in oppressing others and consider how to take responsibility for the oppressive systems in which we as women are differently and hierarchically placed?

Hierarchical Relations among Women

In proposing to begin with where women stand in relation to one another, two concepts are significant: complicity and the interlocking nature of systems of domination. In chapter 4 I noted that when we as feminists engage in 'saving' other women, what we fail to consider is how we are implicated in the subordination of other women. An attention to complicity has not strongly emerged in feminism because, for the most part, we continue to avoid any inquiry into domination and our role in it when we confront issues of difference and diversity. Instead, each of us feels most safe in these discussions anchored in our subordinated position by virtue of our being of colour, disabled, economically exploited, colonized, a lesbian, or a woman. Identifying as part of a marginalized group allows each of us to avoid addressing our position within dominant groups and to maintain our innocence or belief in our non-involvement in the subordination of others. Knowing the difficulties involved in confronting our own role in systems of domination, we may find that being anchored on the margin is more preferable. Yet, if we remain anchored on the margin, the discourse with women subordinated to ourselves stops, and various moves of superiority, notably pity and cultural othering, prevail. We become unable to interrogate how multiple systems of oppression regulate our lives and unable to take effective collective action to change these systems.

Hierarchies among women are maintained in law through a number of universalizing or homogenizing tropes and explanatory frameworks. In the area of violence against women, Catharine MacKinnon argued, as early as 1981, that rape is legally defined as intercourse without consent, hence the importance in rape trials of consent and of the degree of force used. Rape is not defined as violation, a definition more in keeping with how women experience it. One important consequence of viewing rape solely through the lens of consent and force is that it becomes difficult to examine the norms against which we measure what is coercive. Hence, the woman who is coerced into saying yes because to say no would mean risking her marriage is not raped but has instead engaged in a contract. The social terms of the contract that limit her options are not subject to scrutiny. As MacKinnon saw, we sell out such women when we fail to interrogate the context in which choices are made.[3] Law divides women into those who cannot say yes and those who cannot say no. MacKinnon later elaborated on the implications of this division between women in a court of law:

All women are divided into parallel provinces, their actual consent counting to the degree that they diverge from the paradigm case in their category. Virtuous women, like young girls, are unconsenting, virginal, rapable. Unvirtuous women, like wives and prostitutes, are consenting, whores, unrapable. The age line under which girls are presumed disabled from consenting to sex, whatever they may say, rationalizes a condition of sexual coercion which women never outgrow. One day they cannot say yes, and the next day they cannot say no ... As with protective labor laws for women only, dividing and protecting the most vulnerable becomes a device for not protecting everyone who needs it and also may function to target those singled out for special abuse. Such protection has not prevented high rates of sexual abuse of children and may contribute to eroticizing young girls as forbidden.[4]

Margaret Baldwin took up MacKinnon's recognition of categories of women when she argued: 'The fate of a woman's claims for justice, we all seem to know somewhere, crucially depends on her success in proving that she is not, and never has been, a prostitute.'[5] Feminist law reform, Baldwin notes, has not ruptured the 'not a prostitute approach':

In its legal expression, this feminist flight from prostitution seems largely reactive, driven by a tacit recognition that legal regulation of sexual violence and sex discrimination at bottom always functions as some form of judicial review of a man's conclusion that a complaining woman was, in fact, a whore, and therefore a permissible target of misogynist rage, contempt and sexual use.[6]

Restricting the introduction of prior sexual history in rape shield laws 'is designed to defeat the whore status her (a woman's) prior sexual activity would ascribe to her.'[7] Baldwin's work is particularly useful for illustrating the theme of complicity, uncovering, that is, the many stories we tell ourselves in order to maintain the prostitute/not-a-prostitute division between women. She writes, for example, that feminists transform prostituted women into 'other women' when we argue that prostitution is simply an issue of exploitative labour conditions or when we present prostitution as a symbol of the oppression of all women. Such explanations deny the harsh realities of prostitution. In adopting them, we collude in the logic that says if a woman can be seen to be getting something out of sexual violence (most often money but also affection, social approval, etc.), then she has not suffered violence but is instead merely a party to a contract. Defending the logic of contract with respect to prostitution, some feminists argue that prostitutes themselves have made it clear that they view themselves as engaging in a contract. However, as Baldwin and others remind us, we have not created the conditions whereby it would be possible for us to hear the stories of prostituted women who do not make the argument that prostitution is just a job like any other; we are not likely to hear the stories of dead prostituted women whose lives would powerfully speak of the violence. The stories we do hear confirm for us that prostituted women are simply exploited like other women, only sometimes more so.

Three points emerge from Baldwin's critique that are relevant to a consideration of the theme of complicity. First, the status of women who are seen to say no depends on its opposite, women who are seen to say yes. If we did not have a whore, we could not have a virgin, since those categories only have meaning in relation. Thus, in maintaining these categories where they are, a few of us can claim innocence and others are irrevocably confined to guilt. Second, virgin, as many legal scholars have pointed out, is a heavily racialized category.[8] The virgin side of the equation is also unreachable for women with developmental disabilities, many of whom have histories of sexual violence and sexual behaviour and who are often viewed by the court as 'inappropriately sexual,' a theme I discuss in detail later. Third, the operation in law of this dichotomy of virgins and whores inhibits an interrogation into the sources of violence against women and limits what we recognize as violent. We do not ask why prostitution occurs but say instead that it does not occur or occurs as some other thing, most often employment.

The focus on complicity both resembles and is different from some other feminist theorizing about relations between women. Where a complicity approach departs from MacKinnon, Baldwin, and others, for instance, is in how I understand the underlying social arrangements that position women into these two categories. It is not simply that a male view prevails in terms of what constitutes rape and that this arrangement results in some forms of violence being legitimized while others are not. It is also that what happens to one group of women is inextricably linked to what happens to another in interlocking systems of domination. Using pornography as an example, Patricia Hill Collins has powerfully illustrated the theme of interlocking oppressions to demonstrate that the story of pornography begins with slaves on the auction block:

The pornographic treatment of Black women's bodies challenges the prevailing feminist assumption that since pornography primarily affects white women, racism has been grafted onto pornography. African-American women's experiences suggest that Black women were not added into a preexisting pornography, but rather that pornography itself must be reconceptualized as an example of the interlocking nature of race, gender, and class oppression. At the heart of both racism and sexism are notions of biological determinism claiming that people of African descent and women possess immutable biological characteristics marking their inferiority to elite white men. In pornography these racist and sexist beliefs are sexualized. Moreover, for African-American women pornography has not been timeless and universal but was tied to Black women's experiences with the European colonization of Africa and with American slavery. Pornography emerged within a specific system of social class relationships.[9]

The theme of interlocking oppressions, as opposed to additive analysis (whereby some women are worse off), is an important aspect of examining complicity and one that makes it a different analytical framework from other theories of social relations or rights critiques. To take another example, in *Making All the Difference: Inclusion, Exclusion and American Law*, Martha Minow describes a social relations approach as one which rejects either/or constructions and focuses instead on relations, the ways in which exceptional treatment depends on a norm that can itself be questioned.[10] In calling passionately for an emphasis on 'context and particularity'[11] and for rights in relationship, Minow explains in her conclusion that such an approach would require that we ask questions about institutional arrangements and about the distinctions we make between innocents and victims. It would require, for instance, in the case of affirmative action, looking at how the majority have long enjoyed privileged access to jobs. Minow stresses that we need to 'acknowledge our own participation in the meanings of the differences we assign to others.'[12] Minow's critique of rights discourse, and of the legal reasoning that flows from it, is that the framework is an individualized one that does not recognize the interdependency of individuals and the central fact that difference is a relation. Again this is where the complicity approach starts, but it is critically important to characterize these relations as a set of interlocking social arrangements that constitute groups differently, *as subordinate and dominant*. Minow (and others)[13] recognize that autonomy in liberal discourse is essentially a relation of domination when she notes:

The very freedom of the traditional male role – to participate in public life and move in and out of the private family realm – depended upon the traditional female role, which maintained continuity in the family realm and provided some- one – a wife – to be subject to the husband's freely exercised power.[14]

This analysis does not apply to those women whose lives have always been public lives and who have in fact been denied any kind of a tradi- tional female role in the private sphere.[15] It is also an analysis that leads too easily to a minimizing of the role of class exploitation, racism, and ableism in women's lives and to a failure to theorize how these systems sustain one another. When we revise this analysis to incorporate inter- locking oppressions (for example in chapter 1, where Patricia Williams has explored how the power of her great-great-grandfather, a white slave- owner, depended on the absence of choice for her great-great-grandmother, a slave), we uncover the complicity of white men and women interlock- ing with the systems of racism and sexism.[16]

In the realm of disability, there has been a strong tendency to rely on additive analysis rather than to develop an analysis of interlocking oppres- sions. Women with developmental disabilities have been constructed almost universally as vulnerable, a social construction most often used to *explain* tremendous social and sexual violence in their lives.[17] As researchers Masuda and Riddington chillingly put it in their examination of disability and violence: 'It somehow seems more OK to abuse an imperfect child, or someone who really doesn't know what is going on, or is more pow- erless.'[18] In more clinical terms, Charlene Senn reiterates the same point by citing David Finkelhor's theory of sexual abuse, which outlines four salient preconditions of sexual abuse: the adult must be predisposed to abuse; internal inhibitions against abusing must be reduced; external social restraints must be reduced; and the child's own restraints and pro- tection must be overcome. In the last three preconditions, girls and wo- men with developmental disabilities are clearly at greater risk. Adults with a desire to sexually abuse a child, for example, can rationalize that a child or a woman with an intellectual impairment 'would not know what was happening' and, most important, would not be believed if she reported the violence.[19] When we label this social situation as one of the vulnerability of 'special needs groups,' we take the focus away from those who actively and aggressively set out to sexually violate and, again, we fail to ask about the sources of the violence itself.

Feminists have not greatly disrupted this framework of vulnerability and its attendant implications in strategies to limit the operation of sexual stereotypes in rape trials. The idea that women with developmental disabilities (and other groups of women) are specially at risk has been a part of reform efforts to legally restrict the introduction of evidence about past sexual history (rape shield laws) and to clarify the meaning of consent and non-consent. For example, in Canada, the National Action Committee on the Status of Women (NAC), the Women's Legal Education and Action Fund (LEAF), and the National Association of Women and the Law (NAWL) all stated in their lobbying efforts to amend the Criminal Code in 1992 that past sexual history is never relevant and should not be submitted as evidence.[20] These Canadian national feminist organizations also argued that consent cannot be presumed unless reasonable efforts have been made to know whether it has been given; a man's view of consent is not necessarily a woman's and it is a woman's view of consent that should prevail. Although the intention behind these arguments was to ensure that the accused bear a great burden of proof, the focus on consent has sometimes served to de-emphasize the defendant's conduct and responsibility and to entrench a 'reasonable woman' standard into the interrogation of whether or not there has been consent.[21] In seeking to avoid a reasonable woman standard, that is, a standard that sets a normative prescription of what a woman's consent looks like, recent feminist efforts to address differences among women may have ended up minimizing the defendant's conduct and responsibility and limiting the extent to which we can question the sources and boundaries of violence.

Billed the 'No Means No' campaign in Canada in the early 1990s, feminist lobbying clearly emphasized for the first time that some women are more vulnerable to sexual assault than others. NAC called for a preamble to amendments to the Criminal Code that would expressly name the categories of women who had a heightened vulnerability to sexual assault, noting, for example, that 'many women with disabilities because of their dependence on care-givers, difficulty in resisting or expressing their lack of consent and objectification as passive are more vulnerable to sexual assault than able-bodied women.'[22] Arguing that only a small fraction of women, 'determined, optimistic or naive enough to believe that juries will find them worthy of the law's protection,' ever consider turning to the legal system, LEAF sought (but did not get) a clause stipulating that consent cannot be presumed on the basis of membership in a historically disadvantaged group. For LEAF, examples of historically disadvantaged women included 'sex-trade workers,'[23] immigrants and refugees, and lesbians. NAC's list of women in this category included women with disabilities, women of colour, lesbians, domestic workers, 'sex-trade workers,' younger and older women. What is significant about this thesis of the increased vulnerability of women in these groups is that feminist reformers enumerate them specifically in order to argue that the incidence of violence is higher for women and that employment status, disability, language, and culture cannot be used by the accused to presume consent. In other words, the operation of specific stereotypes that come into play when these groups of women are involved should be more heavily scrutinized since the case of non-consent will be harder to make (how will we know she meant to say no when 'she usually says yes'; 'she can't communicate no in a language I understand').

At its core, the argument of greater vulnerability invites a tautology: women from historically disadvantaged groups are more vulnerable because they are more vulnerable. Apart from its lack of clarity, this position does not encourage us to interrogate *how* the risks of sexual violence become magnified for these 'special' groups of women and not for others. Instead, vulnerability is used to argue that such women cannot consent because we cannot know if they have consented. It is thus knowledge of her consent, and not the consequences of a man's actions, that becomes important in this formulation. Less focus is placed on what a man *does*, and his responsibility for the harm he causes, than on the woman's capacity to say yes; a situation I illustrate below in the *Glen Ridge* case.

The use of vulnerability as a construct carries a major risk in the legal context. Pity is the emotional response to vulnerability, a response that does not necessarily lead to respect – that is, to a willingness to change the conditions that hurt people with disabilities. Martha Minow comments that focusing on the special needs of persons with disabilities can be a helpful impulse, but such responses 'fundamentally preserve the pattern of relationships in which some people enjoy the power and position from which to consider – as a gift or act of benevolence – the needs of others without having to encounter their own implication in the social patterns that assign the problems to those others.'[24] Thus, vulnerability, and the pity it gives birth to, are unlikely to lead to respect. Feminists must consider to what extent we are complicitous in making possible pity and not respect when we rely on vulnerability in our law reform strategies.[25] Do we, in focusing on vulnerability, continue to divide women into those who cannot say yes and those who cannot say no, women in this second category being those who might be enmeshed in a contract with the accused (for money, affection, social validation, immigrant status, etc.)? Further, how invested are we, the non-disabled, in our icons of pity?

How can we begin to ask in a court of law what makes the sexual violence in the lives of women with disabilities so permissible and prevalent? To fail to ask the question is to abandon the contextualizing needed in order to uncover sexual violence; it is to privatize. As Frances Lee Ansley has argued about the trend to consider white supremacy as it operates in employment as nothing more than a conflict between two workers (the minority worker versus the innocent white male), the privatization of social issues 'leaves too much out of the picture to yield a just result.'[26] We privatize the social construction of disability when we focus on the vulnerability and incapacity of individual women and not on the social relations that transform a physical or mental condition into a condition of great vulnerability.[27] To be sure, feminists have spoken about these social conditions and mean to call attention to them when we enumerate the groups of women we designate as specially vulnerable. Yet without an explicit theory of interlocking oppressions, without the social contexts of white supremacy, patriarchy, ableism, and class exploitation that position us in different and unequal relation to one another, we are left with the consent framework and legal processes that require caricatures: an arch-villain and a quintessential victim both acting out a private drama. And we are let off the hook in that we do not have to move from pity to respect, that is, we do not have to assume responsibility for the individual and social actions that produce and sustain multiple systems of oppression.

In a bid to get beyond the caricatures, to locate women with developmental disabilities within their social contexts and to move beyond pity, I want to show the operation of subtexts around gender, developmental disability, race, and class in two sexual assault trials – the Canadian *Mohammed* trial and the widely publicized American *Glen Ridge* trial.[28] I argue that in addressing the social construction of these categories, we come nearer to justice. That is, we move beyond consent to responsibility and beyond pity to respect. There are a number of covert (and not so covert) competing subtexts in such cases that operate for both the defence and the prosecution as they mount arguments around consent, arguments that have to do with proving that the woman is either a victim or a slut. These simplified options mask who is doing what to whom and ensure that limited attention is paid to the accused's responsibility for his actions. I would suggest that the logic that drives the consent vehicle and keeps hidden the operation of subtexts results, in the first place, in few cases involving women with developmental disabilities being taken up, since friends, family, the police, and the state all assume that such cases have too many complications to be worth pursuing. In the second place, when they are taken up, convictions are obtained but sentences remain light, reflecting that the harm of the violence has not been fully taken into account.[29] Pity only goes so far.

What Is Not Said

Her Majesty the Queen v. Mahde Mohammed

In the spring of 1992, a twenty-five-year-old Somali refugee man was tried for the crime of sexually assaulting a twenty-year-old white woman with a developmental disability. Mahde Mohammed, the accused, had been in Canada a little over a year and worked alongside of Lisa H., his accuser, at a fast-food restaurant in Toronto, Ontario. The 'facts' of the case are bare. On the night of 6 October 1991, both Lisa and Mahde worked the evening shift. Lisa alleged that at 7:30 pm she was cleaning the last cubicle in the second-floor women's washroom when Mahde entered the cubicle, locked the door, and attempted to rape her. The entire incident supposedly lasted ten to fifteen minutes during which time two customers used the washroom but were not alerted to anything's being amiss. Lisa contended that Mahde stood on the toilet seat, held one hand to her mouth and the other he held first to her breast and then against her pants. She maintained that she eventually succeeded in knocking him down with her elbow. She then descended to the main floor and told a female co-worker, Marianne, 'Just half [the story]. Just he just touch me.'[30] Marianne then allegedly advised Lisa 'to say nothing to nobody,' since she herself intended to ask Mahde if it was true. A week later, Lisa told her male co-worker Richard the whole story and he told her boss Ron who in turn told another boss, Mike, and finally another, Bill. It was Bill who wrote everything down and who took the case to Lisa's counsellor and, ultimately, they all went to the police.[31] Mahde was arrested a short time later. During the trial, differences of fact emerged around work procedures, and Mahde's story turned on how he interpreted these procedures. He alleged that Lisa was in the process of cleaning downstairs so he went upstairs to clean the washrooms. After cleaning the men's washroom, he knocked on the door of the women's washroom. Receiving no answer, he walked in and saw Lisa there. He asked her to come out so he could clean but she refused, inviting him to come in anyway. At this point, Mahde claimed that he announced his intention to come back later when she had left, whereupon Lisa threatened him that if he did not come in there would be consequences.[32]

Race, gender, and developmental disability enter this script in a number of overt, covert and intersecting ways that may have helped to produce the responses to how both of these stories were heard in court. The credibility of witnesses in the rape trial, Kimberlé Crenshaw writes, 'are mediated by dominant narratives about the way that men and women "are."'[33] But the way men and women are, that is, the narratives that socially script them, varies. In this trial, it is not just a man or just a woman, but a Black refugee man and a white woman with a developmental disability, both working as cleaners in a restaurant; their respective characteristics and situations have specific social meanings not in and of themselves but in relation to each other. In court, Mahde appeared as a handsome, sincere young Black man with a hesitant command of English and an intelligent air. Lisa, an extremely overweight young white woman, whose disability was manifest in her half completed sentences and difficulties with details and words, also appeared truthful. Yet her physical appearance in combination with her disability produced certain responses in a society that pathologizes fatness[34] and equates thinness with sexual desirability. There were other significant players both in and out of the courtroom whose characteristics also have social meanings. The judge, a white man, was relatively new to the bench. The Crown attorney, a competent, self-assured man was also white, as was the lawyer for the accused. Among the significant players not officially part of the proceedings were the five white men to whom Lisa told her story, including her counsellor, Mike. The case was tried in Metropolitan Toronto, a city in which racial tensions exist and in which crime is associated with Black males.

Developmental disability entered the trial as an important indicator of credibility almost immediately, and predictably, when the lawyer for the accused apologetically interrupted the opening question put by the Crown attorney:

MR. ABBAS: Excuse me, Your Honor, I don't mean to interrupt my friend. I'm sorry, I thought my friend understood there is a question here of whether or not this witness can be sworn. I was going to ask your honor to conduct an inquiry on the basis that she may be mentally in a position where she cannot be sworn. I'm sorry to my friend, I didn't mean to catch him by surprise here. I think my friend is aware of what I'm talking about. Maybe he can address that.[35]

It was quickly established that Lisa did indeed have some understanding that she was under oath to tell the truth, but her competence was possibly acknowledged at the expense of her credibility, as she explained to the court in childlike phrases that she knew God would punish her if she lied.

Beyond the initial consideration of her competence, the significance of Lisa's disability and its relevance to her story were never explicitly explored by either side during the trial, yet intellectual impairment in a woman was a central subtext in the arguments of both sides. Everyone seemed to know what it meant. The defence built its case on the familiar idea that Lisa was a vengeful woman whose allegation that Mahde assaulted her was made in retaliation for his rejection of her advances.[36] Familiar as the idea of the vengeful woman is, one wonders to what extent this line of argument is rendered more plausible by the assumption that a fat woman with a disability is inherently unrapeable and will stop at nothing to get the male attention usually denied her. As Anne Finger notes, the stereotype of asexuality often applied to women with disabilities also has its opposite: people with disabilities are sometimes seen as 'diseased lusts' and, in the case of women, potential prostitutes.[37] Illogically, the defence's vengeful woman would have to be smart enough to 'cry rape,' a degree of conniving which their earlier questions about Lisa's capacity to comprehend an oath would seem to negate.[38] The Crown prosecutor also relied on Lisa's disability. As he put it to Mahde Mohammed:

I'm going to suggest to you, sir, that your whole testimony today has been a fabrication; that you went into the women's washroom when she was cleaning it and you knew she was mentally retarded, or mentally handicapped, and that in fact you could take advantage of her. Isn't that correct, sir?[39]

Lisa's disability was presented here as proof of Mahde's intent, a line of reasoning similar to the one used in the past against Black men in American courts when the victim in question was white.[40] Even the accused, Mahde Mohammed, however, speculated about Lisa's disability. In reply to a question from the prosecutor about his knowledge of Lisa's disability he stated: 'Well I was not aware of any problem, but I suspected, especially that day when I was working with her.'[41] No one invited him to discuss what exactly he suspected or its relevance to the alleged sexual assault, perhaps because all parties shared a conceptual scheme that categorized intellectual impairment as a problem at best, deviance at worst, at least in the realm of sexuality.

The significance of Lisa's disability and her gender shaped in covert ways how her story was heard. She was depicted by the defence as a woman who has 'problems' with matters of sexuality, an image sustained by the stereotype, once common in psychiatric literature and still prevalent in popular culture, that 'sexual abuse [of persons with an intellectual impairment] was the result of the odd demented offender ... or the seductive activity of precocious children ... reinforcing the illusion of rarity.'[42] Lisa was asked by Abbas, the lawyer for the accused, if she liked boys. He then illegally brought to light her past sexual history in which she once alleged that three boys, known to her through her cousin and who stayed the night at her house, tried to rape her. Abbas also noted that Lisa herself had once been accused of sexual improprieties in an incident of sexual abuse involving a three-and-a-half-year-old child. Neither of these attempts to discredit Lisa departs from well-known patterns of attacking the credibility of women in other rape trials, except for the fact that Lisa's alleged sexual aggression concerns young children. The social worker's statement that Lisa's file revealed that she had indeed been sexually assaulted in the past did little to dispel the image of a woman whose sexuality was uncontrolled and deviant. The social worker attested that Lisa had been counselled about the criminality of having sex with younger people and she was pressed by Abbas to admit that Lisa was described in her file as both a victim and a perpetrator of sexual abuse.[43]

Analogous in many ways to the situation of a prostituted woman attempting to prove she has been raped, a woman with a developmental disability must also overcome the background of sexual violence so common in her life before she can be seen to be vulnerable. She must, in effect, establish her virtue – for the legitimacy of her claim to the court's protection is based on belonging to a group whose virtue must be protected. Virtue, after all, is central to how white bourgeois women are defined – the lady of Victorian society still stands as the epitome of womanhood.[44] Lisa's history, inextricably produced by gender and disability as systems of oppression, reduces her chances for membership in this category. In her case, it is not merely that there were stereotypes to be uncovered, but an actual and complicated sexual history existed that required a deeper contextualizing.

Rape trials, of course, turn on consent, and this one was no exception. The defence attempted to undermine Lisa's story by emphasizing that, by her own account, she did not resist the alleged rape. She did not scream or punch Mahde Mohammed, Lisa explains, '[c]ause I didn't know what he was going to do to me. If I hit him then he hit me back.'[45] Her 'failure to resist,' a strategy well known to many women concerned first of all for their physical survival, might or might not have weakened her story, a variable that depended perhaps on the gender consciousness of those listening. Her narrative, however, was not straightforward about what women do when confronted with violence. Her response was examined in court along with details that included discrepancies in the timing and sequence of events. No one suggested here that Lisa's difficulties with timing may have originated in her disability, a factor well documented in the literature on developmental disabilities.[46]

If the subtexts I have so far alluded to suggest that gender and disability are categories that convey a variety of unacknowledged, hence unexplored assumptions that might have helped to weaken Lisa's story, there were also subtexts that, we might speculate, worked for her. The prosecution's case against Mahde Mohammed relied in the first instance on the idea that he exploited her greater vulnerability as a woman with a developmental disability. The prosecution argued that Mahde's testimony was 'inherently unreasonable' because it was informed by the idea of the vengeful woman.[47] Due in no small way to the pressures of feminists and their success in promoting rape as a political issue, the vengeful woman scenario is now perhaps sufficiently discredited in legal circles[48] as a narrative that, in this trial at least, can be dismissed as nothing more than misogynist invention.

Subtexts must also be uncovered as they affect Mahde Mohammed's story. Two categories merit examination here, although again, neither surfaced explicitly in the courtroom. Mahde Mohammed was a Black man of Somali origin and a refugee. We can only speculate on whether the enduring myth of the Black rapist and the white victim helped fuel either Lisa's allegation or the support she received from her bosses and counsellor (all white males) in pressing the charges. Kristin Bumiller has persuasively argued that the politics of rape reform have taken us to a place wherein life experiences must be reduced to the adversarial Black and white.[49] Feminists concentrate on creating a space in the courts where women's stories can be heard and believed, but a language does not yet exist to describe gender relations in their fullest complexities. When rape is constructed as a balancing of men's and women's interests, there is no room to explore how the myths of a patriarchal, ableist, and racist society intersect in any one scenario. As Bumiller argues, 'an important part of deconstructing the consciousness of rape is revealing the social mechanisms that empower violence against both racial groups and women.'[50] The rape trial remains primarily a scrutiny of the victim and the offender as individuals in an organizing framework of consent. There is thus little exploration of the power relationships that might have created the situation in the first place. The trial of Mahde Mohammed did not uncover, for instance, the circumstances leading up to Lisa's allegation. As a woman with a developmental disability, she did not get to the point of a courtroom trial without the intervention of several people, most of whom in this instance were white and male.

Finally, Mahde Mohammed's story must be interpreted through the lens of his refugee status. A key part of his testimony concerned his observation of work procedures. He was insistent, for example, that Lisa knew, as he did, the policy that when one worker is cleaning downstairs, the other should be cleaning upstairs unless there are many customers: 'We don't go to one washroom and clean together and leave the rest of the area without cleaning,' he replied in response to the prosecutor's questioning as to why they did not work together as a team. Displaying a precise knowledge of workplace procedures, Mahde was then asked what, if anything, he understood by Lisa's smiling invitation to enter the washroom:

She knows about the policy. She work there. She knows we both aren't supposed to be working in the same place and when I saw her insisting to stay inside and she wants me to come in and carry on the job, *anything can happen* [emphasis added]. She could turn around and say I was in the bathroom and he came in.[51]

The prosecutor did not press Mahde to explain what he thought could happen but there are at least three possible meanings to the statement. First, Mahde's statement that 'anything can happen' can be taken to reveal his sense of vulnerability as a refugee claimant. Certainly, a criminal conviction would result in his expulsion from Canada, a possibility that weighs heavily on the mind of any refugee seeking sanctuary. Second, he could have been expressing his vulnerability as a man likely to be accused of rape by a woman, a scenario that carries additional dangers when the man is Black and the woman white. Third, Mahde may have been voicing here the vulnerabilities of a worker of colour who, in a racist climate, can be fired for not following proper work procedures. His sense of vulnerability as a worker would certainly be shared by many workers of colour, and the more so by Somali refugees who report a 90 per cent unemployment rate and who experience considerable racism in Toronto. As a number of studies on racism in employment have revealed, Black workers learn to be extremely vigilant on the job; in the event of their complaining of unfair treatment, for example, it is they, rather than the perpetrators, who are disciplined 50 per cent of the time.[52]

In *R. v. Mohammed*, the accused was acquitted. Mr Justice Brent Knazen found that both Lisa and Mahde were credible and that Lisa's story could not be established beyond a reasonable doubt. He was careful to note that Lisa's developmental handicap 'had nothing to do with any rejection of her evidence' and that he did not rely on the length of time before she reported the incident, her failure to scream, or her past sexual history, all of which he would be legally prohibited from doing in any event. He also stressed that the acquittal did not signal his acceptance of the vengeful woman scenario put forward by the defence. Instead, he concluded:

Mr. Mohammed has given testimony in as clear and straightforward a fashion as Ms. H. did. He, as well, stood up to cross-examination and I cannot find where the truth lies. That is why I said at the outset that the law is clear with respect to the result.[53]

The outcome in *Mohammed* as articulated by Mr Justice Knazen unintentionally suggests my argument around the subtexts. We cannot find where the truth lies when all we have to rely on is 'clear and straightforward' testimony. Such an approach steadfastly ignores the subtexts and multiple meanings and the fact that our responses are both individually and socially produced. In failing to connect our immediate responses to social narratives, we leave ourselves open to the powerful seduction of racist, sexist, and ableist narratives. As Martha Minow writes, one can miscalculate one's capacity to be fair.[54] Traditionally, she observes, we consider the problem of judicial bias as a problem of either being too close to the problem or too far. It is time to find a way to use prior knowledge as well as question assumptions, 'to suspend our conclusions long enough to be surprised, to learn.'[55] In *Mohammed*, the prior knowledge we might have used to explore what needs to be considered in order to hear both Mahde and Lisa has to do with (among other things) social responses to Black men and to fat women with developmental disabilities *in the realm of sexuality*. That both individuals were cleaners in a fast-food restaurant, hence relatively powerless, also could have alerted us to what may have been assumed by the more socially powerful participants in this story.

Bringing to light prior knowledge has been widely assumed to be too problematic, however, particularly when it is knowledge about past sexual history as feminist lobbying efforts indicate. The attorney general of

Ontario, acting on the basis that the Supreme Court of Canada in *Seaboyer; Gayme* has expressly warned about the unspoken sexual myths activated when evidence is adduced about past sexual history, has explicitly instructed his lawyers to work towards limiting such prejudicial effects by limiting the introduction of evidence.[56] This is of course in keeping with the feminist strategy so aptly described by Margaret Baldwin as 'the freeze-frame, miniaturist portrait of the rape victim.'[57] How then do we reconcile the argument I have been making that subtexts are powerfully present (and perhaps not so covert as we might expect – the decision in *Mohammed* is perhaps too careful in noting what was *not* taken into account) and should be brought to light with the argument that such subtexts, particularly when embedded in past sexual history, are too mired in social myths and will only serve to further limit what can be heard in a courtroom? In the *Glen Ridge* rape trial, we can more clearly see what gets suppressed and what is uncovered when developmental disability and gender intersect in the realm of sexual violence. The portrait of the victim in *Glen Ridge* was certainly beyond miniaturist, and predictably, a host of social myths emerged. Yet, I would suggest that, in between the cracks and fissures of sexual history, information about the victim's social life seeped out that could have been more profitably used to bring social issues into focus and to undermine the privileging of consent issues over violence.

From Consent To Responsibility

The Glen Ridge Case

In March 1989, a white teenage girl with a developmental disability was sexually assaulted by a group of young white male high school athletes in the basement playroom of a house in Glen Ridge, New Jersey, an affluent suburb of New York.[58] Two years later a jury found three of the young men guilty of conspiracy and aggravated assault (sentenced to up to fifteen years in a youth detention centre), and a third guilty of conspiracy (sentenced to community service). Two other young men involved were ultimately not tried, one for medical reasons and the other because the parents of the assaulted girl believed that their daughter could not endure another trial. The men sentenced to up to fifteen years had their sentences reduced to indeterminate length, which means that ultimately they could serve as little as twenty months.[59] As I suggested at the beginning of this chapter, *Glen Ridge* may be paradigmatic in that convictions were obtained but sentences appear unusually light.

In *Glen Ridge*, four men sexually assaulted the victim with a baseball bat, a broom handle, and a stick while up to thirteen others watched and urged them on. The violence notwithstanding, the central issue in the case remained consent. Defence lawyers, relying among other things on a taped conversation, argued that the victim was sexually experienced and consented, receiving only minimal help to insert the broom and bat and willingly performing fellatio with another defendant. The prosecution, presenting medical evidence and the corroboration of friends and teachers, argued that the victim was mildly retarded and incapable of freely and truly consenting. Desperate for social approval, she consented in the hope that one of the boys would ask her out for a date. Under New Jersey law, anyone who has sex with a 'mentally defective' person and knows 'or should have known' of the mental condition can be found guilty of sexual assault.[60] Thus, as the nature of developmental disability, either as a biological or a social condition or both, quickly gained prominence during the trial, consent issues around disability were reframed.

Silence about her sexual past was not an option for the victim in *Glen Ridge*. Early in the trial, to the intense dismay of feminist observers, rape shield provisions were lifted. In making this ruling, Mr Justice Burrell Ives Humphreys noted that the state depicted the victim as a 'very vulnerable, open person and that her sexual conduct was not for sexual gratification but rather to gain the affection, love and attention of others,' an argument that required, in his view, that questions be posed about her past sexual history.[61] The implication, of course, is that the court must be able to evaluate whether or not she is the kind of woman who often says yes or one who must always be presumed to be saying no. It was not so much her past sexual history, however, as much as her *social* history of marginalization and oppression that was a necessary part of her story, and these aspects, emerging as they did as a subtext of the central text of consent, made it difficult to put on the table the social context of the accused boys. Specifically, their own histories of domination and entitlement were rendered invisible.

These salient facts emerged about the victim's past in *Glen Ridge*:

1. As a child and young adult, she was socially isolated, frequently scorned and mocked by her peers and treated as 'an oddball.'
2. She once approached varsity football players asking them if they wanted to 'fuck.'
3. She was asked to leave Columbia High School for a number of reasons, but among them was the school's position that it could not guarantee her safety from rape.[62]

4. Her mother testified that she was placed on birth control pills after leaving Columbia High School because of the risk of rape by one student in particular who had placed his hand down her pants and because she had been raped before by an athlete from the school.[63]

5. Her sister testified that as a child the victim was often persecuted by children in the neighbourhood and that two of the accused boys were part of a group of children who got her to eat dog faeces when she was five.

The judge ordered that none of the defendants could be identified before the jury as participants in the dog faeces incident or in the incident when the same boys, as young children, participated in tormenting her at a tennis camp.[64] These facts, and similar testimony, were enlisted by the defence to paint a picture of a woman/child who did not know sexual boundaries, who was in fact 'overly sexed, sexually aggressive' and whose 'genital signals – are greater than normal.'[65] In a phrase, the defence relied upon the 'diseased lust' that is a recurring stereotype of persons with developmental disabilities, the prostitute part of the not-a-prostitute story. The prosecution used the same evidence as part of its case that the victim often did whatever she was asked to do in order to gain social approval. As one medical expert testified, 'her concept is she has to do something to please somebody else.'[66] (That her desire to please often took sexualized forms says a great deal about the intersection of gender and disability in this context.) Stories of the girl's interaction with her peers were therefore of importance only insofar as they shed light on whether her yes meant yes or no. They were not enlisted directly as part of an argument about the violence and degradation of her social environment and how this might help to uncover what happened. Significantly, they were also not a direct part of the social environment of the accused, even though, as one journalist put it, 'it wasn't much of a leap from the dog faeces to the broomstick.'[67]

Stories of social violence thus entered the main text by stealth; they would certainly have contributed to forming the jury's and the judge's overall impressions but they were not framed as the central issues under consideration. Rather, when the victim said to a girlfriend (in a conversation that was secretly taped), 'Yeah, I feel like a whore but it doesn't bother me. I am so lucky. I mean I've been doing this since I was little,' and when she took the stand and said confusedly that she knew she was free to leave the basement scene but didn't, her childhood and young-adult history of violence and degradation helped to contextualize these

words but not to highlight how the boys would have so easily participated in the basement scene in the first place.[68] In other words, they shed
light on consent but not on the responsibility of the defendants.

Although it is not easy to judge from the newspaper accounts the extent
to which the boys' responses to her disability and gender came under
scrutiny, it would appear that they did so mostly within the legal context
of whether or not the boys knew the victim had a developmental disability. While journalists made the connection between sexual violence
and the sports cult of masculine aggression, of which the boys appeared
to be a part, the judge directed the jury to ignore any suggestion that the
boys were connected to a sexually violent lifestyle. It was left to journalists, feminists, and advocates to pursue the stories lying behind the moral
question put by journalist Robert Lipsyte: 'So even if they are all "not
guilty," what were Tyson [a reference to the Mike Tyson trial] and the Glen
Ridge athletes thinking of?'[69] What the athletes were thinking of would
have led the court into the realm of socially produced responses to disability and gender and to a keener appreciation of the sexualized, racialized and gendered forms of subordination. The boys' affluent white background, for example, remained in shadow although some journalists
occasionally grumbled about its significance.[70] Similarly, their social
power as male athletes went largely unscrutinized.

Douglas Biklin, a professor of special education, using language reminiscent of Catharine MacKinnon's early arguments about consent, succinctly put forward how I would suggest we begin to escape the not-a-
prostitute story and move towards an approach that recognizes the
processes of domination and subordination. Questioned by a journalist
about his views on the *Glen Ridge* case, he stated: 'I would always wish
that the core could be argued that she is a person, she was mistreated,
she was violated and this should happen to no one.'[71] Yet, a major difficulty persists with this approach. As law professor James Ellis pointed
out, the problem is that it is difficult to see the violation suffered by the
victim in *Glen Ridge* given that she is not the same kind of valuable woman as are non-disabled women.[72] The dilemma is thus: if the trial could
focus on how the basement scene was socially produced, both the victim
and the accused would come into view[73] and the subtexts would get
named, but the victim comes into view as less than human, full of contradictions, deserving perhaps of our pity but not our respect. As Professor Ruth Luckasson commented: 'Very frequently the victimization of
the mentally retarded is not uncovered. Or if it is uncovered, it is not

taken seriously.'[74] How might we talk about the social context of women with disabilities without reifying the othering that marks this context in the first place?

In an early article on battered women's syndrome, Elizabeth Schneider named a similar dilemma encountered when the full context of victimization is introduced via expert testimony:

> The expert testimony cases are the natural result of the 'differences' approach – the goal of the expert testimony is to explain the content of battered women's *different* experiences and perceptions so that juries can fairly apply the *same* legal standards to them. But the question which the expert testimony cases squarely pose is this: if battered women's experiences are explained as different, can they ever be genuinely incorporated into the traditional standard and understood as equally reasonable? Are these different experiences inevitably perceived as inferior, as 'handicaps'? If so, is it necessary to alter the traditional standard?[75]

What Schneider does not pursue here is: What if these are handicaps in the traditional sense of the word and not as metaphor? In other words, in disability cases, the premise is not that these are women who are different from men but human beings who are biologically different from other human beings. When Schneider notes that the battered woman syndrome 'implies that she is limited because of *her* weakness and *her* problems,' we have to extrapolate that for the woman with a developmental disability this is not an implied analytical frame but one that is overt and central to the case. Thus, if the battered woman syndrome too easily brings to mind 'the seeds of old stereotypes of women in new forms – the victimized and the passive battered woman, too paralysed to act because of her own incapacity,'[76] what can we say for the woman who is indeed paralysed or otherwise 'biologically' (for all biology is inextricably linked to the social sense we make of it) incapable of acting? What seems clear from the *Glen Ridge* case is that we need to find legal mechanisms to bring to the fore how social attitudes condition individual responses – responses not only of the victim but of the accused and of the court. These competing subtexts, if left uninterrogated, prevent us from asking questions about dominant narratives. Additionally, the emphasis on consent to the exclusion of social violence limits how we might connect individual to social responsibility. The specific approaches we consider must materialize women with disabilities not as vulnerable women but as women who are unjustly treated. At least one possibility is hearing expert testimony explicitly on processes of subordination rather than limited to individual psychology. It is the pathologizing of disability that must be resisted.

From Pity to Respect: The Scope of the Problem

In making an argument for uncovering subtexts and moving away from a framework that prioritizes consent issues at the expense of the social histories of oppression and sexual violence, I have run smack into the problem identified by feminist law reformers: how to limit the operation of deeply embedded social stereotypes. In the *Glen Ridge* case, these stereotypes emerged at the intersection of developmental disability and gender, and my proposal for limiting their operation by confronting their social origins head-on, runs the risk of othering the victim of sexual violence to the point where she is pitied but not respected. Given how heavily invested the non-disabled world is in pity – that is, in not recognizing how we have transformed a mental or physical condition into a disadvantage by privileging non-disabled norms – this risk, too, must be explored. As I asked earlier, How far will pity take us in pushing the boundaries of what we recognize to be violent?

Assumptions about intellectual impairment can serve to protect girls (assuming the girl is fourteen years old or older)[7] and women from a further interrogation into their consent. In these decisions, courts infer from developmental disability a vulnerability and degree of intellectual impairment that make moot the question of consent. For example, in *Glen Ridge*, the prosecutor's central activity was the establishment of the victim's vulnerability. The failure to interrogate further into what the connection is between a victim's disability and her responses to sexual violence may, however, serve to mask important details about her context and the harm she has suffered ultimately promoting offender-centred justice. The focus on vulnerability does not stand up well to the complex issues of most cases. In *Mohammed* and in *Glen Ridge*, both women were not quintessential victims; that is, perceived of as blameless. Both had backgrounds of prior sexual violence and what was referred to in the trials as inappropriate sexual behaviour. In *Mohammed*, suppression of Lisa's history of violence affected how we could understand the meaning of certain allusions and 'facts' about Lisa's sexual past, hints intended to portray her as promiscuous. In *Glen Ridge*, the victim's sexual history was explored but evidence about the continuing sexual aggression of the defendants (in one case the defendant had been accused of yet another rape subsequent to the one for which he was being tried) was not allowed.[78] Similarly, in R. v. Shunamon,[79] a seventeen-year-old girl was described as 'of greatly diminished intelligence.'[80] The same brief association of intellectual impairment with response went noted but unexplored in a sentencing decision in R. v. Malbog,[81] in which a thirteen-year-old girl, described as 'somewhat mentally slow,' got lost and took the wrong bus and was offered a ride home by the bus driver when the bus reached the end of the line. Once in his car, the offender began touching the girl in a sexual manner and then stopped in order to go home to change out of his uniform. He then invited her into his residence, but she declined and stayed in the car. After having changed his clothes, he drove the girl to her school and on the way commenced once again to sexually molest her. He asked her to touch him, whereupon, in the words of the decision, 'for some reason, unbeknownst even to her, she said yes, meaning no, and he reached over, took her hand, and placed it on his penis, on the outside of his pants.' She immediately withdrew her hand, and the incident ended. Discussion of her non-consent goes no further than this re-telling in the decision, again because it is assumed that her intellectual impairment sufficiently explained her responses.

The lines blur in cases of developmental disability between medical and social meanings of disability and between sexual and social violence. They require a clear articulation of how power relations produce the responses of nondisabled individuals to persons with disabilities and how the subtexts of race, gender, disability, sexuality and class interlock. Pity will not provide sufficient motivation to pursue these complexities, daunting as they are. We are apt to give up, viewing people with disabilities as having 'a bottomless pit of needs'[82] that the legal system cannot confront. The case of Dr Wilfred Chin, accused of 'fondling' the breasts of a sixteen-year-old girl, C, hospitalized temporarily and described as 'mentally handicapped,' epileptic, and subject to seizures that affect her memory, dramatically illustrates the nature of the complexities we are likely to encounter and why we must find ways to talk about them.[83] Dr Chin was convicted at trial largely on the basis of testimony from a nurse, Barbara Keats, that she saw him 'fondle' C's breasts. No other patient or visitor present in C's room at the time witnessed the event or recalled Dr Chin's presence on the morning of the alleged incident with the exception of T, another patient, whose own disability resulted in memory lapses and confusion. At the heart of the issues during the trial was the testimony of C herself, found by the trial judge to be a 'moody, unpredictable, suggestible, moderately mentally handicapped girl (whose) ...

evidence must be scrutinized with the greatest of care in order to determine whether any part of her evidence is credible.'[84] C's own physician declared her to be unreliable and various nurses corroborated this 'diagnosis' adding that her behaviour was often 'inappropriate and unpredictable.'[85] C's doctor also testified that C was able to understand simply phrased, concrete questions but that the way she would respond to suggestible questions was to be very agreeable. Dr Gossage also asserted that C really had no memory, was easily confused, and had a minimal capacity to deal with abstraction.[86] In the face of these medical assessments, C had no chance at credibility, in spite of the testimony of the nurse who allegedly saw the doctor grope her. Even as a child who potentially had been sexually abused, she was not given the benefit of the doubt because, as one expert in child abuse testified, the accuracy of information obtained from children in these cases depended on whether it is information that is elicited or spontaneously given and C, more so than most children, was declared eminently suggestible.[87]

Like many other girls and women with developmental disabilities, C came from a background of previous allegations of abuse. Her doctor acknowledged this and noted at the same time that events had a tendency to blur in C's memory. C alleged, for instance, that she was sexually assaulted by Dr Chin when she was six months old. If C's medical assessment condemned her to being without voice in the proceedings, her situation as someone bringing a charge against a well-respected and prominent senior pediatrician of the medical community further diminished her credibility. Twenty-nine witnesses testified to Dr Chin's good character. Moreover, the only witness to the alleged incident, Barbara Keats, was confused about a crucial part of her testimony after discussing her evidence with her husband, a hostile witness against Dr Chin. Jim Keats, the principal of the school that C attended, had been making inquiries about Dr Chin in connection with another girl and may have questioned C before she herself initiated the topic. It is important to note that C, like Lisa in R. v. Mohammed and indeed most women with developmental disabilities, was encircled by a number of non-disabled adults who played significant roles in her life, individuals who must have assisted her in pressing charges.

How then can a court begin to thread its way through the maze of multiple contexts in which gender and disability come together here? How can we move beyond consent and pity to responsibility and respect? In finding Dr Chin guilty at the trial level and sentencing him to nine months imprisonment, the court succinctly identified C's vulnerability: 'He [Dr

Chin] knew if C.D. complained, few would believe her as she is highly suggestible.'[88] Yet C's extreme vulnerability cannot be taken as evidence of Dr Chin's intent, as the Crown suggested it might in the case of Mahde Mohammed. In ordering a new trial of Dr Chin, an appeal court therefore stressed the need to establish the credibility of key witnesses. Such a proposal is hardly out of the ordinary but in the case of developmental disability in women, a new trial would then have to include a call to interrogate more closely the conditions of C's life and the interests of those closest to her who played roles in her life related to her disability that have no parallel in the lives of able-bodied women. Who, for example, helped C to formulate the idea of bringing a charge and who helped her carry it through? How much previous sexual violence was there in the past and how might uncovering this history help her to tell her present story? In the event of a new trial, to grant C the full respect of her rights, to treat her as the same kind of woman as other women, requires that we begin with the relationships that shape her life and explore the consequences of her disability not only in the specific incident at hand but also historically. For C to tell her own story, a full contextualization of her life as a woman with a developmental disability needs to be introduced. It is possible that to introduce these stories in a rape trial may damage C's credibility[89] even more, but without them, she may not have a voice at all, and we cannot begin to untangle the relations out of which the allegations emerged nor fully assess C's responses.

Conclusion

Against the background of their complex histories of social and sexual violence, women with developmental disabilities do not face the same difficulties in court in telling their stories as do other women, nor are their difficulties simply greater. The terrain in which rape politics in North America have been played out in the last few years has not provided ways to address their difficulties. For example, as Bumiller writes, the women's movement

has defended a woman's right to be free from sexual violence by dispelling the myths that denigrate her words. The underlying principle is that only when the woman is 'taken for her word' is she given the same treatment as victims of less serious 'nonsexual' crimes. The vision of consent versus nonconsent, however, is incongruent with the conditions of sexual domination that inhibit the voices of victims.[90]

Bumiller enjoins us as feminists to recognize that we need a theory that can account for the structure of violent relationships in women's lives and expose the social conditions that limit what can be said in the rape script.

I have argued here that we must begin with our own complicity: What are the explanations and stories we endorse when we focus on the vulnerability of women with developmental disabilities? When we argue, for instance, that disability makes gender worse, we do not have to face how those systems interlock to produce advantages for some women at the expense of others. Specifically, we do not thereby rupture either the consent or the pity frameworks. To do so, we need to call into question the sources and boundaries of what we call sexual violence and trace the investments we each have in maintaining them where they are.

As a first step, for women with developmental disabilities to tell their stories, we must pave the way for an uncovering of the sometimes conflicting subtexts that so often remain hidden in rape trials, subtexts about the sources of the violence in the lives of girls and women with developmental disabilities. Uncovering these texts means simultaneously challenging the consent framework. As Baldwin has reminded us, however, this does not mean that we try to prove that all women are on the innocent side of the divide. Instead we need to ask why some groups of women are so routinely degraded and brutalized. It is not an answer to say that all women are brutalized or that sexual violence is what men do to women, for this answer serves to minimize what we each do to sustain the systems of domination out of which comes the violence. In particular, it is an explanation that masks the 'disengagement tactics' Margaret Baldwin identified in feminist strategies around prostitution, strategies that maintain that 'prostitution is love, freedom, force or fear: anything but prostitution.'[91] We utilize such strategies when we talk about vulnerability with respect to women with disabilities and when we refuse to examine their sexual histories of violence. The risk, of course, is that a more authentic picture of men's violence and our complicity can be absorbed by an antifeminist agenda that depicts men as the real victims. Risky as it is, we cannot shy away from uncovering the subtexts and our complicity; the stories of women with disabilities must be told, not as stories of vulnerability, but as stories of injustice.

6

Conclusion
To Essentialize or Not to Essentialize:
Is This the Question?

How do we negotiate an intellectually charged space for experience in a way that is not totalizing and essentializing – a space that acknowledges the constructedness of and the differences within our lived experiences while at the same time attending to the inclining, rather than declining, significance of race, class, culture, and gender?

Ann duCille, 'The Occult of True Black Womanhood:
Critical Demeanor and Black Feminist Studies'

Essentialism, Trina Grillo writes,

is the notion that there is a single woman's, or Black person's, or any other groups's experience that can be described independently from other aspects of the person – that there is an 'essence' to that experience. An essentialist outlook assumes that the experience of being a member of the group under discussion is a stable one, one with a clear meaning, a meaning constant through time, space, and different historical, social, political, and personal contexts.[1]

Throughout these essays, I have explored the limitations of an essentialist understanding of women's experiences by focusing on *how* a woman's race, class, sexuality, and physical or mental condition combine in historically specific ways to produce her, and the responses to her, in classrooms and courtrooms. For example, in the preceding chapter, in exploring how a white, middle-class woman with a developmental disability was perceived in a sexual assault trial taking place in a North American city in the 1990s, it became clear that a series of assumptions about the meaning of her gender, race, class, and disability operated simultaneously to obscure the violence in her life. She was not considered to have suffered from the violence to the same extent as would another woman of her race and class who did not have a developmental disability. Disability did not simply combine with gender, race, and class, as bricks piled one on top of the other. Rather, the social response to mental disability *in a woman*, a response that would surely have been different if the woman in question had been Black, or poor, or both, included assumptions about her capacity to know she was being violated, ideas about men's right to women's bodies, and in particular, white men's right to violate with impunity.

The point of anti-essentialism – the complex tracing of the social narratives that script how women experience their gender and how others respond to it – is to determine how to identify and interrupt those assumptions and practices that deny women their human rights. Put another way, the point of anti-essentialism is antisubordination. The tracing of these multiple systems of domination as they come together at one site for different kinds of women helps us to evaluate feminist law reform strategies. For example, rape shield laws restricting the introduction of prior sexual history may work well for many women but can work against women with developmental disabilities, because these laws make it difficult to introduce the social histories of violence that mark the women's lives. Without these social histories of violence – the way, for instance, that a woman with developmental disabilities often has a long history of being sexually abused and assaulted by men around her – it is difficult to make sense of her behaviour and the behaviour of others to her. We cannot begin to evaluate how laws work for women, or don't work, without understanding that gender comes into existence through race, class, sexuality, and physical or mental capacity.

In identifying the multiple narratives that script women's lives, we come to see that women are socially constituted in different and unequal relation to one another. It is not only that some women are considered to be worth more than other women, but that the status of one woman depends on the subordinate status of another woman in many complex ways. To take just one example, a middle-class woman gains her respectability, hence her value, from a number of sources, among them the social status she gains from not cleaning her own house, and not engaging in paid work to clean the houses of others. These sources of her status are not merely in representation, that is, in how she is likely to be perceived. They are also material. The houses of the middle class *are* cleaned by working-class women, and more often than not by Black women and women of colour. Here the material and ideological arrangements of patriarchy, class exploitation, and white supremacy combine in uneven ways to structure relations among women. While these oppressive systems do not come together in ways that ensure that socially advantaged women can successfully press their claims in court (there are still powerful narratives that work against them), belonging to the dominant race, class or culture does alter the forms of marginalization women encounter in the justice system.

Given the many ways in which women are implicated in one another's lives, anti-essentialism as a methodology takes us well beyond a politics of inclusion. That is, we can no longer devise political strategies that start with something we might call women's experience, on to which we would then graft the special strategies that would apply to women with disabilities, women of colour, or lesbians. To do so is to install a norm that privileges one group of women at the expense of others. A more fruitful approach is to ascertain how, at specific sites, patriarchy, white supremacy, and capitalism interlock to structure women differently and unequally. When we pursue these shifting hierarchical relations, we can begin to recognize how we are *implicated* in the subordination of other women. Our strategies for change then have less to do with being inclusive than they have do with being accountable.

What would a politics of accountability look like? Clearly it begins with anti-essentialism and the recognition that there is no one stable core we can call woman's experience. Equally important, it is a politics guided by a search for the ways in which we are complicitous in the subordination of others. A feminist politics of accountability cannot proceed on the assumption that as women we are uninvolved in the subordination of others. If we take as our point of departure that systems of domination interlock and sustain one another, we can begin to identify those moments when we are dominant and those when we are subordinate. Our implication in various systems of domination means that there are several ways in which we can perform ourselves as dominant at the same time that we understand ourselves to be engaging in liberatory politics. For example, Western middle-class women benefit from those economic and political processes that produce immigrant and refugee women from the South. When we engage in political action, for example efforts to use international law to protect women from male violence, we cannot understand the context in which this violence takes place without examining how our own positions of middle-class respectability help to sustain and produce such violence. In the search for appropriate strategies, we will need to examine those systems which benefit us, as well as those which subordinate us. As Western women we perform ourselves as dominant when we engage in a politics of saving other women. Instead of seeking to save women we consider less fortunate than ourselves, we might begin to organize against the racism that structures migration and flight, and that continues to structure the lives of women fleeing to the North.

Obviously, such political projects cannot get underway if we do not *recognize* our own habits of dominance and our complicity in systems of domination. A goal of this book has been to develop our capacity to engage in this kind of re-visioning through a critical appraisal of the social construction of gender, race and class. The anti-essentialism that is the thrust of much of what I have argued enjoyed considerable popularity in many academic circles over the past five years. Of late, however, it has become increasingly clear that the honeymoon is over and the critics of anti-essentialism, who are by no means a unified group, have begun to assert themselves. In this last chapter, I want to explore some of the criticisms directed at anti-essentialist approaches and reiterate my conclusion that feminist politics must pursue the charting of hierarchical relations among women if we are to change the world.

Criticisms of anti-essentialist approaches have come from feminists and others. Some concerns have taken the form of a general condemnation of anti-essentialists who rely on postmodernism. There is also a more specific charge from within feminism that an anti-essentialist approach is politically ineffective and slides too easily into a disparagement of white women. As these criticisms suggest, the salient question is, 'To essentialize or not to essentialize?' I want to suggest here that this question must be asked alongside of another: How does essentialism or anti-essentialism contribute to antisubordination?

Anti-essentialists who rely on postmodernism have been criticized for the apparent contradiction between seeing identity as socially constructed in multiple ways and maintaining, nonetheless, that there are identifiably oppressed groups; that there is, as Fanon wrote, 'a fact of Blackness.'[2] Keenan Malik, for instance, articulates the gist of this concern when he argues that a postmodern understanding of difference can lead to the position that all identities have equal validity. One could not, therefore, make an objective assessment that specific groups of people are oppressed by others. Like many others who fear that anti-essentialism leaves us hopelessly stuck in a relativist position, Malik suggests that we have to return to 'real social and economic mechanisms.' In his words, we 'require a standard of significance to distinguish between real or significant facts and irrelevant ones' although such a standard has to be historically specific.[3] This standard must enable us to name inequality, for example, as a by-product of capitalism, and enable us to chart the specific groups that are oppressed under capitalism.

In this book, while I have relied on postmodern theories for understanding the construction of subjectivity, I tried to keep a modernist eye on domination. Who is dominating whom is not a question I reply to with the answer that we are all constituted as simultaneously dominant and subordinate. While we *are* all simultaneously dominant and subordinate, and have varying degrees of privilege and penalty, this insight is not the most relevant when we are seeking to end specific hierarchies at specific sites. For example, when we confront the whiteness of the academy and note that an overwhelming majority of professors are white, we cannot change this situation by responding that white professors also belong to subordinate groups – some are women, some are disabled, some are lesbians. Such a response amounts to a statement that race does not matter, an outright denial of the impact of white supremacy on the lives of people of colour.

Thus, my own pursuit of anti-essentialism has often required the kind of historically specific standard to which Malik refers, even though I do not understand postmodernism to be as dangerously relativist as he does. Throughout this work, I have talked about dominant and subordinate groups as though they exist, and I have named patriarchy, white supremacy and capitalism as three systems that interlock to structure women, differently, in subordinate positions. I have therefore operated under the assumption that to have white skin is to have privilege, for example, but noted repeatedly that the significance of this privilege could only be ascertained when we considered how privileges combine with penalties in specific situations to produce hierarchies of women. The work I have presented here is mainly a tracing of the production of these hierarchies, utilizing postmodern tools about the constitution of subjectivity, in order to determine how we might disrupt these systems of subordination. This approach is not one unanimously endorsed by Western feminists, and it is to their criticisms that I now turn.

Anti-essentialism Isn't What It Used to Be

In the last few years, among feminist academics with whom I have common cause and, frequently, a shared conceptual framework of anti-essentialism, I have encountered a slightly different critique of anti-essentialism than the one expressed by Malik. In prestigious feminist journals and books, various writers have suggested that the project to talk about race and gender oppression in the same breath, as an anti-essentialist analysis would require, is terribly flawed. The core of what is wrong, these writers suggest, is that in the rush away from gender essentialism, theorists attending to the significance of both race and gender have simply essentialized differences. This charge of essentialism is usually directed at people of colour and at antiracist projects. It is primarily a claim that gender essentialism has been replaced by race essentialism.

For some writers, the effort to attend to how race and gender interlock has also resulted in a malicious depiction of white women as villains. Others express a yearning for the good old days when the description of women's oppression possessed 'the oomph that gender packs'[4] or the 'cultural authority'[5] that was gained from speaking of an essential female subject. Naomi Shor, in mourning the sisterhood and solidarity that a common description of women's oppression could provide, illustrates this response. She writes:

I would argue that such a commonality, however tenuous, however contested, however limited in its geopolitical sphere of application, did exist in the early days of feminism and did make possible some of its greatest gains.[6]

Equally nostalgic for the time when feminist politics did not pay attention to race, Jane Roland Martin suggests in an article published in the leading feminist journal *Signs*, that white women scholars are having to endure an exceedingly chilly academic climate produced by those who judge white women's scholarship by a harsher standard than that applied to men's scholarship.[7] Quoting Nancy Miller, Martin writes that white women scholars now live in fear – a fear of other women's critiques. It is clear that Martin and Miller are referring to women of colour, although there are many white women scholars who make antiracist critiques. Martin's resentment is shown when she asserts that clearly the academy became more comfortable for those who had previously been excluded while it became an exceedingly chilly research climate for white feminists.[8]

No less a scholar than Catharine MacKinnon, who has otherwise enabled us to think so deeply about the social construction of gender and on whose work I have often relied, has declared that there is a widespread and abhorrent 'trivialization of the white woman's subordination.'[9] Anyone who suggests that white women are also privileged, MacKinnon proclaims, is bent on 'dis-identification with women.' Aiming low, she claims that all such critics really want is to be in a group that includes men.[10] To call this a backlash and leave it at that is unhelpful. Instead, I want to re-examine what lies behind the words (the direct thrusts as well as the more refined ones), of some of these eminent feminist scholars who think that the anti-essentialist project of theorizing women's differences has gone so terribly awry. I will argue that recent claims that anti-racist projects are simply essentializing race in place of gender are made by those who, as Paul Gilroy has put it, are 'insufficiently alive to the lingering power of specifically racialized forms of power and subordination.'[11]

Although most scholars concerned with the failings of current attempts to deal with differences among women do not go to the lengths of MacKinnon and Martin, in accusing women of colour of undermining white women, the more muted criticism, that differences are now being essentialized, conceals a similar resentment of the race-ing of gender and a denial of the social context of racism. One such example can be found in a widely acclaimed feminist text. Christina Crosby, a women's studies scholar, in an article for the influential anthology *Feminists Theorize the Political*, which contains the work of many prominent feminist scholars, begins her criticism of the way we currently 'deal' with differences by asserting that

'differences' are now spoken everywhere in the academy. The demand to specify, to mark the (now familiar) differences of race, class, and gender is part of a general call for diversity, pluralism, for a multicultural academy. In research and teaching, in writing or awarding grants, in admitting students, in hiring and promoting faculty, one must now deal with differences.[12]

It is difficult not to see in these words a scholarly version of the complaint articulated by the conservative Right that minority demands have simply gone too far and that political correctness has taken hold. Many academic and legal institutions have remained steadfast in their position that race and class must not count. So steadfast are they in their claim to neutrality that, in many institutions, the numbers of faculty members of colour have not changed for a decade and, in some, have even dropped.[13] There is a deep refusal to 'deal with difference,' and a marked complacency about the rising incidents of racist violence in and out of the academy. But Crosby is right is one respect. Diversity, while not in everyone's budget, is at least on everyone's lips. Some of those speaking, however, are anxious to declare obsolete the concern with difference (we are all humans, equally meritorious, etc.) or to speak in the language of human resources and the corporate world, of an ominous management of diversity.

Claiming to be a member of the team that is devoted to 'building for differences,' Crosby argues that the problem today is that we have taken a very old unreflective stance towards difference. Just as we once made the mistake of understanding women's identity as preordained, something we would just have to discover and could confidently say applied to all women, so now we understand differences as pre-given. The question used to be 'Who am I?' but this has given way to 'Who are we?'[14] Difference has become an essence to be recognized rather than a process, a social and historical construction, to be deconstructed.

It is hard to disagree with Crosby when she notes that there is much to worry about when we rely on a theory of identity that remains so determinedly ahistorical and essentialist. Differences, she maintains, cannot be seen as self-evident; we must ask how they are socially produced. Crosby argues that we must be able to get from the particular to the universal, so that each of us does not remain trapped in our own particularism. Until recently, I would have enthusiastically endorsed what I believed was a call to attend to the production of the categories of race, class, and gender and how they interlock. I am now much more guarded, but not because I dispute the constructedness of categories or the complexities of their operation in and through one another.

A sense of racial entitlement surrounds these arguments, as though the academy is naturally white and must now remake itself in ways too foreign to contemplate. I have begun to notice that those who complain that we now see differences as pre-given assume that women of colour have won significant gains in the academy. When Jane Roland Martin maintains that in the rush to be non-essentialist, we have constructed 'the trap of pre-determined categories' and that we have unduly privileged race and class as fundamental variables,[15] I am reminded that this is the same person who thinks that the academy is comfortable for women of colour and chilly for white women academics. In other words, those who are complaining of differences being essentialized are also minimizing the continuing effects of white supremacy in the lives of people of colour and making the assumption that their presence in the academy is disruptive.

The danger in making the argument that differences are now essentialized is to miscalculate how far we have actually come on the road of racial equality. We risk ignoring the relentless whiteness of the academy and thus the social context in which our descriptions of inequality are *heard*. It has been far too easy to confuse an argument about the construct-edness of all identities with the view that the oppression of specific groups of peoples does not exist. I found to my dismay that when, in my grad-uate seminars and in my writing, I noted that races, like nations, are ima-gined,[16] meaning that our understanding of race is socially constructed and historically specific, what some of my white readers and listeners understood was that *racism* is imagined.

The Canadian scholar Patricia Marchak exemplifies this kind of denial of racism in the university when she discusses the difficulties of defining race:

A more precise biological definition (of race) is not of much use since, with the massive mixing of peoples of all gene pools, the human population is not divided into groups demarcated by distinctive physical characteristics. The term 'race' is thus not very helpful, *and its extension 'racism' is somewhat ambiguous* [emphasis added].[17]

Racism is, of course, anything but ambiguous to its victims, but a social con-struction approach can easily be harnessed by those who do not experi-ence racism to deny its existence.

Encountering this reaction among colleagues has led George Dei to com-ment:

I have seen, although never understood why, some colleagues enclose race in quotation marks. All social concepts lack scientific validity. Terms like gender, race, and class are concepts that society has chosen to engage in conversations. They are socially constructed categories whose meanings are historically specific and change in different political and cultural contexts. They are contested notions and yet it is race that appears in quotation marks. Why?[18]

One wonders what, or more to the point, who, is really being bracketed by the inverted commas? Is the assumption that race is not really a signi-ficant determinant of status, whereas gender or sexual orientation is? The popular expression of this sentiment can be seen in such arguments as put forward by *Toronto Star* columnist Frank Jones, who writes approv-ingly of sociologist Evelyn Kallen's opinion that the people most stigma-tized today are gay men and lesbians. Whereas 'bias against racial groups is steadily being chipped away by research showing that, genetically, humans regardless of race, are almost identical,' Jones reports that sociologists such as Kallen and her husband, David Rees Hughes, are of the opinion that 'prejudice against homosexuality' is 'especially hard to crack because it is reinforced by some religious groups.'[19] Jones's views, and those of other writers who would deny what Dei describes as 'the wrath of oppressive practices which continue to signify skin colour as racial difference,'[20] contribute greatly to the notion of hierarchies of oppression and discourage in this way the solidarity that might be possible with a better analysis of interlocking oppression.

Ironically, since the denial of racism is easily accomplished with the conceptual tools of social construction, those scholars who put their stock in gene pools and 'prejudice,' rather than racist practices, now stand side by side with those scholars who reject such analytical frameworks and who are more alert to the enduring power of racism. Christina Crosby is a scholar who acknowledges that it 'is impossible to exaggerate the importance of the critique of feminism's (*white* feminism's) exclusions, the ways in which the supposedly universal category of "woman" was constituted.' Yet she immediately qualifies this statement with a critique of African-American feminist Audre Lorde's call for a recognition of the significance of race. Crosby notes:

However importantly feminism has been modified, specifying differences and 'describing minority experiences' is not going to transform women's studies at the level of theory, that is, enable it to break through the circle of ideology. For that circle is vicious precisely because it is elastic and expansive though resolutely closed. While Hartsock has taken seriously Lorde's call for a theory which can deal with differences, Lorde herself, in appealing to the 'fact' of 'the differences between us' as the corrective to feminist theory, is suggesting, however polemically, that facts speak for themselves. The *relationship*, then, between 'the real' and knowledge of the real, between 'facts' and theory, history and theory is occluded even as women's studies seeks to address the problem of theoretical practice. Lorde's intervention, and a host of other critiques of 'racist feminism' have broken up an oppressively singular feminism, but much of U.S. women's studies is still bound to an empiricist historicism which is the flip side of the idealism scorned and disavowed by feminisms.[21]

Speaking about racial difference, then, is not going to start the revolution. When Crosby takes Audre Lorde to task for talking about difference as though it were a fact and not a process, a crucial piece of history has been omitted. The fact of difference is, for Lorde, the reality of tremendous racial oppression. Lorde was mostly talking to white women about this fact and she was uncompromising in her insistence that the categories of race, class, gender, and sexuality are interlocked. The question of audience is a crucial one here.[22] Lorde had to remind her audience of the difference that skin colour makes since they were unlikely to keep this in mind.[23]

The way we talk currently about differences is most assuredly socially produced and specific to our historical moment, but that moment continues to be one in which white supremacy is alive and well and deeply influencing how subordinate groups talk about their difference and the way in which they are heard. We still cannot speak out loud about the complexities of racial identities without risking that the oppressive contours of racism will be denied. How do we distinguish a denial of racism from the argument that we cannot speak of social construction and facts of oppression in the same breath?

Critics of what are variously called 'the problem of difference,' identity politics, ethnic particularism, or race essentialism have argued that we need to return to a concept of the universal, although most of those making this argument acknowledge that the old image of the Enlightenment's universal man, rational, and autonomous, has to be refashioned.[24] For Naomi Shor, a well-known white academic, the problem of difference today is that, in the move away from universalism, we have turned to a particularism that is dangerous, narrow, and exclusive. Her complaint, like most of this kind, focuses on racial differences. Simply put, the complaint is that in our bid to move beyond universalism and gender essentialism (two slightly different ideas for some),[25] we have come to a dreadful and dangerous place of race essentialism and regressive ethnic enclaves. In a sobering paragraph, in which the name Auschwitz invokes the genocide of European Jewry, Shor writes:

If Auschwitz dealt the Enlightenment ideal of universalism – a notion rejected by fascism – a death blow, what may pass for the repetition of Auschwitz, the ongoing ethnic cleansing in Bosnia Herzegovina, has if not revived universalism, then called into question the celebration of particularisms, at least in their regressive ethnic form.[26]

Significantly, it is only in a footnote attached to the end of this quote, that Shor completes the progression of signs that begins with Auschwitz (where Nazis clearly did not believe in a universal humanity), moves to Bosnia, and ends, cryptically, with a footnote that references a point made by Cornel West, a Black scholar who writes that the new cultural politics of difference is about trashing the monolithic and the homogeneous in the name of diversity and multiplicity. Since West warns of ethnic chauvinism at the same time as he decries a faceless universalism,[27] and is clearly in favour of the new cultural politics of difference, it is unclear whether Shor means to indicate that he endorses her position. Certainly, many Black scholars share her concerns about the dangers of particularism, but they also note, usually in the same sentence, the persistence of racism and the need to counter its destructive effects.[28] Patricia Hill Collins, responding to a reviewer's criticism that her book *Black Feminist Thought* is built on the notion of a unitary or essential Black subject, noted that she deliberately decided not to focus on diversity among Black women. To do so, she countered, would have made them disappear as subjects, a tendency that is all too prevalent in a racist society.[29]

It can be argued that when white feminists essentialized gender, they were making a similarly strategic move. Strategic essentialism, however, is less of a defence at sites where it is employed by dominant groups in order to exclude subordinate groups, for example, when white women employ essentialism in order to privilege their own experience of gender. Collins's essentializing also could not be justified if it were to be applied at a site where power and access are granted to Black subjects who most closely fit the standard she sets for Blackness. For example, she could not rely on a unitary Black subject in an all-Black organization where the interests of Black lesbians were being disregarded.

Recognizing differences and multiplicities cannot be automatically conflated with a terrible celebration of particularisms or a self-serving essentialism. I doubt that Shor would say that all articulations of difference lead to Bosnia, but the risk is clearly present and it is a risk that makes most of our hearts skip a beat. If paying attention to race can take us to Auschwitz and Bosnia, let us stamp out the evil before it is full-grown. I can read such passages no other way in spite of the author's numerous distractions, philosophical detours, and earnest declarations of being really and truly in favour of diversity. This is a different kind of critique than the one made by women of colour to white women that a homogeneous description of women's oppression re-centres white women and leaves racism unexamined. Shor's critique speaks to something more terrible than a maintenance of the status quo. It is addressed to us 'ethnics' who would speak of our differences in so essentialist a fashion, or perhaps, who would speak of our differences at all. In this way, as Ann duCille has noted of the response to Black women scholars, legitimate complaints about oppression and attempts to resist are dismissed as anti-intellectual identity politics.[30] That this is the case in as refined a criticism as Shor's is evident in her vague references to the misery caused by identity politics,[31] to 'all we have lost' as a result of it[32] (begging the question, Who has lost what?), and to the good old days of 1970s feminism.

Along with bell hooks, I am suspicious of those who warn of the dangers of identity politics, race essentialism, or ethnic particularism without paying attention to the specific relations of domination and subordination in any one context, and without contextualizing the responses subordinate groups make to domination, thus distinguishing acts of resistance from acts of domination.[33] As hooks suggests in her assessment of Diana Fuss's exploration of the misuses of essentialism by minority students in the classroom, critiques of identity politics may be 'the new, chic way to silence students from marginal groups.'[34]

In a white-dominated classroom or courtroom, those who talk about their differences are likely to be heard as essentialist, while those who listen to the talk about differences get to sit in judgment. In such a scenario, those who judge have a better chance of appearing calm, confident, all knowing, and in control, while the natives, pleading their case, can only be described as restless.[35] Without taking into account the context of persistent and destructive racism, it is possible to equate Black women's desire to set up a counter-canon of Black women's writings with the universalizing of Enlightenment thinkers who did not think Black people could have access to their notion of the universal. Similarly, only in failing to keep the realities of white supremacy front and centre could one see, as Christina Crosby does, in Audre Lorde's 'fact of difference,' a similarity to the willingness of Charlotte Brontë's white heroines so eager to make themselves into universal subjects.[36]

We can and we must transcend these positions and we must do so by talking about how we are implicated in the 'particularisms,' which I *will* put in quotation marks. I am not suggesting that articulations of difference by subordinate groups remain beyond critique, but that those making this critique closely examine their own subject positions. Who is describing and assessing the realities of whom, how do we hear these descriptions and what relations do they secure? Shor declares that her goal is a revised universal that 'would include all those who wish to be included, and that would above all afford them the opportunity to speak universal while not relinquishing their difference(s).'[37] This goal is unreachable because our differences are precisely what cannot be acknowledged without confronting the fact of domination. What has prevailed in the views I have so far been discussing is that dominant groups have been arguing from a point of subordination, a position of innocence and non-implication in systems of oppression. It is white women who are really disparaged, these scholars argue, and it is they who are the outsiders in the academy today.

As I noted in my introduction, the point of theorizing differences among women is not for the sake of inclusion but for the sake of antisubordination. There is little chance of disturbing relations of domination unless we consider how they structure our subject positions. What most distinguishes the critics discussed in this chapter is their inattention to these relations, an inattention that has led to a denial of the continuing effects of white supremacy (for example, the erroneous view that women of colour now have most of the jobs in the academy and get all the grants), claims of mutuality between vastly different contexts (Auschwitz, Bosnia, and attempts to establish a counter-canon of Black women's writings), and an arrogance of subject position that does not ask about the sources of the yearning for the good old days of lost sisterhood and the rush to critique how women of colour essentialize differences but not how white women do. What all of these features secure is innocence, a determined non-involvement in the social relations being analyzed.

Before we can determine how far we can go, either in essentializing or not essentializing, we need to examine how we explain to ourselves the social hierarchies that surround us. We need to ask: Where am I in this picture? Am I positioning myself as the saviour of less fortunate peoples? as the progressive one? as more subordinated? as innocent? These are moves of superiority and we need to reach beyond them. I return here to my notion of a politics of accountability as opposed to a politics of inclusion. Accountability begins with tracing relations of privilege and penalty. It cannot proceed unless we examine our complicity. Only then can we ask questions about how we are understanding differences and for what purpose.

Notes

Introduction: Looking White People in the Eye

1 Frantz Fanon, *Black Skin, White Masks* (New York: Grove Press 1967). Originally published in French under the title *Peau Noire, Masques Blancs* (Paris: Éditions du Seuil 1952).

2 Robert Young, *Colonial Desire: Hybridity in Theory, Culture and Race* (London: Routledge 1995), 161.

3 Homi K. Bhabha, *The Location of Culture* (London: Routledge 1994), 41, 42.

4 Fanon, *Black Skin, White Masks*, 231.

5 Bhabha, *The Location of Culture*, 41–3.

6 Stuart Hall, 'The After-life of Frantz Fanon: Why Fanon? Why Now? Why *Black Skin, White Masks?*' in Alan Read, ed., *The Fact of Blackness: Frantz Fanon and Visual Representation* (Seattle: Bay Press 1996), 18–19.

7 bell hooks, *Black Looks: Race and Representation* (Boston: South End Press 1992), 22.

8 Ibid., 23.

9 Ibid., 24.

10 Ibid.

11 Inderpal Grewal, *Home and Harem: Nation, Gender, Empire, and the Cultures of Travel* (Durham: Duke University Press 1996), 11.

12 Ibid., 12.

13 Edward W. Said, *Covering Islam: How the Media and the Experts Determine How We See the Rest of the World* (New York: Pantheon 1981).

14 Simon Watney has written of the demonizing of Africa through the social construction of AIDS as an African disease that has contaminated Europe and North America. 'Missionary Positions: AIDS, "Africa," and Race,' in Russell Ferguson, Martha Gever, Trinh T. Minh-ha, and Cornel West, eds.,

Out There: Marginalization and Contemporary Cultures (Cambridge, MA: The New Museum of Contemporary Art and the MIT Press 1990), 89–106.

15 See Homa Hoodfar, 'The Veil in Their Minds and on Our Heads: The Persistence of Colonial Images of Muslim Women,' *Resources for Feminist Research / Documentation sur la recherche féministe* 22, nos. 3/4 (Fall/Winter 1993), 5–18.

16 Daliah Setarah, 'Women Escaping Genital Mutilation – Seeking Asylum in the United States,' *UCLA Women's Law Journal* 6, no. 1 (1995), 126.

17 Ibid., 131. The sheer numbers of legal articles on female genital surgeries and the popularity of this theme among graduate students selecting topics for research are indicators of the place female genital surgeries have in the scholarly imagination. See chapter 5.

18 Rupert Ross, *Dancing with a Ghost: Exploring Indian Reality* (Markham, ON: Octopus Publishing Group 1992); R. Ross, *Returning to the Teachings: Exploring Aboriginal Justice* (Toronto: Penguin 1996).

19 Ross, *Dancing with a Ghost*, 4.

20 Focusing on sight and the politics of the gaze arguably excludes people who are blind. It would be interesting to consider the extent to which people who are sight or hearing-impaired absorb dominant messages. For example, if one does not actually see racist images of people of colour, or hear them, is one more immune to their racist content? Similarly, does a blind person have fewer racist responses because she cannot see that a person is Black?

21 Sherene Razack, 'Schooling Research on South and East Asian Students: The Perils of Talking about Culture,' *Race, Class and Gender* 2, no. 3 (Spring 1995), 67–82.

22 Christine Sleeter, 'How White Teachers Construct Race,' in Cameron McCarthy and Warren Chrichlow, eds., *Race, Identity and Representation in Education* (New York and London: Routledge 1993), 157–71.

23 For an incisive critique of the appropriation of Aboriginal practices, see Ward Churchill, *Indians Are Us? Culture and Genocide in Native North America* (Toronto: Between the Lines 1994).

24 Chandra Mohanty, 'On Race and Voice: Challenges for Liberal Education in the 1990s,' *Cultural Critique* 14 (Winter 1991), 181.

25 Coco Fusco, 'The Other History of Intercultural Performance,' *The Drama Review* 38, no. 1 (1994), 145.

26 I attempt to use the concept of space in a forthcoming work on prostitution. That is, the actual spaces where prostitution takes place come into existence through capitalist, patriarchal, and white supremacist practices and, simultaneously, these spaces uphold capitalism, white supremacy, and patriarchy.

27 Trinh T. Minh-ha, *Woman, Native, Other: Writing Postcoloniality and Feminism*

(Bloomington: Indiana University Press 1989); Patricia Hill Collins, *Black Feminist Thought: Knowledge, Consciousness, and the Politics of Empowerment* (Boston: Unwin Hyman 1990).

28 Anne McClintock, *Imperial Leather: Race, Gender and Sexuality in the Colonial Contest* (London and New York: Routledge 1995).

29 Ann Laura Stoler, 'Carnal Knowledge and Imperial Power: Gender, Race, and Morality in Colonial Asia,' in Micaela di Leonardo, ed., *Gender at the Crossroads: Feminist Anthropology in the Post-Modern Era* (Berkeley: University of California Press 1991), 71.

30 Ibid., 70.

31 Sara Suleri, *The Rhetoric of English India* (Chicago: University of Chicago Press 1992).

32 Reina Lewis, *Gendering Orientalism: Race, Femininity, and Representation* (London: Routledge 1996).

33 For a review of intersectionality theorists in law, see Trina Grillo, 'Anti-Essentialism and Intersectionality: Tools to Dismantle the Master's House,' *Berkeley Women's Law Journal* 10, no. 1 (1995), 16–30.

34 Cynthia Enloe, *Bananas, Beaches and Bases: Making Feminist Sense of International Politics* (London: Pandora Press 1989), 185.

35 Abigail B. Bakan and Daiva Stasiulis, 'Making the Match: Domestic Placement Agencies and the Racialization of Women's Household Work,' *Signs: Journal of Women in Culture and Society* 20, no. 2 (1995), 303–35.

36 Mary Louise Fellows and Sherene Razack, 'The Race to Innocence: Confronting Hierarchical Relations among Women,' *Iowa Journal of Gender, Race and Justice*, forthcoming.

37 Mary Louise Pratt, *Imperial Eyes: Travel Writing and Transculturation* (London and New York: Routledge 1992), 7.

38 Lewis, *Gendering Orientalism*, 4.

39 See Himani Bannerji, ed., *Returning the Gaze: Essays on Racism, Feminism and Politics* (Toronto: Sister Vision Press 1993).

40 Rey Chow, *Woman and Chinese Modernity: The Politics of Reading between the East and West* (Minneapolis: University of Minnesota Press 1991), 23.

41 Edward W. Said, *Culture and Imperialism* (New York: Alfred Knopf 1993), xviii.

42 Sherene Razack, *Canadian Feminism and the Law: The Women's Legal Education and Action Fund and the Pursuit of Equality* (Toronto: Second Story Press 1991).

43 David Theo Goldberg, *Racist Culture: Philosophy and the Politics of Meaning* (Oxford: Blackwell 1993).

44 Linda Martin Alcoff, 'Philosophy and Racial Identity,' *Radical Philosophy* 75 (Jan/Feb 1996), 5.

45 Trinh, *Woman, Native, Other*, 149.

46 For a discussion of how this unfolded at one feminist conference, see Mary Louise Fellows and Sherene Razack, 'Seeking Relations: Law and Feminism Roundtables,' *Signs: Journal of Women and Culture in Society* 19, no. 4 (1994), 1048–83.

47 One exception is Martha Minow's work, *Making All the Difference: Inclusion, Exclusion, and American Law* (Ithaca: Cornell University Press 1990).

48 Ibid., 174.

49 George J. Sefa Dei, 'African-Centred Schools in North America: Going Beyond the Polemic,' in *Anti-Racism Education: Theory and Practice* (Halifax: Fernwood Press 1996).

50 See Joy Mannette, ed., *Elusive Justice: Beyond the Marshall Inquiry* (Halifax: Fernwood Press 1992).

51 Chow, *Woman and Chinese Modernity*, 17.

1: 'The Cold Game of Equality Staring'

1 Trinh T. Minh-ha, *Woman, Native, Other: Writing, Postcoloniality and Feminism* (Bloomington: Indiana University Press 1989), 54.

2 Alan Borovoy, *The Fundamentals of Our Fundamental Freedoms* (Ottawa: Canadian Labour Congress 1979).

3 For a discussion of these stereotypes, see Gina Marchetti, *Romance and the 'Yellow Peril': Race, Sex, and Discursive Strategies in Hollywood Fiction* (Berkeley: University of California Press 1993); Richard Fung, 'Looking for My Penis: The Eroticized Asian in Gay Video Porn,' in Bad Object Choices, eds., *How Do I Look? Queer Film and Video* (Seattle: Seattle Bay Press 1991), 145–60. For a discussion of the operation of these stereotypes in the law see Cynthia Kwei Yung Lee, 'Beyond Black and White: Racializing Asian Americans in a Society Obsessed with O.J.,' *Hastings Women's Law Journal* 6, no. 2 (Summer 1995), 165–207.

4 Sherene Razack, 'Revolution from Within: Dilemmas of Feminist Jurisprudence,' *Queen's Quarterly* 97, no. 3 (Autumn 1990), 401.

5 Joan C. Williams, 'Culture and Certainty: Legal History and the Reconstructive Project,' *Virginia Law Review* 76, nos. 1–4 (1990), 719.

6 Kenneth L. Karst, 'Woman's Constitution,' *Duke Law Journal* 3 (June 1984), 447–508.

7 See Razack, 'Revolution from Within,' for a fuller discussion.

8 William Kymlicka, *Liberalism, Community, and Culture* (Oxford: Clarendon Press 1989).

9 Sherene Razack, *Canadian Feminism and the Law: The Women's Legal Education and Action Fund and the Pursuit of Equality* (Toronto: Second Story Press 1991), 23.

10 See, for example, William Kymlicka, 'Individual and Community Rights,' in Judith Baker, ed., *Group Rights* (Toronto: University of Toronto Press 1994), 17–33.

11 Razack, *Canadian Feminism and the Law.*

12 Rheal Seguin and Rod Mickleburgh, 'Nancy B. Judge Balanced 2 Codes,' *The Globe and Mail* (Toronto), 7 January 1992, A4.

13 Jenny Morris, *Pride Against Prejudice: Transforming Attitudes to Disability* (London: Women's Press 1991), 42.

14 Carol Pateman, *The Sexual Contract* (Stanford: Stanford University Press 1988), 8.

15 Patricia Williams, *The Alchemy of Race and Rights: Diary of a Law Professor* (Cambridge: Harvard University Press 1991), 131.

16 Ibid., 21.

17 Ibid., 19.

18 Toni Morrison, *Playing in the Dark: Whiteness and the Literary Imagination* (Cambridge: Harvard University Press 1992), 64.

19 See Robert A. Williams, Jr., 'Taking Rights Aggressively: The Perils and Promise of Critical Legal Theory for Peoples of Color,' *Law and Inequality* 5 (1987), 130; Elizabeth M. Schneider, 'The Dialectic of Rights and Politics: Perspectives from the Women's Movement,' *New York University Law Review* 61 (October 1986), 599.

20 Pateman, *The Sexual Contract*, 16.

21 Jane Flax, *Thinking Fragments: Psychoanalysis, Feminism and Postmodernism in the Contemporary West* (Berkeley: University of California Press 1990), 181.

22 Michel Foucault, 'Two Lectures,' in Colin Gordon, ed., Colin Gordon, Leo Marshall, John Mepham, and Kate Soper, trans., *Power/Knowledge: Selected Interviews and Other Writings, 1972–1977* (New York: Pantheon Books 1980), 88–9.

23 Ibid., 96.

24 Valerie Walkerdine, *Schoolgirl Fictions* (London: Verso Press 1990), 18.

25 Foucault, 'Two Lectures,' 92.

26 Biddy Martin, 'Feminism, Criticism and Foucault,' in Irene Diamond and Lee Quinby, eds., *Feminism and Foucault: Reflections on Resistance* (Boston: Northeastern University Press 1988), 17.

27 Walkerdine, *Schoolgirl Fictions*, 36.

28 Jennifer Nedelsky, 'Law, Boundaries and the Bounded Self,' *Representations* 30 (Spring 1990) 169.

29 Flax, *Thinking Fragments*, 182.

2: The Gaze from the Other Side

I would like to thank the many colleagues and friends who sustained this critical reflection, including Dwight Boyd, Irene Bujara, Homa Hoodfar, Ruth Roach

Pierson, and Judith Whitehead. Special thanks to Dominique Boisvert for the many conversations that prompted this article in the first place.

1 Mari J. Matsuda, 'Public Response to Racist Speech: Considering the Victim's Story,' *Michigan Law Review* 87 (1989), 2322.
2 Trinh T. Minh-ha, 'Not You/Like You: Post-Colonial Women and the Interlocking Questions of Identity and Difference,' in Gloria Anzaldúa, ed., *Making Face, Making Soul: Creative and Critical Perspectives of Women of Color* (San Francisco: an aunt lute foundation book 1990), 373.
3 See Arun Mukherjee, ed., *Sharing Our Experience* (Ottawa: Canadian Advisory Council on the Status of Women 1993).
4 Toni M. Massaro, 'Empathy, Legal Story-telling, and the Rule of Law: New Words, Old Wounds?' *Michigan Law Review* 87 (August 1989), 2099.
5 Ibid.
6 Kim Lane Scheppele, 'Foreword: Telling Stories,' *Michigan Law Review* 87 (August 1989), 2079.
7 Richard Delgado, 'When a Story Is Just a Story: Does Voice Really Matter?' *Virginia Law Review* 76, no. 9 (1990), 95.
8 Matsuda, 'Public Response,' 2326.
9 Mari J. Matsuda, 'Looking to the Bottom: Critical Legal Studies and Reparations,' *Harvard Civil Rights–Civil Liberties Law Review* 22 (1987), 324.
10 Massaro, 'Empathy, ' 2105.
11 Sherene Razack, *Canadian Feminism and the Law: The Women's Legal Education and Action Fund and the Pursuit of Equality* (Toronto: Second Story Press 1991).
12 Robin West, 'Jurisprudence and Gender,' *University of Chicago Law Review* 55, no. 1 (Winter 1988), 70.
13 *FWTAO v. Tomen* formed the basis of a Charter challenge and a human rights complaint. For a discussion of the initial Charter challenge in 1987, see Razack, *Canadian Feminism and the Law,* 74–81. In 1991, the Federal Court of Appeal denied FWTAO the right to appeal the decision made at a lower level to reject its claims. The Court declared the by-law a private regulation and not one approved by the Lieutenant-Governor. The Charter does not apply to private regulations. See *FWTAO v. Tomen* (1991), 50 O.A.C. 158 (S.C.C.). When the case progressed through the Human Rights Commission, a Board of Appeal saw the by-law establishing FWTAO as discriminatory and not justifiable as a special program. FWTAO appealed this decision to the Divisional Court of Ontario. A decision rendered in 1995 also rejected their claims although the minority opinion suggested that the by-law was not in fact discrimination but a distinction without a disadvantage. See *Ontario Human Rights Commission et al. v. Ontario Teachers' Federation et al.* Ontario Court (Divisional Court), File No. 271/94, 273/94. Unreported decision, 21 June 1995.

14 Razack, *Canadian Feminism and the Law*, 78.

15 Patricia Monture-Angus, *Thunder in My Soul: A Mohawk Woman Speaks* (Halifax: Fernwood 1995), 35.

16 16 For a fuller discussion, see Razack, *Canadian Feminism and the Law*, chaps. 3 and 4.

17 Norma Alarcón, 'The Theoretical Subject(s) of This Bridge Called My Back and Anglo-American Feminism,' in Gloria Anzaldúa, ed., *Making Face, Making Soul. Haciendo Caras. Creative and Critical Perspectives by Women of Color* (San Francisco: an aunt lute foundation book 1990), 357.

18 Massaro, 'Empathy,' 2127.

19 Matsuda, 'Public Response,' 2322.

20 Ibid., 2327.

21 Ibid., 2362.

22 Ibid., 2364.

23 Kathleen Weiler, *Women Teaching for Change: Gender, Class and Power* (New York: Bergin and Garvey 1988), 5.

24 Henry Giroux, *Theory, Resistance, and Education* (South Hadley, MA: South Hadley Press, Bergin and Garvey, 1983), 19, cited in Weiler, *Women Teaching for Change*, 22.

25 Weiler, *Women Teaching for Change*, 22–3.

26 Valerie Walkerdine, 'On the Regulation of Speaking and Silence: Subjectivity, Class and Gender in Contemporary Schooling,' in Carolyn Steedman, ed., *Language, Gender and Childhood* (London: Routledge and Kegan Paul 1985), 204.

27 Ibid., 228–9.

28 Ibid., 238.

29 Paolo Freire, *Pedagogy of the Oppressed* (New York: Continuum Publishing 1970).

30 Some of this questioning, but with little in-depth study of the power of the educators and theorists in the First World, is undertaken in Peter McLaren and Peter Leonard, eds., *Paulo Freire: A Critical Encounter* (London and New York: Routledge 1993), 5. Indeed, the contributors to the book, with the exception of a brief reflection by bell hooks, are all men and overwhelmingly European.

31 Charles Paine, 'Relativism, Radical Pedagogy and the Ideology of Paralysis,' *College English* 50, no. 6 (1989), 558.

32 Salomón Magendzo, 'Popular Education in Nongovernmental Organizations: Education for Social Mobilization?' *Harvard Educational Review* 60, no. 1 (February 1990), 50.

33 Ricardo Zuniga, 'La Gestion Amphibie,' *Revue internationale d'action communautaire* 19 (1988), 158.

34 Ibid., 162.

35 Gayle Greene and Coppélia Kahn, 'Feminist Scholarship and the Social Con-
    struction of Woman,' in Gayle Greene and Coppélia Kahn, eds., *Making a Dif-
    ference: Feminist Literary Criticism* (London: Routledge 1985), 25.
36 Gloria Anzaldúa, *Borderlands/La Frontera* (San Francisco: Spinsters/an aunt
    lute foundation book 1989), 78.
37 Ibid., 80.
38 Bettina Aptheker, *Tapestries of Life* (Amherst: University of Massachusetts Press
    1989), 254.
39 Elizabeth Ellsworth, 'Why Doesn't This Feel Empowering? Working Through
    the Repressive Myths of Critical Pedagogy,' *Harvard Educational Review* 59,
    no. 3 (August 1989), 297–324.
40 I have used the word *ethical* to describe a collective reflection on the moral
    values we each hold. An ethical vision informs our politics in the sense that
    it is a shared sense of what is right and what is wrong.
41 Ellsworth, 'Why Doesn't This Feel Empowering?' 301.
42 Ibid., 305.
43 Uma Narayan, 'Working Together Across Differences: Some Considerations
    on Emotions and Political Practice,' *Hypatia* 3, no. 2 (Summer 1988), 31–47.
44 Monture-Angus, *Thunder in My Soul*, 67.
45 This issue is taken up at length by Mary Louise Fellows and Sherene Razack
    in 'The Race to Innocence: Confronting Hierarchical Relations among Women,'
    Iowa Journal of Gender, Race and Justice, forthcoming.
46 For an in-depth discussion of this concept, see Audre Lorde, *Sister Outsider*
    (New York: The Crossing Press 1984), 110.
47 Mechthild Hart, 'Critical Theory and Beyond: Further Perspectives on Eman-
    cipatory Education,' *Adult Education Quarterly* 40, no. 3 (Spring 1990), 135.
48 Lynet Uttal, 'Nods That Silence,' in Anzaldúa, ed., *Making Face, Making Soul*,
    318.
49 Monture-Angus, *Thunder in My Soul*, 18–19.
50 Richard Brosio, 'Teaching and Learning for Democratic Empowerment: A
    Critical Evaluation,' *Educational Theory* 40, no. 1 (Winter 1990), 75.
51 Iris Marion Young, *Justice and the Politics of Difference* (Princeton: Princeton
    University Press 1990), 235.
52 Carolyn Steedman, *Landscape for a Good Woman: A Story for Two Lives* (London:
    Virago 1986), 79.
53 Maria Lugones, 'Hablando cara a cara/Speaking Face to Face: An Exploration
    of Ethnocentric Racism,' in Anzaldúa, ed., *Making Face, Making Soul*, 49.
54 Ibid.
55 Trinh, *Woman, Native, Other*, 88.
56 Ibid.

57 Monture-Angus, *Thunder in My Soul*, 16.
58 Ibid., 28.
59 Trinh, 'Not You/Like You,' 373.
60 Gayatri Chakravorty Spivak, 'The Problem of Cultural Self-Representation,' in Sarah Harasym, ed., *The Post-Colonial Critic: Interviews, Strategies, Dialogues* (New York and London: Routledge 1990), 57.
61 Trinh, *Woman, Native, Other*, 40.
62 Ibid., 43.
63 Ibid., 41.
64 Anzaldúa, *Borderlands/La Frontera*, 80.
65 Ibid., 82.
66 Spivak, 'The Postmodern Condition: The End of Politics?' in Harasym, ed., *The Post-Colonial Critic*, 30.
67 Spivak, 'Strategy, Identity, Writing,' in Harasym, ed., *The Post-Colonial Critic*, 42.
68 Kimberlé Crenshaw, 'Whose Story Is It Anyway? Feminist and Antiracist Appropriations of Anita Hill,' in Toni Morrison, ed., *Race-ing Justice, En-Gendering Power: Essays on Anita Hill, Clarence Thomas and the Construction of Social Reality* (New York: Pantheon Books 1992), 404.
69 Trinh, *Woman, Native, Other*, 90.
70 Spivak, 'Strategy, Identity, Writing,' in Harasym, ed., *The Post-Colonial Critic*, 47.

3: What Is to Be Gained by Looking White People in the Eye?

I would like to thank Kathleen Gallivan for her outstanding legal research and critical skills. Yvonne Bobb Smith, Jacqueline Castel, and Donna Jeffery provided valuable research assistance, and they, along with Barbara Buckman, Irene Bujara, Hélène Moussa, and Ruth Roach Pierson, endured many conversations, read the draft, and enthusiastically supported me in this research. The revised version of this chapter relied heavily on the research skills and insight of Bonita Lawrence to whom I am very grateful for her many scholarly reminders that Aboriginal women cannot be understood in the same analytical framework used for women of colour.

1 The Aboriginal peoples of Canada include Indian, Métis, and Inuit peoples. *Indian* typically refers to Aboriginal people entitled to be registered as Indians (Status Indians) according to the *Indian Act of Canada*, although there are many people of Indian ancestry not entitled to register under the Act for a variety of reasons. Metis refers to Aboriginal peoples of mixed blood, although the

Métis National Council does not recognize the existence of Métis peoples 'outside the historic homeland of Ontario, the Prairies, B.C. and the North,' a definition that would exclude the Labrador Métis Association. For this discussion, see 'Innu Question Labrador Metis Status,' *Windspeaker*, October 1996, 2. Inuit refers to Aboriginal peoples known formerly as Eskimos. The word *Native* is also used to refer to Indian, Métis, and Inuit peoples. In this chapter, I have not used the term Indigenous which some would argue is the most historically correct term. See Janice Acoose/Misko-Kisikawihkwe (Red Sky Woman), *ISKWEWAK–Kah' Ki Yaw Ni Wahkomakanak: Neither Indian Princesses Nor Easy Squaws* (Toronto: Women's Press 1995), 13.

2 Rupert Ross, *Dancing with a Ghost: Exploring Indian Reality* (Markham, ON: Octopus Publishing Group 1992).

3 Ken MacQueen, 'Academia Goes for the Judicial Jugular,' *The Toronto Star*, 18 December 1992, A4.

4 In Canada, many Aboriginal children were forcibly removed from their homes and taken away to residential schools run by the Catholic church. Allegations of rampant sexual and physical abuse are increasingly common and many cases have been proven. Bishop O'Connor was eventually convicted of sexual assault. See *R. v. O'Connor*, [1996] B.C.J. No. 1663, Vancouver Registry No. CC920617, British Columbia Supreme Court, Vancouver, British Columbia, Oppal J. Heard: July 3, 4, 5, 8, 9, 10, 1996, Judgment: filed 25 July 1996.

5 *R. v. O'Connor*, excerpts of proceedings at trial, 2 December 1992, (B.C.S.C.), 16.

6 Fauzia Rafiq, ed., *Toward Equal Access: A Handbook for Service Providers Working with Survivors of Wife Assault* (Ottawa: Immigrant and Visible Minority Women Against Abuse 1991).

7 Sunera Thobani, 'There Is a War on Women: A Desh Pradesh Workshop,' *Rungh: A South Asian Quarterly of Culture, Comment and Criticism*, Pt. 1, nos. 1/2 (1993), 12.

8 Patricia Monture-Angus, *Thunder in My Soul: A Mohawk Woman Speaks* (Halifax: Fernwood Publishing 1995), 147.

9 John O. Calmore, 'Critical Race Theory, Archie Shepp, and Fire Music: Securing an Authentic Intellectual Life in a Multicultural World,' *Southern California Law Review* 65, no. 5 (1992), 2185.

10 See Philomena Essed, *Understanding Everyday Racism: An Interdisciplinary Theory* (Newbury Park, CA: Sage Publications 1991), 14; and Calmore, 'Critical Race Theory,' 2131.

11 Essed, *Understanding Everyday Racism*, 44.

12 Ibid., 43.

13 Ibid., 30.

14 Homi K. Bhabha, 'A Good Judge of Character: Men, Metaphors, and the Common Culture,' in Toni Morrison, ed., *Race-ing Justice, En-Gendering Power: Essays on Anita Hill, Clarence Thomas and the Construction of Social Reality* (New York: Pantheon Books 1992), 235.

15 Arthur Brittan and Mary Maynard, *Sexism, Racism, and Oppression* (Oxford: Basil Blackwell 1984), 19.

16 Bhabha, 'A Good Judge of Character,' 232.

17 Dwight Greene, 'Abusive Prosecutors: Gender, Race and Class Discretion and the Prosecution of Drug-Addicted Mothers,' *Buffalo Law Review* 737 (1991), 39, cited in Calmore, 'Critical Race Theory,' 2136.

18 *Delgamuukw v. Her Majesty the Queen*, Reasons for Judgement of the Hon. Chief Justice Allan McEachern, British Columbia Supreme Court, No. 0843, Smithers, and Vancouver, B.C., 8 March 1991, 129.

19 Gisday Wa and Delgam Uukw, *The Spirit in the Land. Statements of the Gitksan and Wet'suwet'en Hereditary Chiefs in the Supreme Court of British Columbia 1987–1990* (Gabriola, BC: Reflections 1992), 96.

20 Tracey Tyler, 'Are Judges Guilty of Gender Bias? The Jury's Out,' *The Toronto Star*, 2 December 1992, A1, A17.

21 Ontario Native Women's Association, *Report on Aboriginal Family Violence* (Thunder Bay, ON: ONWA 1989), 3.

22 *Native Women's Association of Canada, Gail Stacey-Moore and Sharon McIvor and Her Majesty the Queen, The Right Honourable Brian Mulroney and the Right Honourable Joe Clark* in Re the Referendum Act, file no. T2283-92, 18 September 1992, applicants' memorandum of fact and law in the Fed. Ct. (Trial Division) 17. NWAC does not represent all native women and some groups, for example Pakuutit, the Inuit Women's Association, claim that NWAC does not speak for them.

23 *Native Women's Association of Canada and Her Majesty the Queen*, Reasons for judgment, 11 June 1992, Mahoney J.A. (Fed. C.A.), 7. For the final appeal to Federal court protesting the outcome of the constitutional talks (events after 20 August 1992, see *Native Women's Assn. of Canada v. Canada* 1993, 1, *Federal Court Reports* (Ottawa: Queen's Printer, 1993), 171–86 and D-4 (Court of Appeal).

24 Monture-Angus, *Thunder in My Soul*, 171.

25 Ibid., 173.

26 Beverly Sellars, cited in Sherene Razack and Mary Louise Fellows, 'Seeking Relations,' *Signs: Journal of Women in Culture and Society* 19, no. 4 (1994), 1154–5.

27 Madeleine Dion Stout, 'Fundamental Changes Needed to End Violence,' *Windspeaker*, 7–20 November 1994, 10.

28 Canada, Royal Commission on Aboriginal Peoples, *Final Report* (Ottawa: Supply and Services Canada 1996), 66.

29 Ontario Native Women's Association, *Report*, 23.

30 Ibid., 50.

31 Lorraine Courtrille, *Abused Aboriginal Women in Alberta: The Story of Two Types of Victimization* (Edmonton: Misener-Margetts Women's Resource Centre 1991), 23.

32 Northwest Territories Status of Women Council, 'We Must Take Care of Each Other: Women Talk about Abuse' (discussion paper, 1990), 26–7.

33 Canadian Council on Social Development and Native Women's Association of Canada, *Voices of Aboriginal Women: Aboriginal Women Speak Out about Violence* (Ottawa: Canadian Council on Social Development 1991), 25–6.

34 Canada, *Report of the Aboriginal Justice Inquiry of Manitoba*, Volume 1: *The Justice System and Aboriginal People* (Winnipeg: Queen's Printer 1991), 485.

35 Ibid., 507.

36 Ibid., 498–501.

37 For a timely discussion of this theme and the ways in which incarceration of Aboriginal women destroys Aboriginal women and communities see Elizabeth Cook-Lynn, 'The Big Pipe Case,' in *Why I Can't Read Wallace Stegner and Other Essays* (Madison: University of Wisconsin Press 1996).

38 Sharon Marcus, 'Fighting Bodies, Fighting Words: A Theory and Politics of Rape Prevention,' in Judith Butler and Joan Scott, eds., *Feminists Theorize the Political* (New York: Routledge 1992), 392.

39 Kristin Bumiller, 'Fallen Angels: The Representation of Violence against Women in Legal Culture,' in M.A. Fineman and N.S. Thomadsen, eds., *At the Boundaries of Law* (New York: Routledge 1991), 97.

40 Jennifer Wriggins, 'Rape, Racism, and the Law,' *Harvard Women's Law Journal* 6 (1983), 121.

41 See Ward Churchill, *Indians Are Us? Culture and Genocide in Native North America* (Toronto: Between the Lines 1994).

42 Emma Laroque, cited in *Report of the Aboriginal Justice Inquiry of Manitoba*, 479. See also, Acoose, *ISKWEWAK*.

43 See Lee Maracle, *I Am Woman* (North Vancouver: Write-on Publishers 1988), 71–7.

44 Teressa Nahanee, 'Sexual Assault of Inuit Females: A Comment on "Cultural Bias,"' in Julian V. Roberts and Renate M. Mohr, eds., *Confronting Sexual Assault: A Decade of Legal and Social Change* (Toronto: University of Toronto Press 1994), 192–204. This article was published after Nightingale's study (see note 45) but existed in draft form at the same time as the latter.

45 Margo Nightingale, 'Judicial Attitudes and Differential Treatment: Native Women in Sexual Assault Cases,' *Ottawa Law Review* 23, no. 1 (1991), 71–98.

46 There are obviously parallels here to how intoxicated non-Aboriginal victims

of sexual assault are treated, but I would argue that the pervasiveness of the stereotype of the drunken Indian ensures that, for the judiciary and for society, Aboriginal women's intoxication offsets the harm of sexual assault.

47 Note that consent is not an issue in the case of rape of a girl under fourteen years of age. For a fuller discussion see Nightingale, 'Judicial Attitudes,' 92–4.

48 Ibid., 92–3.

49 *Report of the Aboriginal Justice Inquiry of Manitoba*, 400–1.

50 It has been suggested that Bourassa's original attraction to a community disposition in *R. v. Naqitarvik* stemmed, in fact, from his special concern for the survival of a small and fragile Arctic Inuit community (Jim Bell, 'The Violating of Kitty Nowdluk,' *Arctic Circle* (July/August 1991), 32–8.

51 *R. v. T.(J.J.)*, judgment delivered orally, 26 April 1989, Tallis J.A., Vancise and Gerwing J.A. concurring (C.A. Sask), 8.

52 *R. v. Whitecap (R.T.) and Whitecap (D.M.)*, judgment delivered orally, 5 January 1989, Gerwing J.A., Tallis J.A. concurring. Wakeling J.A. in dissent (C.A. Sask.).

53 *R. v. Okkuatsiak. Nfld. & P.E.I.R.* 65 (1987), 234. This challenge was later discontinued due to a lack of funding.

54 *R. v. J. (E.)*, court file no. 90-06337, judgment delivered orally, 15 March 1991, Madison J. (S.C. Yukon).

55 Nahanee, 'Sexual Assault of Inuit Females,' 195.

56 Ibid., 196.

57 Twenty-nine cases prior to 1989 and ten cases from 1989 to 1992 confirm Nightingale's conclusions on sexual assault cases in predominantly Northern jurisdictions.

58 *R. v. M. (G.O.). Canadian Criminal Cases* 54 (3rd), 1990 (S.C.NWT.), 81.

59 *R. v. Ritchie*, court file no. CC39/87, Reasons for Sentence, 2 March 1988, Houghton CCJ (County Ct.B.C.) 1.

60 *R. v. J. (H.)*, court file no. 1095FC, Reasons for Sentence, 17 January 1990, Barrett J. (Pr. C. B.C.) 1.

61 Ross, *Dancing with a Ghost*, 2.

62 Ibid., 2.

63 Ibid.

64 Ibid., 4.

65 Ibid., 6.

66 Ontario Native Women's Association, *Report on Aboriginal Family Violence*.

67 Heino Lilles, 'A Plea for More Human Values in Our Justice System,' *Queen's Law Journal* 17 (1992), 328–49, and Heino Lilles, 'Some Problems in the Administration of Justice in Remote and Isolated Communities,' *Queen's Law Journal* 15 (1990), 327–44. Note that the word *disadvantaged* implies that the problem is one of bad luck. There is thus no agent of domination, whereas

to say oppressed implies that oppressors exist. Patricia Monture-Angus also notes that when we conceptualize changes in the legal system as changes we must make for the benefit of disadvantaged groups, what is implied is benevolence and not, therefore, a change that is for the benefit of all people. See Monture-Angus, *Thunder in My Soul*, 27.

68 Lilles, 'Some Problems,' 330.

69 Ibid., 343.

70 Ibid., 330.

71 A chart of Native and white value systems is popular among judges in their training sessions and is also used by some sexual assault centres in their recent bid to understand cultural differences. One handout used by the Hamilton Sexual Assault Centre correctly attributes the original description of Native values to Mr Justice Thomas Berger, *Northern Frontier, Northern Homeland: The Report of the Mackenzie Valley Pipeline Inquiry*, Volume 1 (Ottawa: Supplies and Services Canada 1977), 93–9. The Berger Report was highly influential and remains a frequently cited description of Native culture.

72 Lilles, 'Some Problems,' 341.

73 Ideas for Aboriginal justice systems and community-based initiatives have been advanced for some time in Canada, particularly by Aboriginal communities themselves. Most recently, the Law Reform Commission has cautiously endorsed the idea. While the Commission is careful to explore potential difficulties, gender-based concerns are not among these (Law Reform Commission of Canada, 1991, 16–23). *The Report of the Aboriginal Justice Inquiry of Manitoba* concluded more strongly that a separate Aboriginal justice system was required but stressed also that Aboriginal self-government and the settlement of land claims were necessary steps before justice could be served. The concerns of Aboriginal women are addressed in this Report.

74 *Report of the Aboriginal Justice Inquiry of Manitoba*, 27. An example of this approach in a non-sexual assault case is the case of *R. v. Moses*, again in the North, in which a young Aboriginal man was found guilty of carrying a baseball bat with the intent to assault a police officer. The judge in this case, very concerned about the 'gross inequities in opportunities, social resources, and social conditions,' utilized a community developed approach to sentencing to conclude that the accused 'is not a hardened, habitual criminal' but an 'emotionally disturbed, severely handicapped sexual-abuse survivor with no skills or support system to escape repeatedly tumbling into crime.' The healing circle, in this case, was intended to 'protect the community from the grip of alcohol and crime' by presenting the young man with a series of community supports. See *R. v. Moses. Canadian Criminal Cases* 71 (3d), 1992 (Terr. Ct. Yukon), 347–85.

75 *R. v. P. (J.A.)*, 6 C.R. 4th(1991), 126; *R. v. P. (J.A.). Northwest Territories Reports (1991)* 305.

76 Ibid., 315.

77 Ibid., 317.

78 Lilles, 'A Plea for more Human Values,' 330.

79 *R. v. Hoyt*. Reasons for Sentence, 18 July 1991, Lilles C.J.T.C. (Terr. Ct. Yukon), 17.

80 *R.v. Hoyt*. Oral reasons for judgment, 17 January 1992, Taggert, Lambert, and Hollinrake (C.A.Yukon).

81 Jan Forde, Paula Pasquali, and Alexis Peterson, 'A Victim-Centered Approach,' *Yukon News*, 12 July 1991, 7.

82 *R. v. J. (E.)*, court file no. 90-06337 judgment delivered orally, 15 March 1991, Madison J.(S.C. Yukon); *R. v. Kowch*, court file no. 87-4661, 20 March 1989, (S.C. Yukon); *R. v. Roach*, court file no. 523.87, 8 December 1987, (S.C. Yukon); *R. v. Vaneden*. Reasons for Sentence, 1 February 1988, Ilnicki J. (Terr. Ct. Yukon).

83 Forde, Pasquali, and Peterson, 'A Victim-Centered Approach,' 7.

84 Talal Asad, 'The Concept of Cultural Translation in British Social Anthropology,' in James Clifford and George E. Marcus, eds., *Writing Culture: The Poetics and Politics of Ethnography* (Berkeley: University of California Press 1986), 163.

85 Lila Abu-Lughod, 'Writing against Culture,' in Richard Fox, ed., *Recapturing Anthropology: Working in the Present* (Santa Fe, NM: School of American Research Press 1991), 162.

86 Dion Stout, 'Fundamental Changes Needed to End Violence,' 10.

87 Ibid., 143.

88 Royal Canadian Mounted Police Public Complaints Commission, *Public Hearing into the Complaint of Kitty Nowdlok-Reynolds: Commission Report*. Prepared by Allan Williams, Q.C., S. Jane Evans, and Lazarus Arreak (Vancouver, 1992).

89 Ibid., 47.

90 The suggestion that we should presume that racism exists in such a context unless disproven has been strenuously resisted in the Canadian context. A report prepared for the Ontario Human Rights Commission suggested that because racism is the norm, the tendency to assume an accused is not racist skews the process of investigation. Donna Young, 'The Donna Young Report: The Handling of Race Discrimination Complaints at the Ontario Human Rights Commission' (Toronto: Ontario Human Rights Commission, 1992). The recommendations contained in the Donna Young Report were rejected by the attorney-general, Marion Boyd. Boyd told reporters that this amounted to tampering with an investigation; see Richard Mackie and Gay Abbate, 'Boyd Rejects Human Rights Report on Racism,' *The Globe and Mail (Toronto)*, 15 July 1993, A14.

91 James Youngblood 'Sakej' Henderson, 'The Marshall Inquiry: A View of the Legal Consciousness,' in Joy Mannette, ed., *Elusive Justice* (Halifax: Fernwood Publishing 1992), 37.

92 Ibid., 41.

93 Joy Mannette, 'The Social Construction of Ethnic Containments: The Royal Commission on the Donald Marshall Jr. Prosecution,' in Mannette, ed., *Elusive Justice*, 65.

94 Ibid., 68.

95 Ibid., 72.

96 Bhabha, 'A Good Judge of Character,' 235.

97 Yasmin Jiwani, 'To Be and Not to Be: South Asians as Victims and Oppressors in the *Vancouver Sun*,' *Sanvad* 5, no. 45 (August 1992), 14.

98 Ibid., 14.

99 *R. v. E. G.*, Ontario Appeal Cases 20, 379, 1987 (C.A. Ont.) 379.

100 *R. v. S. (D.D.).*, Reasons for Sentence, 2 November 1988, Langdon J. (Prov. Ct. Ont.) 15; *R. v. L.(K.)*, Reasons for Sentence, 18 September 1989, Meyers J. (P.C. Man.), 3.

101 *R. v. Drozdkik*, court file no. CC870536, Reasons for Sentence, 31 March 1988, Boyd J. (County Ct.B.C.), 5.

102 Mobina Jaffer, *Is Anyone Listening? Report of the British Columbia Task Force on Family Violence* (Vancouver: n.p. 1992), 20.

103 Nakanyike Musisi and Fakiha Muktar, *Exploratory Research: Wife Assault in Metropolitan Toronto's African Immigrant and Refugee Community* (Toronto: Canadian African Newcomer Aid Centre of Toronto 1992), 22.

104 Katirai Mahboubeh, *Assessing the Needs of Alternative Services for Culturally Diverse Assaulted Women* (Hamilton, ON: Interval House of Hamilton-Wentworth 1991), 5.

105 Rafiq, ed., *Toward Equal Access*, 12.

106 Tereza Coutinho, 'Culture,' in Rafiq, ed., *Toward Equal Access*, 49.

107 Thomas McCarthy, 'Doing the Right Thing in Cross-Cultural Representation,' review essay of James Clifford, *The Predicament of Culture*; James Cliford and George E. Marcus, eds., *Writing Culture*; and George E. Marcus and Michael M.J. Fischer, *Anthropology as Culture Critique*, Ethics 102, no. 3 (1992), 645.

108 Jo-Ellen Asbury, 'African-American Women in Violent Relationships: An Exploration of Cultural Differences,' in Robert L. Hampton, ed., *Violence in the Black Family: Correlates and Consequences* (Hampton, MA: Lexington Books 1987), 90–105, as cited in Evelyn L. Barbee, 'Ethnicity and Woman Abuse in the United States,' in Carolyn Sampselle, ed., *Violence Against Women: Nursing Research, Education and Practice Issues* (New York: Hemisphere Publishing 1992), 153–65.

109 *R. v. O'Connor.* (B.C.S.C), 2 December 1992, excerpts of proceedings at trial, 33. See note 4 for the final decision in this case.

110 Ibid., 16.

111 Ibid., 18.

112 *R. v. O'Connor and Aboriginal Women's Council, Canadian Association of Sexual Assault Centres, Disabled Women's Network Canada, the Women's Legal Education and Action fund and the Canadian Mental Health Association,* written reasons for judgment of application for intervenor status, 30 June 1993, Taylor J.A., Wood J.A., Hoolinrake, J.A., Rowles, J.A. and Prowse, J.A. concurring (C.A.B.C.). The result of these efforts was that, although the court allowed the defence access to the materials in question, the court laid out the steps required for this to happen to ensure that in future such a practice would be rare.

4: Policing the Borders of Nation

This paper was first presented at the Critical Race Theory Workshop, June 1994, in Miami, Florida. I would like to thank Robert Chang for his comments. Since then, Mary Louise Fellows and Homa Hoodfar have been generous with their insights. Geraldine Sadoway and Constance Nakatsu generously shared their legal files and perspectives, and Judith Ramirez of the Immigration and Refugee Board facilitated access to the Board's public material. Without the careful research assistance of Kathleen Gallivan, Kirsten Roger, and, especially, Gabrielle Hezekiah and Helle-Mai Lenk, this paper could not have been completed.

1 Deborah Cheney, 'Valued Judgments? A Reading of Immigration Cases,' *Journal of Law and Society* 20, no. 1 (1993), 23.

2 'Racialized: any and all significance extended, both explicitly and silently by racial reference, over discursive expression and practice. Further, "racist" will always be made to invoke those exclusions prompted or promoted by racial reference or racialized significance, whether such exclusions are actual or intended, effects or affects of racial and racialized expression.' David Theo Goldberg, *Racist Culture: Philosophy and the Politics of Meaning* (Cambridge: Blackwell 1993), 2.

3 I use the term *Third World* throughout this chapter, although it reproduces the idea of a geographical space that is merely underdeveloped only in so far as it is oppositionally constituted to the First World. I continue to use it, however, to stress that this constitution represents a relation of domination. For a history of the term, and its possible oppositional uses, see Goldberg, *Racist Culture*, 155.

4 For a discussion of the space myths of Canada as the true North, pure and

more innocent than the U.S., see Rob Shields, *Place on the Margins: Alternative Geographies of Modernity* (New York: Routledge 1991), 162–206.

5 Elizabeth Cook-Lynn, *Why I Can't Read Wallace Stegner and Other Essays* (Madison: University of Wisconsin Press 1996), 31.

6 Gayatri Chakravorty Spivak, 'Acting Bits/Identity Talk,' *Cultural Inquiry* 18 (Summer 1992), 781.

7 Michael Omi and Howard Winant, 'On the Theoretical Concept of Race,' in Cameron McCarthy and Warren Crichlow, eds., *Race, Identity and Representation in Education* (New York: Routledge 1993), 3.

8 Canada, Immigration and Refugee Board, *Guidelines Issued by the Chairperson Pursuant to Section 65 (3) of the Immigration Act (1993)*.

9 '"Convention refugee"

(a) by reason of a well-founded fear of persecution for reasons of race, religion, nationality, membersip in a particular social group or political opinion,

(i) is outside the country of the person's nationality and is unable or, by reason of that fear, is unwilling to avail [her]self of the protection of that country, or
(ii) not having a country of nationality, is outside the country of the person's former habitual residence and is unable or, by reason of that fear, is unwilling to return to that country,

(b) has not ceased to be a Convention refugee ...'

Canada, *An Act to Amend the Immigration Act, 1976 and to Amend Other Acts in Consequence Thereof*, R.S.C. 1985, c. 1–2, 2(1).

10 Some of the most recent are Nancy Kelly, 'Gender-Related Persecution: Assessing the Asylum Claims of Women,' *Cornell International Law Journal* 26 (1993), 625; Pamela Goldberg, 'Any Place But Home: Asylum in the United States for Women Fleeing Intimate Violence,' *Cornell International Law Journal* 26 (1993), 565; Heather Potter, 'Gender-based Persecution: A Challenge to the Canadian Refugee Determination System,' *Dalhousie Journal of Legal Studies* 3 (1994), 81–104; Audrey Macklin, 'Refugee Women and the Imperative of Categories,' *Human Rights Quarterly* 17 (1995), 213.

11 A. Sivanandan, 'U.K. Commentary: Signs of the Times: An Interview with A. Sivanandan by Paul Grant,' *Race and Class* 33, no. 4 (1992), 68.

12 Edward W. Said, *Orientalism* (New York: Vintage Books 1979).

13 Goldberg, *Racist Culture*, 174.

14 Ibid., 150.

15 I have chosen to use the word imperial rather than colonial even though, as Goldberg has suggested, imperialism connotes a direct rule of subjugation and colonialism an indirect one. My intent is to drive home that the relations of domination present in Canada's regulation of its borders resembles the direct subordination characteristic of imperial regimes. Canadian politicians, even those on the Left, are apt to pride themselves on the fact that Canada is not an imperial nation, a gesture intended to deny the relations of racial domination as they exist today, notably those between Canada and its Aboriginal populations.

16 Robert Carr, 'Crossing the First World/Third World Divides: Testimonial, Transnational Feminisms and the Postmodern Condition,' in Inderpal Grewal and Caren Kaplan, eds., *Scattered Hegemonies: Postmodernity and Transnational Feminist Practices* (Minneapolis: University of Minnesota Press 1994), 157.

17 Ibid., 159.

18 Ibid., 155.

19 Joanna Kerr, 'Introduction, ' in Joanna Kerr, ed., *Ours by Right: Women's Rights as Human Rights* (London: Zed Books Ltd. 1993), 4.

20 Charlotte Bunch, 'Women's Rights as Human Rights: An International Lobbying Success Story,' *Human Rights Tribune*. Special Issue. *UN World Conference on Human Rights* 2, no. 1 (June 1993).

21 Ibid., 30.

22 Rebecca J. Cook, 'Women's International Human Rights Law: The Way Forward, ' *Human Rights Quarterly* 15 (1993), 242–3.

23 The activities of the Jamaican feminist collective Sistren stand out as an example of educational efforts around the debt crisis, activities that privilege gender without abandoning a regional political analysis, which stresses the origins of the crisis in Western hegemony.

24 Martha Mahoney, 'Whiteness and Women, in Practice and Theory: A Reply to Catharine MacKinnon,' *Yale Journal of Law and Feminism* 5, no. 2 (1995), 217; Erin Edmonds, 'Mapping the Terrain of Our Resistance: A White Feminist Perspective on the Enforcement of Rape Law,' *Harvard BlackLetter Journal* 9 (1992), 43.

25 Catharine A. MacKinnon, 'From Practice to Theory or What Is a White Woman Anyway?' *Yale Journal of Law and Feminism* 4, no. 13 (1991), 15.

26 Catharine A. MacKinnon, 'Turning Rape into Pornography: Postmodern Genocide,' *Ms.* 4 (July/August 1993), 27.

27 Catharine A. MacKinnon, 'On Torture: A Feminist Perspective on Human Rights,' in Kathleen E. Mahoney and Paul Mahoney, eds., *Human Rights in the Twenty-First Century: A Global Challenge* (The Netherlands: Kluwer Academic Publishers 1993), 21; Bunch, 'Women's Rights as Human Rights,' 30.

28 Vasuki Nesiah, 'Towards a Feminist Internationality: A Critique of U.S. Feminist Legal Scholarship,' *Harvard Women's Law Journal* 16 (Spring 1993), 202.

29 David L. Neal, 'Women as a Social Group: Recognizing Sex-based Persecution as Grounds for Asylum,' *Columbia Human Rights Law Review* 20, no. 1 (1988), 207.

30 Neal, 'Women as a Social Group,' 207; Karen Bower, 'Recognizing Violence Against Women as Persecution on the Basis of Membership in a Particular Social Group,' *Georgetown Immigration Law Journal* 7, no. 1 (1993), 173; Linda Cipriani, 'Gender and Persecution: Protecting Women under International Refugee Law,' *Georgetown Immigration Law Journal* 7, no. 3 (1993), 511. Also see Kristin E. Kandt, 'United States Asylum Law: Recognizing Persecution Based on Gender Using Canada as a Comparison,' *Georgetown Immigration Law Journal* 9, no. 1 (1995), 137.

31 Neal, 'Women as a Social Group,' 209.

32 Cipriani, 'Gender and Persecution,' 513.

33 See, for example, Valerie Oosterveld, 'Refugee Status for Female Circumcision Fugitives: Building a Canadian Precedent,' *University of Toronto Faculty of Law Review* 51, no. 2 (1993), 277; Robbie D. Steele, 'Silencing the Deadly Ritual: Efforts to End Female Genital Mutilation,' *Georgetown Immigration Law Journal* 9, no. 1 (1995), 105; Blake M. Guy, 'Female Genital Excision and the Implications of Federal Prohibition,' *William and Mary Journal of Women and the Law* 2, no. 1 (1995), 125.

34 Isabelle R. Gunning, 'Arrogant Perception, World-travelling and Multicultural Feminism: The Case of Female Genital Surgeries,' *Columbia Human Rights Law Review* 23, no. 2 (1991–2), 247. See also, Hope Lewis, 'Between Irua and "Female Genital Mutilation": Feminist Human Rights Discourse and the Cultural Divide,' *Harvard Human Rights Journal* 8 (1995), 32.

35 Karen Engle, 'Female Subjects of Public International Law: Human Rights and the Exotic Other Female,' *New England Law Review* 26 (1992), 1509.

36 Guy, 'Female Genital Excision,' 152.

37 Layli Miller Bashir, 'Female Genital Mutilation in the Unites States: An Examination of Criminal and Asylum Law,' *Journal of Gender and the Law* 4 (1996), 419.

38 Simon Watney, 'Missionary Positions: AIDS, "Africa," and Race,' in Russell Ferguson, Martha Gever, Trinh T. Minh-ha, and Cornel West, eds., *Out There: Marginalization and Contemporary Cultures* (New York and Boston: The New Museum of Contemporary Art and The MIT Press 1990), 89.

39 The Female Genital Mutilation Legal Community Committee, 'Brief to the Parliamentary Standing Committee on Justice and Legal Affairs, re: Bill C-27, Section 268, Subsection (3) & (4),' November 26, 1996.

40 Annie Bunting, 'Theorizing Women's Cultural Diversity in Feminist International Human Rights Strategies,' *Journal of Law and Society* 20, no. 1 (1993), 15.

41 Mahoney, 'Whiteness and Women,' 227.

42 Nurjehan Mawani, 'Introduction to the Immigration and Refugee Board Guidelines on Gender-Related Persecution,' *International Journal of Refugee Law* 5, no. 2 (1993), 244.

43 Felicité Stairs and Lori Pope, 'No Place Like Home: Assaulted Migrant Women's Claims to Refugee Status and Landings on Humanitarian and Compassionate Grounds,' *Journal of Law and Social Policy* 6 (1990), 200–1; the testimony of Lori Pope to the Subcommittee of Bill C-86, *Canada Parliament. House Legislative Committee on Bill C-86. Proceedings. 34th Parliament, 3rd Session, 1992* (Ottawa: Queen's Printer of Canada Publishing, Supply and Services 1992) No. 12, 9, 15.

44 Romeo Kaseram, '"My Husband Will Kill Me" Trinidadian Wife Seeks Refuge from Violent Marriage,' *Indo Caribbean World (Toronto)*, 2 September 1992, 1.

45 Cited in Ramabai Espinet, 'How Doularie Became "A Survivor,"' *Indo Caribbean World (Toronto)*, 7 October 1992, 1.

46 For example, the discussion of the case of Parmati Ramsabach on the *CTV News* broadcast of 9 March 1993.

47 Homa Hoodfar, 'The Veil in Their Minds and on Our Heads: The Persistence of Colonial Images of Muslim Women,' *Resources for Feminist Research/Documentation sur la recherche féministe* 22, nos. 3/4 (Fall/Winter 1993), 5; Yasmin Jiwani, 'To Be and Not to Be: South Asians as Victims and Oppressors in the *Vancouver Sun*,' *Sanvad* 5, no. 45 (August 1992), 13.

48 John Ward Anderson and Molly Moore, 'Women Doomed to Life of Misery,' *The Toronto Star*, 4 April 1993, A6.

49 John Ward Anderson, 'Phantoms of the Census Forms,' *The Toronto Star*, 5 April 1993, A15.

50 Molly Moore, 'Thousands Sold as Prostitutes Each Year,' *The Toronto Star*, 6 April 1993, A15.

51 Julia Preston, 'Burying Children Routine for Mothers in Rural Brazil,' *The Toronto Star*, 5 April 1993, A15.

52 Susan Okie, 'Mutilation and Rape "Normal" for Girls,' *The Toronto Star*, 5 April 1993, A15.

53 Molly Moore, 'The Start of a Social Revolution,' *TheToronto Star*, 18 April 1993, A21.

54 Caryle Murphy, 'Slowly, Islamic Women Trade the Veil for White Collars,' *The Toronto Star*, 7 April 1993, A15.

55 Jiwani, 'To Be and Not to Be,' 47.

56 Heather Bird, 'Why Not Open the Doors?,' *The Ottawa Sun*, 14 April 1994, 11.

57 Ted Byfield, 'Ottawa Now Takes On "White Woman's Burden,"' *The Financial Post*, 20 March 1993, S31.

58 Barbara Amiel, 'The Female Refugee: A Fraudulent Concept,' *Macleans* 106, no. 3 (March 1993), 9.

59 Editorial, *The Toronto Sun*, 14 March 1993, C1.

60 Teun A. van Dijk, *Elite Discourse and Racism*, Sage Series on Race and Ethnic Relations (Newbury Park, CA: Sage Publications, Inc. 1993), 69.

61 Hon. Bernard Valcourt (Minister of Employment and Immigration), House of Commons, *Debates*, 19 June 1992, 12456.

62 van Dijk, *Elite Discourse and Racism*, 111.

63 United Nations, *Convention and Protocol Relating to the Status of Refugees*, Final Act of the United Nations Conference of Plenipotentiaries on the Status of Refugees and Stateless Persons and the Text of the 1951 Convention Relating to Refugees, Resolution 2198 adopted by the General Assembly and the Text of the 1967 Protocol Relating to the Status of Refugees, United Nations, 1983, Article 1A(2): 12 and 39. Incorporated into Canada's *Immigration Act*.

64 Table de Concertation de Montréal pour les Réfugiés, *Consultation on Refugee Women Claimants. Report* (Fulford Hall, 1444 Union, Montréal, 1993).

65 James C. Hathaway (assisted by Anne MacMillan), *Rebuilding Trust. Report of the Review of Fundamental Justice in Information Gathering and Dissemination at the Immigration and Refugee Board of Canada*. Submitted to the Chairperson, Immigration and Refugee Board of Canada, December 1993.

66 One training initiative (held in February 1994) focused on Islamic sharia law and its impact on women; an earlier one trained Board members on the concept of women's rights as human rights (IRB, Press Communiqué, 7 March 1993).

67 Canada, Immigration and Refugee Board, 'The Guidelines on Women Refugee Claimants Fearing Gender-Related Persecution: Update,' 25 November 1996.

68 From 1993, when the *Guidelines* came into effect, until September 1996, there were 1,134 gender persecution claims of which 624 were accepted, 510 rejected, and the others withdrawn or pending. This represents slightly over half the claimants being granted asylum. Canada, Immigration and Refugee Board, 'The Guidelines on Women Refugee Claimants Fearing Gender-Related Persecution: Update,' 25 November 1996.

69 *V. (A.P.)*, 18 November 1992, Court File Number: T92-03227. C.R.D.D. No. 318 at 11. The panel member who made the argument in this case, Jack Davis, continues to make it, the Charter of Rights and Freedoms and the *Guidelines* notwithstanding. See the discussion of Aisha below. See also, C.R.D.D. T93-00104, T93-09539. Toronto, Ontario. J. Davis and M. Qureshi. Heard: 7 July 1993. Decision: 29 October 1993. Reasons for decision.

70 *M. (X.K.)*, [1994] C.R.D.D. No. 78. No. U93-09791. Toronto, Ontario. E.R. Smith and B. Menkir. Heard: 20 October 1993 and 13 January 1994. Decision: 13 January 1994. Reasons for decision.

71 *C. (X.N.)*, [1993] C.R.D.D. No. 28 No. U92-08714. Toronto, Ontario. H. Maraj and M. Shecter. Heard: 11 March 1993. Decision: 4 June 1993. Reasons for decision.

72 Ibid., 5.

73 Neal, 'Women as a Social Group,' 239.

74 C.R.D.D. T93-07375. Toronto, Ontario. K.S. Desai and N.L. Cheeseman. Heard: 27 September 1993. Decision: 18 January 1994. Reasons for decisions.

75 Ibid., 4.

76 *I. (G.F.) (Re).*, [1993] C.R.D.D. No. 114. No. T92-09592. Toronto, Ontario. M.V. Toth and A. Dualeh. Heard: 25 March 1993. Decision: 14 September 1993. Reasons for decision.

77 C.R.D.D. M92-13594. Ottawa, Ontario. E. Harker and J. MacPherson. Heard: 20 April and 15 June 1993. Decision: 13 September 1993. Reasons for decision.

78 C.R.D.D. U93-01178, U93-01179, U93-01180. Toronto, Ontario. B.L. Thomas and D.J. Whitfield. Heard: 5 February 1993. Decision: 16 March 1993. Reasons for decision.

79 Ruttenberg argues that domestic violence against Black women is viewed as less harmful because of the stereotype of tough Black women. She cites Sharon Angella Allard who explores how the image of Black women as strong and angry excludes them from the battered woman syndrome defence which requires viewing the woman as helpless and fragile. Miriam H. Ruttenberg, 'A Feminist Critique of Mandatory Arrest: An Analysis of Race and Gender in Domestic Violence Policy,' *The American University Journal of Gender and the Law* 2 (1994), 185. See also Sharon Angella Allard, 'Rethinking Battered Woman Syndrome: A Black Feminist Perspective,' *UCLA Women's Law Journal* 19, no. 1 (1991), 193–4.

80 With the elimination of the initial hearing stage, claimants now go to a single refugee determination ruling, normally before a panel of two members, although a claimant can consent to one. Only one member needs to decide in favour of the claimant. However, a unanimous decision is required if there are reasonable grounds to believe that a claimant has, without valid reason, destroyed or disposed of personal identity papers or has, during the course of the claim, visited the country from which he or she is fleeing. There is also a fast track process where a claim can be determined by one member without a hearing in cases where there is a high probability that a hearing will result in a positive decision. *Immigration and Refugee Board News Release*, 20 May 1994.

81 For a discussion of the representation of Indian women in Trinidad, see Ramabai Espinet, 'Representation and the Indo-Caribbean Woman in Trinidad and Tobago,' in Frank Birbalsingh, ed., *Indo-Caribbean Resistance* (Toronto: TSAR Publications 1992), 42–61.

82 A federal court agreed with an adjudicator who had earlier concluded that Mayers had been subject to domestic abuse and that Trinidadian women subject to such abuse constituted a group requiring protection from persecution. *Mayers, Marcel v. Minister of Employment and Immigration* (1992), 97 D.L.R. (4th) 729 (F.C.A.).

83 C.R.D.D. U93-07891, U93-07892, U93-07893, U93-07894. (Toronto, Ontario). Submissions of counsel, 9 December 1993. Counsel: G. Sadoway. (Sadoway, 'Submission,' 1).

84 Ibid., 5.

85 Ibid.

86 Linda Martin Alcoff and Laura Gray, 'Survivor Discourse: Transgression or Recuperation?,' *Signs: Journal of Women in Culture and Society* 18 (1993), 285.

87 Ibid.

88 C.R.D.D. U93-07891, U93-07892, U93-07893, U93-07894. Toronto, Ontario. Submissions of counsel, 9 December 1993. Counsel: G. Sadoway. (Sadoway, 'Submission,' 6).

89 Ibid., 7.

90 Ibid., 7–8.

91 However, the Caribbean Association for Feminist Research and Action (CAFRA) reported that in June 1990, 1,200 protection orders were issued and a conviction was obtained in 60 per cent of the cases. This rate suggests that problems persist but that, clearly, legal strategies do exist and can be successfully utilized. CAFRA, 'Regional Meeting on Women, Violence and the Law: A Provisional Report,' based on a conference held in St. Augustine, Trinidad and Tobago, January 1991. Date of Report unknown.

92 C.R.D.D. U93-07891, U93-07892, U93-07893, U93-07894. Toronto, Ontario. Submissions of counsel, 9 December 1993. Counsel: G. Sadoway. (Sadoway, 'Submissions,' 31).

93 Geraldine Sadoway, interview by author, Toronto, Ontario, 14 January 1994. Transcript on file with author.

94 Roberta Clarke, interview by author, Port-of Spain, Trinidad, 11 January 1994. Transcript on file with author.

95 Elizabeth M. Schneider, 'Describing and Changing: Women's Self-Defense Work and the Problem of Expert Testimony on Battering,' *Women's Rights Law Reporter* 14 (Spring/Fall 1992), 226.

96 C.R.D.D. C93-00223. (Calgary, Alberta). (Place of hearing also listed as Win-

nipeg, Manitoba.) Reasons for decision. J.E. Wieler and H.S. Pawa. Heard: 25 October 1993. Decision: 31 December 1993. (Date of decision also listed as 12 January 1994.) Reasons for decision, 3.

97 Hoodfar, 'The Veil,' 15.

98 Kimberlé Crenshaw has argued that these tropes were not available for Anita Hill, whereas Clarence Thomas could call upon the spectre of the lynched Black man. Kimberlé Crenshaw, 'Whose Story Is It, Anyway? Feminist and Antiracist Appropriations of Anita Hill,' in Toni Morrison, ed., *Race-ing Justice, En-Gendering Power: Essays on Anita Hill, Clarence Thomas and the Social Construction of Reality* (New York: Pantheon Books 1992), 418.

99 *Harper v. The Queen* (Ministry of Employment and Immigration) Rothstein J., p. 10 F.C.J. 212 action 93-T-41 [unreported decision].

100 Ingrid Harper and The Queen (Minister of Employment and Immigration) Ont. Ct. (G.D.), 11 January 1993, *Affidavit* 47.

101 *R. (U.R.) (Re).*, [1994] C.R.D.D. No. 69. No. T93-01306. Toronto, Ontario. J. Morrison and S.G. Flintoff. Heard: 14 October 1993. Decision: 29 April 1994. Reasons for decision.

102 C.R.D.D. U93-07212. Toronto, Ontario. Transcript of hearing. G. Carsen and A. Leistra. Decision: 3 December 1993. (Transcript, 2.)

103 C.R.D.D. U93-07212. Toronto, Ontario. G. Carsen and A. Leistra. Decision: 3 December 1993. Reasons for decision, 6.

104 Ibid.

105 *N. (L.Y.) (Re).*, [1993] C.R.D.D. No. 55 No. U93-02026. Toronto, Ontario. E.R. Smith and P. Stratton. Heard: 31 March 1993. Decision: 13 May 1993. Reasons for decision.

106 Ibid., Reasons for decision, 7.

107 *A. (I.E.) (Re).*, [1993] C.R.D.D. No. 111 No. T93-03535. (Toronto, Ontario.) Reasons for decision. Y. Shymko and M. Qureshi. Heard: 22 April 1993. Decision: 30 July 1993.

108 James Ferguson, 'Jamaica: Stories of Poverty,' *Race and Class* 34, no. 1 (1992), 70.

109 V. Salter and Women's Mediawatch, 'Jamaica's Position on Domestic Violence,' *Women's Mediawatch*, 29 December 1994.

110 Ibid.

111 C.R.D.D. T93-08347. Toronto, Ontario. E.A. Grice and M.Y. Mouammar. Heard: 26 October 1993. Decision: 19 January 1994. Reasons for decision; C.R.D.D. M93-03388, M93 03391. Montréal, Québec. M. Hébert and D. Raymond. Heard: 7 October 1993. Decision: 2 December 1993. Reasons for decision; *K. (L.M.) (Re).*, [1994] C.R.D.D. No. 68 T93-08122. Toronto, Ontario. S.G. Flintoff and N.H. Jiwan. Heard: 13 December 1993. Decision: 16 February 1994. Reasons for decision.

112 C.R.D.D. T93-08347. E.A. Grice and M.Y. Mouammar. Toronto, Ontario. Heard: 26 October 1993. Decision: 19 January 1994. Reasons for decision.

113 *K. (L.M.) (Re).*, [1994] C.R.D.D. No. 68 T93-08122. Toronto, Ontario. S.G. Flint-off and N.H. Jiwan. Heard: 13 December 1993. Decision: 16 February 1994. Reasons for decision.

114 C.R.D.D. M93-03388, M93-03391. Montréal, Québec. M. Hébert and D. Raymond. Heard: 7 October 1993. Decision: 2 December 1993. Reasons for decision.

115 See, for example, *Q(X.B.) (Re)*, [1990] C.R.D.D. No. 216; *W.(C.X.) (Re)*, [1991] C.R.D.D. No. 483.; *X. (W.N.) (Re)*, [1991] C.R.D.D. No. 752.; *K.(T.J.)(Re)*, [1992] C.R.D.D. No. 248.

116 C.R.D.D. T89-04608, T89-04609, T89-04610, T89-04611, Sarzotti, Nig, 22 May 1990, listed in *Reflex*: Special Issue 1 (September 1992) at 5.

117 *Minutes of A Hearing of the Refugee Division Held in Montréal, Québec*, file no. M91-04822, 22 August 1991, 11.

118 Immigration and Refugee Board (24 September 1991) Montréal, Québec: 3.

119 The articles are too numerous to mention. See for example, Jacquie Miller, 'A Feminist Refugee,' *The Ottawa Citizen*, 4 September 1992, A2.

120 See Edward Broadbent, 'Le statut de réfugié et les femmes,' *La Presse*, 30 déc. 1992, 30.

121 See Editorial, 'Women as Refugees,' *Edmonton Journal*, 22 December 1992, A8.

122 See Hoodfar, 'The Veil.'

123 Hoodfar documents how Western feminists from Kate Millett to contemporary Canadian feminists in Montréal (where Nada's case was heard) can see little else about Muslim women besides their location in an oppressive culture. (Ironically, in over eighty interviews with young veiled women, she charts a very high level of everyday racism encountered by this group from Western men and women noting that 'Western responses to Muslim women, filtered through an Orientalist frame, effectively limit how Muslim women might creatively resist the regulation of their bodies and their lives.') See Hoodfar, 'The Veil,' 15.

124 Personal Information Form of File T-92-07219, on file with Constance Nakatsu, Toronto, Ontario.

125 Laurence Deonna, *Le Yemen que j'ai vu* (Paris: Lausanne-Arthaud 1982).

126 Goldberg, *Racist Culture*, 157.

127 C.R.D .D. T92-07219, 14 Feb. 1994.

128 C.R.D.D. T93-12198, T93-12199, T93-12197. Toronto, Ontario. J. Ramirez and J. McCaffrey. Heard: 10 May 1994. Decision: 13 July 1994. Newspaper articles continue to refer to this case. See Ellie Tesher, 'Mutilation of Girls Must Be Stopped,' *The Toronto Star*, 10 May 1995, A2.

129 *Newsworld*, CNN broadcast, April 1995.
130 C.R.D.D. C93-00433. Calgary, Alberta. J.E. Wieler and E.T. Lazo. Heard: 28 October 1993. Decision: 3 December 1993. Reasons for decision.
131 Ibid., 3.
132 Ibid., 7.
133 *W. (Z.D.) (Re).*, [1993] C.R.D.D. No. 3. No. U92-06668. Toronto, Ontario. E.R. Smith and N. Daya. Heard: 13 November 1992. Decision: 19 February 1993. Reasons for decision.
134 *W. (Y.J.) (Re).*, [1994] C.R.D.D. No. 91. Nos. M92-09034, M92-09035, M92-09036. Montréal, Québec. D.N. Doray and L. Dorion. Heard: 15 February and 1 June 1993. Decision: 28 February 1994. Reasons for decision.
135 Ibid., 19.
136 See chapter 5.
137 Sadoway, Interview, 9.
138 Ibid.
139 Lydia Liu, 'The Female Body and Nationalist Discourse: The Field of Life and Death Revisited,' in Grewal and Kaplan, eds., *Scattered Hegemonies*, 45.
140 Ibid., 49.
141 Cheney, 'Valued Judgements?' 35.
142 It is difficult to judge the extent to which the *Guidelines* have resulted in large numbers of women claimants succeeding with their claims. The acceptance rate continues to be slightly more than half of the claims submitted. Although this would seem to signal a high acceptance rate, we must take into account how few women make it to Canadian shores at all and examine in more detail, as I have been arguing, who gets in and on what basis. In 1995, out of 362 finalized claims on the basis of gender persecution, 212 were positive, and in 1996, out of 305 finalized claims, 149 were positive (IRB, Standards, Analysis and Monitoring Branch, March 1997). Given the current government's determination to lower the refugee quota, and to police more vigorously the nation's border, we can only guess at how these directives have begun to affect the adjudication of gender-persecution claims. Of the twenty nine gender persecution cases available from the database of cases selected in February 1996 by the IRB for publication in its journal *Reflex*, seventeen were positive, twelve negative. Of the positive decisions, twelve had either strong components of ethnic or tribal fighting (Somalia), a cultural component such as FGM, Hudood ordinances, or sentences of lashes in Iran. The remaining positive cases included a determination that the Guyanese, Brazilian and Venezualan, Polish, Jamaican and Vincentian governments were unwilling or unable to protect women from domestic violence. In these cases, however, the batterer usually had some state power, that is, as a high ranking police officer. The negative

cases included Iranian women who could only show their disagreement with the regimes dress regulations; Tamil women, including a seventy-six-year-old woman, who were deemed able to avail themselves of an internal flight alternative; Middle-Eastern women with stories that their families disapproved of their having married without their consent, and Central American cases where the political persecution was not obvious. It is of course impossible to conclude that there are definitive tendencies confirming the trends I have noted in this chapter. Successful claims, it might be said, require a clearly marked cultural context that can be described as brutally oppressive towards women, a connection to a minority, or persecution by a powerful man. See Nurjehan Mawani, Chairperson, IRB, 'Notes for Remarks to the Women's Canadian Club of Edmonton,' Edmonton, Alberta, 11 April 1995, and *Reflex* (February 1996), IRB Documentation Centre, Ottawa, Ontario. For the announcement of two new initiatives aimed at limiting the right of appeal and ensuring the speedy removal from Canada of claimants whose claims have been rejected, see the Minister of Citizenship and Immigration, 'Press Release,' 19 December 1996.

5: From Pity to Respect

I would like to thank Kathleen Gallivan for her research assistance and for her careful, critical reading of the draft of this chapter and Mary Louise Fellows for countless discussions around the difference impasse, for her insight into the limitations of accepting consent as a defence of violence, and for her unfailing encouragement and support.

1 Shirley Masuda with Jillian Riddington, *Meeting Our Needs: An Access Manual for Transition Houses* (Toronto: DisAbled Women's Network Canada 1990), ix.
2 Mary Louise Fellows and Sherene Razack, 'Seeking Relations: Law and Feminism Roundtable,' *Signs: Journal of Women in Culture and Society* 19, no. 4 (1994), 1048. We have pursued the concept of the difference impasse further in our article 'The Race to Innocence: Confronting Hierarchical Relations among Women,' *Iowa Journal of Gender, Race and Justice*, forthcoming.
3 Catharine MacKinnon, 'Sex and Violence: A Perspective,' in Catharine MacKinnon, *Feminism Unmodified: Discourses on Life and Law* (Cambridge, MA: Harvard University Press 1987), 91.
4 Catharine MacKinnon, *Toward a Feminist Theory of the State* (Cambridge, MA: Harvard University Press 1989), 175–6.
5 Margaret Baldwin, 'Split at the Root: Prostitution and Feminist Discourses of Law Reform,' *Yale Journal of Law and Feminism* 47, no. 5 (1992), 81.

6 Ibid.

7 Ibid., 69.

8 See, for example, Regina Austin, 'Black Women, Sisterhood, and the Difference/
Deviance Divide,' *New England Law Review* 26 (1992), 887; Kristin Bumiller,
'Fallen Angels: The Representation of Violence against Women in Legal Cul-
ture,' in Martha Fineman and Nancy Thomadsen, eds., *At the Boundaries of
Law* (New York: Routledge 1991), 95; Jennifer Wriggins, 'Rape, Racism, and
the Law,' *Harvard Women's Law Journal* 6 (1983), 103.

9 Patricia Hill Collins, *Black Feminist Thought: Knowledge, Consciousness, and the
Politics of Empowerment* (Boston: Unwin Hyman 1990), 170.

10 Martha Minow, *Making All the Difference: Inclusion, Exclusion, and American
Law* (Ithaca: Cornell University Press 1990).

11 Ibid., 215.

12 Ibid., 390.

13 See Jennifer Nedelsky, 'Law, Boundaries and the Bounded Self,' *Representations* 30 (Spring 1990), 162; Carole Pateman, *The Sexual Contract* (Stanford:
Stanford University Press 1988).

14 Minow, *Making All the Difference*, 276.

15 An example of women in this category are Aboriginal women whose children
have often been forcibly removed and sent to residential schools or to live
with white families, and women with disabilities who have been subjected to
various sterilization measures. For a discussion of these practices, see Beverley
Sellars and Laura Hershey's discussion in Fellows and Razack 'Seeking Relations,' 1064.

16 For a fuller discussion, see chapter 1 in this volume, 'The Cold Game of Equality Staring,' and Patricia Williams, *The Alchemy of Race and Rights: Diary of a
Law Professor* (Cambridge: Harvard University Press 1991), 19.

17 There is little doubt that women with developmental disabilities experience
sexual violence to a greater degree than most other groups. *Vulnerable,* a study
of sexual abuse and people with an intellectual handicap, examined several
Canadian and American studies and found rates of sexual abuse and assault
four times greater than the national average. Charlene Y. Senn, *Vulnerable:
Sexual Abuse and People with an Intellectual Handicap* (Downsview, ON: The
G. Allan Roeher Institute 1989), 4–8. The statistics notwithstanding, many
researchers and activists have suggested that a conspiracy of silence exists
around sexual violence against people with developmental disabilities. Asch
and Fine speculate that many women with developmental disabilities are
sterilized 'to keep the effects of rape from the public eye.' Adrienne Asch and
Michelle Fine, 'Introduction: Beyond the Pedestals,' in Adrienne Asch and
Michelle Fine, eds., *Women with Disabilities: Essays in Psychology, Policy, and*

Politics (Philadelphia: Temple University Press 1988), 23. Certainly some of the impetus for forced sterilization, often unarticulated but disturbingly close to the surface, comes from the fear that a child or woman with a developmental disability is unusually vulnerable either to rape or to an unrestrained sexuality. Legal analysts discussing sterilization, for example, are often overly preoccupied with the 'burden' that disability imposes on non-disabled people. They identify, for example, the 'intolerable' strain on the family who cares for a woman with a developmental disability whose sexuality is not controlled. See, for example, the Honorable Bertha Wilson, 'Women, the Family, and the Constitutional Protection of Privacy,' *Queen's Law Journal* 17 (1992), 18; Elizabeth S. Scott, 'Sterilization of Mentally Retarded Persons: Reproductive Rights and Family Privacy,' *Duke Law Journal* (1986), 845; M. Anne Bolton, 'Whatever Happened to Eve?' *Manitoba Law Journal* 17 (1978), 219–26; Margaret A. Shone, 'Mental Health-Sterilization of Mentally Retarded Persons–*Psarens Patriae* Power,' in 'Notes of Cases,' *Canadian Bar Review* 66 (1987), 639.

18 Masuda and Riddington, *Meeting Our Needs*, 3.
19 David Finkelhor, *Child Sexual Abuse* (New York: The Free Press 1984), cited in Senn, *Vulnerable*, 12.
20 National Action Committee on the Status of Women, 'Justice for Women: A Brief on Bill C-49, An Act to Amend the Criminal Code (Sexual Assault),' 14 May 1992 (Toronto: National Action Committee 1992); Women's Legal Education and Action Fund, 'Submission of LEAF to the Legislative Committee on Bill C-49, An Act Respecting Sexual Assault' (Toronto: LEAF 1992); National Association of Women and the Law, 'A Brief on Bill C-49,' (Ottawa: NAWL 1992).
21 I am indebted to Mary Louise Fellows for helping me articulate this point.
22 NAC, 'Justice for Women,' 4.
23 I have put this term in quotation marks in order to express my disagreement with it. It leads too easily to the view that prostitution is primarily an issue of employment and not violence.
24 Minow, *Making All the Difference*, 219.
25 In many cases of sexual violence involving girls and women with developmental disabilities, legal practitioners display a casual unreflective use of the disability label to connote vulnerability. In fourteen such cases collected by the Metro Action Committee on Public Violence Against Women and Children, the courts continue to use words to describe developmental disability that many members of that community find offensive. 'Mental handicap' is the most frequently used term, but one also finds 'feeble-minded,' 'slow-witted,' and imprecise descriptions of deficiency, diminished intelligence, and impairment. While the offensiveness of the terms used is occasionally shocking, it

is the uses to which they are put that are of paramount interest. In all fourteen decisions, the connection between developmental disability and increased vulnerability was made as though to signal an awareness of a greater abuse of trust, but this awareness does not manifest itself in stronger sentences.

26 Frances Lee Ansley, 'Stirring the Ashes: Race, Class and the Future of Civil Rights Scholarship,' *Cornell Law Review* 74 (September 1989), 994. Cheryl I. Harris, 'Whiteness as Property,' *Harvard Law Review* 106, no. 8 (1993), 1784, has also argued that in the context of the affirmative action debate, privatization of the issues, the descent into 'the warp of sin and innocence' takes the focus away from distributive justice. Thus the affirmative action debate becomes one of who harmed whom and who should be made to pay for it as opposed to a consideration of claims in the context of racism. Within this latter framework, the question then becomes: In a fair world, absent of racism, who would be entitled to what? Hence white individuals would not be entitled to claim benefits they acquired in a racist world and Black individuals would be entitled to benefits that would have accrued to them in a racially fair world. The past and present practices of white supremacy are thus considered when evaluating claims for justice.

27 Minow, *Making All the Difference*, 174, also makes this point when she argues that when difference is thought to reside in the person rather then in the social context, we are able to ignore our role in producing it.

28 I have selected these two cases because they help me to illustrate what I mean about subtexts. Although I cannot argue that they are paradigmatic, I strongly suspect they are.

29 Ruth Luckasson has suggested that one telling indicator of the devaluing of the harm suffered by persons with developmental disabilities when they are victims of crime is the tendency to label crimes against them euphemistically, for example, to call the crime abuse or neglect when it is in fact torture, discrimination when it is hate crime, and mercy killings when it is murder. See her 'People with Mental Retardation as Victims of Crime,' in Ralph Conley, Ruth Luckasson, and George Bouthilet, eds., *The Criminal Justice System and Mental Retardation: Defendants and Victims* (Baltimore: Paul H. Brookes Publishing Co. 1992), 211.

30 *R. v. Mohammed*, 30 April 1992 (Toronto, Ontario Court, Provincial Division), 31.

31 Ibid., 32.

32 Ibid., 49–50.

33 Kimberlé Crenshaw, 'Whose Story Is It Anyway? Feminist and Antiracist Appropriations of Anita Hill,' in Toni Morrison, ed., *Race-ing Justice, En-Gendering Power: Essays on Anita Hill, Clarence Thomas and the Social Construction of Reality* (New York: Pantheon Books 1992), 408.

34 For an account of how fatness is lived as a disability that gives rise to a number of stereotypes, see Carol Schmidt, 'Do Something about Your Weight,' in Susan E. Browne, Debra Connors, and Nanci Stern, eds., *With the Power of Each Breath: A Disabled Women's Anthology* (Pittsburgh: Cleis Press 1985), 248.

35 *R.V. Mohammed*, 5.

36 Ibid., 38.

37 Anne Finger, 'Claiming All of Our Bodies: Reproductive Rights and Disability,' in Browne et al., eds., *With the Power of Each Breath*, 303.

38 Marilyn Frye observes that oppressed peoples frequently find themselves in a double bind – 'situations in which options are reduced to very few and all of them expose one to penalty, censure or deprivation.' She offers as one example of the double bind the situation of women penalized for both sexual activity and sexual inactivity with men. The choice is between being labelled a whore or being labelled frigid or sexually abnormal (since heterosexuality is the norm). Marilyn Frye, 'Oppression,' in Margaret L. Andersen and Patricia Hill Collins, eds., *Race, Class, and Gender: An Anthology* (Belmont, CA: Wadsworth 1992), 38–9.

39 *R.V. Mohammed*, 56.

40 Jennifer Wriggins notes in 'Rape, Racism, and the Law,' *Harvard Women's Law Journal* 6 (1983), 111, that American 'courts even applied special doctrinal rules to Black defendants accused of the rape or attempted rape of white women. One such rule allowed juries to consider the race of the defendant and victim in drawing factual conclusions as to the defendant's intent in attempted rape cases.'

41 *R.V. Mohammed*, 52.

42 Senn, *Vulnerable*, vi.

43 *R.V. Mohammed*, 44.

44 Anne McClintock, *Imperial Leather: Race, Gender and Sexuality in the Colonial Contest* (New York: Routledge 1995).

45 *R.V. Mohammed*, 26.

46 Senn, *Vulnerable*, 69.

47 *R.V. Mohammed*, 60.

48 *Re: Seaboyer v. The Queen; Re Gayme and the Queen*, [1991] 2 S.C.R. 577 at 690. Although the majority decision does not discredit motive to fabricate evidence, Madam Justice L'Heureux-Dubé, in dissent, explicitly rejected the possibility of a vengeful woman. She comments that any use of past sexual history 'depends for its relevance on certain stereotypical visions of women, that they lie about sexual assault, and that women who allege sexual assault often do so in order to get back in the good graces of those who may have her sexual conduct under scrutiny.' For a fuller discussion of this aspect of

Seaboyer, see Peggy Kobly, 'Rape Shield Legislation: Relevance, Prejudice and Judicial Discretion,' *Alberta Law Review* 30 (1992), 988.

49 Kristin Bumiller, 'Rape as a Legal Symbol: An Essay on Sexual Violence and Racism,' *University of Miami Law Review* 42, no. 1 (1987), 75, 88.

50 Ibid., 88.

51 *R.V. Mohammed*, 56.

52 Social Planning Council of Metropolitan Toronto, *A Time for Change: Moving through Discrimination in Employment* (Toronto: The Council 1989); Philomena Essed, *Understanding Everyday Racism: An Interdisciplinary Theory* (Newbury Park, CA: Sage Publications 1991).

53 *R.V. Mohammed*, 60.

54 Martha Minow, 'Stripped Down like a Runner or Enriched by Experience: Bias and Impartiality of Judges and Jurors,' *William and Mary Law Review* 33 (1992), 1201, 1204.

55 Ibid., 1215.

56 Province of Ontario, Ministry of the Attorney General, *Crown Policy Manual*, Policy #SO-2, 15 January 1994.

57 Baldwin, 'Split at the Root,' 71.

58 All information referred to has been gleaned from the *New York Times*, which covered the case exhaustively for more than a year. The material I rely upon is therefore sometimes speculative and second hand. In the absence of the actual court transcript, I still find the newspaper accounts useful in that they enable me to illustrate a possible scenario. A journalist's account of the case can be found in Peter Laufer, *A Question of Consent: Innocence and Complicity in the Glen Ridge Rape Case* (San Francisco: Mercury House 1994).

59 Robert Hanley, 'One Is Freed in Sex Attack in Glen Ridge,' *The New York Times*, 29 January 1994, 24, Metro edition.

60 Joseph Sullivan, 'New Jersey High Court Sets Rules on Mental Handicap in Sex Cases,' *The New York Times*, 5 May 1991, 44.

61 Mr Justice Burrell Ives Humphreys quoted in Robert Hanley, 'Judge Rules Sexual History Is Admissible in Trial,' *The New York Times*, 29 August 1992, 21.

62 Robert Hanley, 'Counsellor Says Woman in Abuse Case Sought Affection to Gain Friends,' *The New York Times*, 9 December 1992, 6.

63 Robert Hanley, 'Accuser's Mother Testifies in Sexual Assault Trial,' *The New York Times*, 18 November 1992, 5.

64 Robert Hanley, 'Sister Calls Woman in Assault Case Pliable,' *The New York Times*, 11 November 1992, 6.

65 Robert Hanley, 'Glen Ridge Abuse Trial Struggles with Two Images of the Accuser,' *The New York Times*, 1 December 1992, 5.

66 Dr Susan Esquilin, quoted in Robert Hanley, 'Witness in Abuse Trial Calls Accuser Vulnerable,' *The New York Times*, 29 October 1992, 8.

67 Anna Quindlen, 'Public and Private: 21 going on 6,' *The New York Times*, 13 December 1992, 4.

68 Reported by Robert Hanley, 'Prosecutors Introduce Secret Tapes at Sex-Assault Trial,' *The New York Times*, 30 October 1992, 6.

69 Robert Lipsyte, 'Must Boys Always Be Boys?' *The New York Times*, 12 March 1993, 7.

70 See for example, Lisa W. Foderaro, 'Glen Ridge Worries It Was Too Forgiving to Athletes,' *The New York Times*, 12 June 1989, 1, in which the town is described as white, Christian, and sport-loving, but also anti-Semitic; Elizabeth Miller-Hall and Robert Laurino, 'Revoke Bail, Prosecutor Says to Court,' *The New York Times*, 23 March 1993, 6.

71 Douglas Biklin, quoted by Catherine S. Mannegold, 'A Rape Case Worries Advocates for the Retarded,' *The New York Times*, 14 March 1993, 3.

72 James Ellis, quoted in Mannegold, ibid.

73 My suggestion that we pursue a more detailed description of the victim and the accused in their social context and move away from consent issues to violence may be seen here as incompatible with the chief objective of a trial which is a determination of guilt or innocence. A discussion of social context may be seen as more relevant to a sentencing hearing. I would respond, however, that issues arising from the social context, issues of the sources of violence, contribute greatly to the finding that is reached at the trial. I would not suggest then that they are best postponed to sentencing.

74 Ruth Luckasson, quoted in Catherine S. Mannegold, 'Bracing for a Message From Glen Ridge Jury,' *The New York Times*, 7 March 1993, 42.

75 Elizabeth M. Schneider, 'Describing and Changing: Women's Self-Defence Work and the Problem of Expert Testimony on Battering,' *Women's Rights Law Reporter* 14 (Spring/Fall 1992), 232.

76 Ibid., 235.

77 In Canada, consent is not a defence in any sexual offence against a child less than fourteen years old, *Criminal Code*, sec. 139 (1).

78 Legal rules often promote this decontextualization. For example, in *R. v. L (J.C.)* (1987) 36, C.C.C. (3d), a trial judge took notice of a context of repeated sexual violence inflicted by the offender on the victim, his daughter. On appeal, however, the court reduced the sentence from four years to three on the basis that sentencing must reflect the gravity of the specific offense for which L. (J.C.) was being tried, namely, the one incident for which he is charged. All other offenses were only alleged and thus could not have an impact on the sentence meted out since the offender has not been tried for them. Simi-

larly, in *R. v. Duffney* (1986), 61 Nfld. & P.E.I.R. at 178, involving a father who sexually assaulted his daughter over a number of years, a trial judge wrote:

> I am not going to attempt to calculate the number of times that these assaults took place because we don't have evidence that is tied to a specific period of time. When the complainant referred to it having taken place twenty or thirty times over a period of probably four years, we have to be very careful in interpreting that as an accurate statement, because that is a wide range anyway, twenty to thirty times in a period of four years. That isn't the time that is covered anyway. The accused himself in his statement that was put in evidence referred to two or three times, something like that.

79   19 Nov. 1986, Halifax S.C.C. 01487 (N.S.C.A.)
80   Ibid. I cannot of course confirm that this was true without an examination of the transcript of the trial.
81   28 April 1989, Edmonton 8803/3048C3 (Alta. Crt QB) 2–5.
82   Minow, *Making All the Difference*, 143, quotes this phrase from Robert Burt, who makes the point in his essay on *Halderman v. Pennhurst State School & Hosp.* that initially all nondisabled parties in the case were able to come together but could not ultimately sustain this cooperation 'over the long haul as the neediness of the vulnerable, inscrutable retarded people seemed to grow endlessly toward insatiability.' Robert Burt, 'Pennhurst: A Parable,' in Robert H. Mnookin, ed., *In the Interest of Children: Advocacy, Law Reform, and Public Policy* (New York: W.H. Freeman 1985), 324.
83   *R. v. Chin*, 23 February 1989, Vancouver CA008543 (B.C.C.A.).
84   Ibid., 6.
85   Ibid.
86   Ibid., 7.
87   Ibid.
88   *R.v. Chin*, 4 December 1987, Kamloops 204/0529 (B.C.S.C.), 1.
89   Research studies have suggested that the introduction of evidence about prior sexual history makes it more likely that the complainant will be not believed. See Peggy Kobly, 'Rape Shield Legislation: Relevance, Prejudice and Judicial Discretion,' *Alberta Law Review* 30 (1992), 991.
90   Bumiller, 'Rape as a Legal Symbol,' 76–7.
91   Baldwin, 'Split at the Root, ' 119.

6: Conclusion: To Essentialize or Not to Essentialize

1   Trina Grillo, 'Anti-Essentialism and Intersectionality: Tools to Dismantle the Master's House,' *Berkeley Women's Law Journal* 10, no. 1 (1995), 19.

2 Frantz Fanon, 'The Fact of Blackness,' in James Donald and Ali Rattansi, eds., *'Race,' Culture and Difference* (London: The Open University Press 1992), 220.

3 Keenan Malik, 'Universalism and Difference? Race and the Postmodernists,' *Race and Class* 37, no. 3 (Jan–March 1996), 13.

4 Caroline Forell, 'Essentialism, Empathy, and the Reasonable Woman,' *University of Illinois Law Review* 4 (1994), 813.

5 Naomi Shor, 'French Feminism Is a Universalism,' *Differences* 7, no. 1 (Spring 1995), 42.

6 Ibid., 28.

7 On this point, I would have to agree. We generally have a higher standard for those who claim to be our allies.

8 Jane Roland Martin, 'Methodological Essentialism, False Difference, and Other Dangerous Traps,' *Signs: Journal of Women in Culture and Society* 19, no. 3 (1994), 630.

9 Catharine MacKinnon, 'From Practice to Theory, or What Is a White Woman Anyway?' *Yale Journal of Law and Feminism* 4, no. 1 (1991), 20.

10 Ibid., 21.

11 Paul Gilroy, *The Black Atlantic* (Cambridge, MA: Harvard University Press 1993), 32.

12 Christina Crosby, 'Dealing with Differences,' in Judith Butler and Joan Scott, eds., *Feminists Theorize the Political* (New York: Routledge 1992), 131.

13 In my institution we are four in a faculty body of one hundred and twenty and the academy is anything but comfortable for us or students of colour. Indeed, it has become less physically safe as the number of incidents of Black students and faculty being threatened and assaulted rises.

14 Crosby, 'Dealing with Differences,' 135.

15 Martin, 'Methodological Essentialism,' 647.

16 For a discussion of this concept see Benedict Anderson, *Imagined Communities: Reflections on the Origins and Spread of Nationalism* (London: Verso 1983); Edward W. Said, *Orientalism* (New York: Vintage Books 1979); Paul Gilroy, *There Ain't No Black in the Union Jack* (London: Hutchinson 1987); and Homi K. Bhabha, *The Location of Culture* (London: Routledge 1994).

17 Patricia Marchak, *Racism, Sexism, and the University: The Political Science Affair at UBC* (Montreal: McGill-Queens University Press 1996), 79. I am grateful to Sheryl Nestel for bringing this to my attention.

18 George J. Sefa Dei, 'The Politics of Educational Change: Taking Anti-Racism Education Seriously' (unpublished manuscript).

19 Frank Jones, 'Answer These Questions on Prejudice,' *The Toronto Star*, 24 February 1997, C4.

20 Ibid., 14.

21 Crosby, 'Dealing with Differences,' 136.

22 This insight comes from a conversation with Mary Louise Fellows.

23 Lorde writes about her experiences in white feminist circles of the early 1980s in *Sister Outsider* (New York: The Crossing Press 1984).

24 Shor cites several prominent thinkers who argue this way, including several French feminists, Cornel West, Seyla Behabib, Nancy Miller, and others. Although I cannot do so here in depth, I argue that there is a qualitative difference in the way many scholars of colour call for a revised universalism and the way some white feminists interpret this goal. The latter often indirectly mean a universal and unraced woman, as the writings of French feminists and of Shor herself indicate, when paying attention to race is considered essentialism or ethnic chauvinism.

25 Shor makes the distinction between universalism and essentialism an important point in her article, giving the example of Simone de Beauvoir, who believed in a universal human nature but knew that men had defined this in such a way that women had no access to it. For Shor, de Beauvoir knew that all women did not share a common feminine nature and she was extremely hostile to the idea of an eternal feminine. She was not therefore a gender essentialist (see 'French Feminism,' 24). As much as this distinction is valid in de Beauvoir, Shor describes 'certain communities of feminist theorists,' namely those who wanted to build a counter-canon of Black women's writing as making universalizing moves (p. 25). She also notes that the reason for returning to universalism is that in giving it up, feminists of the 1970s gave up commonality and political clout. Here, it seems to me that the distinction between universalism and essentialism has collapsed in her work.

26 Shor, 'French Feminism,' 28.

27 Cornel West, 'The New Cultural Politics of Difference,' in Russell Ferguson, Martha Gever, Trinh T. Minh-ha, and Cornel West, eds., *Out There: Marginalization and Contemporary Culture* (New York and Boston: The New Museum of Contemporary Art and The MIT Press 1990), 34.

28 See Stuart Hall, 'New Ethnicities,' in James Donald and Ali Rattansi, eds., *'Race,' Culture and Difference* , 252; Gilroy, *The Black Atlantic* , 32; West, 'The New Cultural Politics,' 29; Grillo, 'Anti-Essentialism,' 24.

29 Patricia Hill Collins, cited in Beverley Balos and Mary Louise Fellows, *Law and Violence Against Women: Cases and Materials on Systems of Oppression* (Durham, NC: Carolina Academic Press 1994), 65.

30 Ann duCille, 'The Occult of True Black Womanhood: Critical Demeanor and Black Feminist Studies,' *Signs: Journal of Women in Culture and Society*, 19, no. 3 (1994), 606.

31 Shor, 'French Feminism,' 29.

32 Ibid., 41.
33 bell hooks, *Teaching to Transgress* (New York: Routledge 1994), 83.
34 Ibid.
35 No better explication of whose voices are heard as native exists than Trinh T. Minh-ha's *Woman, Native, Other: Writing Postcoloniality and Feminism* (Bloomington: Indiana University Press 1989).
36 Crosby begins and ends her article with the example of Lucy Snowe, Brontë's heroine in *Villette*, who gains access to the male universal by remaking herself.
37 Shor, 'French Feminism,' 41.

Bibliography

Abu-Lughod, Lila. 'Writing against Culture.' In *Recapturing Anthropology: Working in the Present*, ed. Richard Fox, 137–62. Santa Fe, NM: School of American Research Press, 1991.

Acoose, Janice/Misko-Kisikawihkwe (Red Sky Woman). *ISKWEWAK- Kah'Ki Yaw Ni Wahkomakanak: Neither Indian Princesses Nor Easy Squaws*. Toronto: Women's Press, 1995.

Alarcón, Norma. 'The Theoretical Subject(s) of This Bridge Called My Back and Anglo-American Feminism.' In *Making Face, Making Soul: Creative and Critical Perspectives of Women of Color*, ed. Gloria Anzaldúa, 356–69. San Francisco: an aunt lute foundation book, 1990.

Alcoff, Linda Martin. 'Philosophy and Racial Identity.' *Radical Philosophy* 75 (Jan/Feb 1966): 5–14

Alcoff, Linda, and Laura Gray. 'Survivor Discourse: Transgression or Recuperation?' *Signs: Journal of Women in Culture and Society* 18, no. 2 (1993): 260–90.

Allard, Sharon Angella. 'Rethinking Battered Woman Syndrome: A Black Feminist Perspective.' *UCLA Women's Law Journal* 19, no. 1 (1991): 191–207.

Amiel, Barbara. 'The Female Refugee: A Fraudulent Concept.' *Maclean's* 106, no. 3 (March 1993), 9.

Anderson, Benedict. *Imagined Communities: Reflection on the Origins and Spread of Nationalism*. London: Verso, 1995.

Ansley, Frances Lee. 'Stirring the Ashes: Race, Class and the Future of Civil Rights Scholarship.' *Cornell Law Review* 74 (September 1989): 994–1076.

Anzaldúa, Gloria. *Borderlands/La Frontera*. San Francisco: Spinsters/an aunt lute foundation book, 1989.

–, ed. *Making Face, Making Soul: Creative and Critical Perspectives on Women of Color*. San Francisco: an aunt lute foundation book, 1990.

Appleby, Yvon. 'Disability and "Compulsory Heterosexuality."' In *Heterosexuality:*

A Feminism and Psychology Reader, ed. Sue Wilkinson and Celia Kitzinger, 266–9. Newbury, CA: Sage Publications, 1993.

Aptheker, Bettina. *Tapestries of Life*. Amherst: University of Massachusetts Press, 1989.

Asad, Talal. 'The Concept of Cultural Translation in British Social Anthropology.' In *Writing Culture: The Poetics and Politics of Ethnography*, ed. James Clifford and George E. Marcus, 141–64. Berkeley: University of California Press, 1986.

Asbury, Jo-Ellen. 'African-American Women in Violent Relationships: An Exploration of Cultural Differences.' In *Violence in the Black Family: Correlates and Consequences*, ed. Robert L. Hampton, 90–105. Hampton, MA: Lexington Books, 1987.

Asch, Adrienne, and Michelle Fine. 'Introduction: Beyond the Pedestals.' In *Women with Disabilities: Essays in Psychology, Policy, and Politics*, ed. Adrienne Asch and Michelle Fine, 1–37. Philadelphia: Temple University Press, 1988.

Atoki, Morayo. 'Should Female Circumcision Continue to Be Banned?' *Feminist Legal Studies* 3, no. 2 (1995): 223–35

Austin, Regina. 'Black Women, Sisterhood and the Difference/Deviance Divide.' *New England Law Review* 26 (1992): 877–87.

Baldwin, Margaret. 'Split at the Root: Prostitution and Feminist Discourses of Law Reform.' *Yale Journal of Law and Feminism* 47, no. 5 (1992): 47–120.

Bakan, Abigail B., and Daiva Stasiulis. 'Making the Match: Domestic Placement Agencies and the Racialization of Women's Household Work.' *Signs: Journal of Women in Culture and Society* 20, no. 2 (1995): 303–35.

Bannerji, Himani, ed. *Returning the Gaze: Essays on Racism, Feminism and Politics*. Toronto: Sister Vision Press, 1993.

Balos, Beverley, and Mary Louise Fellows. *Law and Violence Against Women: Cases and Materials on Systems of Oppression*. Durham, NC: Carolina Academic Press, 1994.

Barbee, Evelyn L. 'Ethnicity and Woman Abuse in the United States.' In *Violence Against Women: Nursing Research, Education and Practice Issues*, ed. Carolyn Sampselle, 153–65. New York: Hemisphere Publishing, 1992.

Bashir, Layli Miller. 'Female Genital Mutilation in the United States: An Examination of Criminal and Asylum Law.' *American University Journal of Gender and the Law* 4 (1996): 415–54.

Bell, Jim. 'The Violating of Kitty Nowdluk.' *Arctic Circle* (July/August 1991): 32–8.

Berger, Thomas. *Northern Frontier, Northern Homeland: The Report of the Mackenzie Valley Pipeline Inquiry*. Ottawa: Supply and Services Canada, 1977.

Bhabha, Homi K. 'A Good Judge of Character: Men, Metaphors, and the Common Culture.' In *Race-ing Justice, En-Gendering Power: Essays on Anita Hill, Clarence Thomas and the Construction of Social Reality*, ed. Toni Morrison, 232–50. New York: Pantheon Books, 1992.

– *The Location of Culture*. London: Routledge, 1994.

Bolton, M. Anne. 'Whatever Happened to Eve?' *Manitoba Law Journal* 17 (1978): 219–26.

Borovoy, Alan. *The Fundamentals of Our Fundamental Freedoms*. Ottawa: Canadian Labour Congress, 1979.

Bower, Karen. 'Recognizing Violence against Women as Persecution on the Basis of Membership in a Particular Group.' *Georgetown Immigration Law Journal* 7, no. 1 (1993): 173–206.

Brittan, Arthur, and Mary Maynard. *Sexism, Racism and Oppression*. Oxford: Basil Blackwell, 1984.

Brosio, Richard. 'Teaching and Learning for Democratic Empowerment: A Critical Evaluation.' *Educational Theory* 40, no. 1 (Winter 1990): 69–81.

Bumiller, Kristin. 'Rape as a Legal Symbol: An Essay on Sexual Violence and Racism.' *University of Miami Law Review* 42, no. 1 (1987): 75–91.

– 'Fallen Angels: The Representation of Violence against Women in Legal Culture.' In *At the Boundaries of Law*, ed. Martha A. Fineman and Nancy Thomadsen, 95–112. New York: Routledge, 1991.

Bunch, Charlotte. 'Women's Rights as Human Rights: An International Lobbying Success Story.' *Human Rights Tribune*. Special Issue. *UN World Conference on Human Rights* 2, no. 1 (June 1993).

Bunting, Annie. 'Theorizing Women's Cultural Diversity in Feminist International Human Rights Strategies.' *Journal of Law and Society* 20, no. 1 (1993): 6–22.

Burt, Robert. 'Pennhurst: A Parable.' In *In the Interest of Children: Advocacy, Law Reform, and Public Policy*, ed. Robert H. Mnookin, 320–44. New York: W.H. Freeman, 1985.

Calmore, John O. 'Critical Race Theory, Archie Shepp and Fire Music: Securing an Authentic Intellectual Life in a Multicultural World.' *Southern California Law Review* 65, no. 5 (1992): 2129–230.

Canada. *An Act to Amend the Immigration Act, 1976 and to Amend Other Acts in Consequence Thereof*, 21 July 1988.

Canada. Immigration and Refugee Board. *Guidelines Issued by the Chairperson Pursuant to Section 65(3) of the Immigration Act*. Ottawa: Supply and Services Canada, 1993.

Canada. Immigration and Refugee Board. 'The Guidelines on Women Refugee Claimants Fearing Gender-Related Persecution: Update.' Ottawa: Supply and Services Canada, 1996.

Canada. Minister of Citizenship and Immigration. Press Release: 'Minister Robillard Announces an Initiative to Create a New Resettlement from Abroad Class and Two Others Aimed at Tightening Up the Removal Process.' Montreal, Quebec, 19 December 1996.

Canada. Royal Commission on Aboriginal Peoples. *Final Report*. Ottawa: Supply and Services Canada, 1996.

Canada. *Report of the Aboriginal Justice Inquiry of Manitoba*. Volume 1: *The Justice System and Aboriginal People*. Winnipeg: Queen's Printer, 1991.

Canadian Council on Social Development and Native Women's Association of Canada. *Voices of Aboriginal Women: Aboriginal Women Speak Out about Violence*. Ottawa: Canadian Council on Social Development, 1991.

Caribbean Association for Feminist Research and Action. 'Regional Meeting on Women, Violence and the Law: A Provisional Report based on a conference in St. Augustine, Trinidad and Tobago, January 1991.'

Carr, Robert. 'Crossing the First World/Third World Divides: Testimonial, Transnational Feminisms and the Postmodern Condition.' In *Scattered Hegemonies: Postmodernity and Transnational Feminist Practices*, ed. Inderpal Grewal and Caren Kaplan, 153–72. Minneapolis: University of Minnesota Press, 1994.

Cheney, Deborah. 'Valued Judgments? A Reading of Immigration Cases.' *Journal of Law and Society* 20, no. 1 (1993): 23–38.

Chow, Rey. *Woman and Chinese Modernity: The Politics of Reading between the East and West*. Minneapolis: University of Minnesota Press, 1991.

Churchill, Ward. *Indians Are Us? Culture and Genocide in Native North America*. Toronto: Between the Lines, 1994.

Cipriani, Linda. 'Gender and Persecution: Protecting Women under International Refugee Law.' *Georgetown Immigration Law Journal* 7, no. 3 (1993): 511–48.

Collins, Patricia Hill. *Black Feminist Thought: Knowledge, Consciousness, and the Politics of Empowerment*. Boston: Unwin Hyman, 1990.

Cook, Rebecca J. 'Women's International Human Rights Law: The Way Forward.' *Human Rights Quarterly* 15 (1993): 230–61.

Cook-Lynn, Elizabeth. *Why I Can't Read Wallace Stegner and Other Essays*. Madison: University of Wisconsin Press, 1996.

Courtrille, Lorraine. *Abused Aboriginal Women in Alberta: The Story of Two Types of Victimization*. Edmonton: Misener-Margetts Women's Resource Centre, 1991.

Coutinho, Tereza. 'Culture.' In *Toward Equal Access: A Handbook for Service Providers Working with Survivors of Wife Assault*, ed. Fauzia Rafiq, 49–64. Ottawa: Immigrant and Visible Minority Women Against Abuse, 1991.

Crenshaw, Kimberlé. 'Whose Story Is It, Anyway? Feminist and Antiracist Appropriations of Anita Hill.' In *Race-ing Justice, En-Gendering Power: Essays on Anita Hill, Clarence Thomas and the Social Construction of Reality*, ed. Toni Morrison, 402–40. New York: Pantheon Books, 1992.

Crosby, Christina. 'Dealing with Differences.' In *Feminists Theorize the Political*, ed. Judith Butler and Joan Scott, 130–43. New York: Routledge, 1992.

Dei, George J. Sefa. 'African-Centred Schools in North America: Going Beyond the Polemic.' In *Anti-Racism Education: Theory and Practice*. Halifax: Fernwood Publishing, 1996.

Delgado, Richard. 'When a Story Is Just a Story: Does Voice Really Matter?' *Virginia Law Review* 76 (1990): 95–111.

Deonna, Laurence. *Le Yemen que j'ai vu*. Paris: Lausanne-Arthaud, 1982.

Dion Stout, Madeleine. 'Fundamental Changes Needed to End Violence.' *Windspeaker* (7–20 November 1994), 10.

duCille, Ann. 'The Occult of True Black Womanhood: Critical Demeanor and Black Feminist Studies.' *Signs: Journal of Women in Culture and Society* 19, no. 3 (1994): 591–628.

Edmonds, Erin. 'Mapping the Terrain of Our Resistance: A White Feminist Perspective on the Enforcement of Rape Law.' *Harvard BlackLetter Journal* 9 (1992): 43–100.

Ellsworth, Elizabeth. 'Why Doesn't This Feel Empowering? Working Through the Repressive Myths of Critical Pedagogy.' *Harvard Educational Review* 59, no. 3 (August 1989): 297–324.

Engle, Karen. 'Female Subjects of Public International Law: Human Rights and the Exotic Other Female.' *New England Law Review* 26 (1992): 1509–26.

Enloe, Cynthia. *Bananas, Beaches and Bases: Making Feminist Sense of International Politics*. London: Pandora Press, 1989.

Espinet, Ramabai. 'Representation and the Indo-Caribbean Woman in Trinidad and Tobago.' In *Indo-Caribbean Resistance*, ed. Frank Birbalsingh, 42–61. Toronto: TSAR Publications, 1992.

Essed, Philomena. *Understanding Everyday Racism: An Interdisciplinary Theory*. Newbury, CA: Sage Publications, 1991.

Fanon, Frantz. *Black Skins, White Masks*. New York: Grove Press, 1967.

– 'The Fact of Blackness.' In *Race, Culture and Difference*, ed. James Donald and Ali Rattansi, 220–40. London: The Open University Press, 1992.

Fellows, Mary Louise, and Sherene Razack. 'Seeking Relations: Law and Feminism Roundtables.' *Signs: Journal of Women in Culture and Society* 19, no. 4 (1994): 1048–83.

– 'The Race to Innocence: Confronting Hierarchical Relations among Women.' *Iowa Journal of Gender, Race and Justice*. Forthcoming.

Female Genital Mutilation Legal Community Committee. 'Brief to the Parliamentary Standing Committee on Justice and Legal Affairs, Re Bill C-27, Section 268, Subsection (3) & (4).' 26 November 1996.

Ferguson, James. 'Jamaica: Stories of Poverty.' *Race and Class* 34, no. 1 (1992): 61–72.

Finger, Anne. 'Claiming All of Our Bodies: Reproductive Rights and Disability.' In *With the Power of Each Breath: A Disabled Women's Anthology*, ed. Susan E. Browne, Debra Connors, and Nanci Stern, 292–307. Pittsburgh: Cleis Press, 1985.

Finkelhor, David. *Child Sexual Abuse*. New York: The Free Press, 1984.

Flax, Jane. *Thinking Fragments: Psychoanalysis, Feminism and Postmodernism in the Contemporary West*. Berkeley: University of California Press, 1990.

Forell, Caroline. 'Essentialism, Empathy, and the Reasonable Woman.' *University of Illinois Law Review* 4 (1994): 769–817.

Foucault, Michel. 'Two Lectures.' In *Power/Knowledge: Selected Interviews and Other Writings, 1972–1977*, ed. Colin Gordon, trans. Colin Gordon, Leo Marshall, John Mepham, and Kate Soper, 78–108. New York: Pantheon Books, 1980.

Frank, Joshua B. 'IJ Grants Asylum to Citizen of Sierra Leone Who Suffered Forced Female Genital Mutilation.' *Georgetown Immigration Law Journal* 9, no. 3 (1995): 613–17.

Freire, Paulo. *Pedagogy of the Oppressed*. New York: Continuum Publishing, 1970.

Frye, Marilyn. 'Oppression.' In *Race, Class and Gender: An Anthology*, ed. Margaret L. Andersen and Patricia Hill Collins, 37–41. Belmont, CA: Wadsworth, 1992.

Fung, Richard. 'Looking for My Penis: The Eroticized Asian in Gay Video Porn.' In *How Do I Look? Queer Film and Video*, ed. Bad Object Choices, 145–60. Seattle: Bay Press, 1991.

Fusco, Coco. 'The Other History of Intercultural Performance.' *The Drama Review* 38, no. 1 (1994): 143–54.

– *English Is Broken Here: Notes on Cultural Fusion in the Americas*. New York: The New Press, 1995.

Gilroy, Paul. *There Ain't No Black in the Union Jack*. London: Hutchinson, 1987.

– *The Black Atlantic*. Cambridge, MA: Harvard University Press, 1993.

Goldberg, David Theo. *Racist Culture: Philosophy and the Politics of Meaning*. Cambridge: Blackwell, 1993.

Goldberg, Pamela. 'Any Place but Home: Asylum in the United States for Women Fleeing Intimate Violence.' *Cornell International Law Journal* 26 (1993): 565–604.

Greatbatch, Jacqueline. 'The Gender Difference: Feminist Critiques of Refugee Discourse.' *International Journal of Refugee Law* 14 (1989): 518–27.

Greene, Dwight. 'Abusive Prosecutors: Gender, Race and Class Distinction and the Prosecution of Drug-Addicted Mothers.' *Buffalo Law Review* 737 (1991): 737–802.

Greene, Gayle, and Coppélia Kahn. 'Feminist Scholarship and the Social Construction of Woman.' In *Making a Difference; Feminist Literary Criticism*, ed. Gayle Greene and Coppélia Khan, 1–36. London: Routledge, 1985.

Grewal, Inderpal. *Home and Harem: Nation, Gender, Empire, and the Cultures of Travel*. Durham: Duke University Press, 1996.

Grillo, Trina. 'Anti-Essentialism and Intersectionality: Tools to Dismantle the Master's House.' *Berkeley Women's Law Journal* 10, no. 1 (1995): 16–30.

Gunning, Isabelle R. 'Arrogant Perception, World-travelling and Multicultural Feminism: The Case of Female Genital Surgeries.' *Columbia Human Rights Law Review* 23, no. 2 (1991–1992): 189–248.

Guy, Blake M. 'Female Genital Excision and the Implications of Federal Prohibition.' *William and Mary Journal of Women and the Law* 2, no. 1 (1995): 125–69.

Hall, Stuart. 'The New Ethnicities.' In *'Race,' Culture and Difference*, ed. James Donald and Ali Rattansi, 252–59. London: The Open University Press, 1992.

– 'The After-Life of Frantz Fanon: Why Fanon? Why Now? Why *Black Skin, White Masks?*' In *The Fact of Blackness: Frantz Fanon and Visual Representation*, ed. Alan Read, 13–37. Seattle: Bay Press, 1996.

Harris, Cheryl I. 'Whiteness as Property.' *Harvard Law Review* 106, no. 8 (1993): 1710–91.

Hart, Mechthild. 'Critical Theory and Beyond: Further Perspectives on Emancipatory Education.' *Adult Education Quarterly* 40, no. 3 (Spring 1990): 125–38.

Hathaway, James C. (assisted by Anne MacMillan). *Rebuilding Trust. Report of the Review of Fundamental Justice in Information Gathering and Dissemination at the Immigration and Refugee Board of Canada*. Canada: Immigration and Refugee Board, 1993.

Henderson, James Youngblood 'Sakej'. 'The Marshall Inquiry: A View of the Legal Consciousness.' In *Elusive Justice*, ed. Joy Mannette, 35–62. Halifax: Fernwood, 1992.

Hoodfar, Homa. 'The Veil in Their Minds and on Our Heads: The Persistence of Colonial Images of Muslim Women.' *Resources for Feminist Research/Documentation sur la recherche féministe* 22, nos. 3/4 (Fall/Winter 1993): 5–18.

hooks, bell. 'Eating the Other.' In *Black Looks, Race and Representation*, 21–39. Boston: South End Press, 1992.

– *Teaching to Transgress*. New York: Routledge, 1994.

Indra, Doreen. 'Gender: A Key Dimension of the Refugee Experience.' *Refugee* 6 (1987): 3–4.

Jaffer, Mobina. *Is Anyone Listening? Report of the British Columbia Task Force on Family Violence*. Vancouver: n.p., 1992.

Jiwani, Yasmin. 'To Be and Not to Be: South Asians as Victims and Oppressors in the *Vancouver Sun*,' *Sanvad* 5, no. 45 (August 1992): 13–15.

Kandt, Kristin E. 'United States Asylum Law: Recognizing Persecution Based on Gender Using Canada as a Comparison,' *Georgetown Immigration Law Journal* 9 no. 1 (1995): 137–80.

Karst, Kenneth L. 'Woman's Constitution.' *Duke Law Journal* 3 (June 1984): 447–508.

Kelly, Nancy. 'Gender-Related Persecution: Assessing the Asylum Claims of Women.' *Cornell International Law Journal* 26 (1993): 625–74.

Kerr, Joanna. 'The Context and the Goal.' In *Ours by Right: Women's Rights as Human Rights*, ed. Joanna Kerr, 3–9. London: Zed Books, 1993.

Kobly, Peggy. 'Rape Shield Legislation: Relevance, Prejudice and Judicial Discretion.' *Alberta Law Review* 30 (1992): 988–1017.

Kymlicka, William. *Liberalism, Community, and Culture*. Oxford: Clarendon Press, 1989.

– 'Individual and Community Rights.' In *Group Rights*, ed. Judith Baker, 17–33. Toronto: University of Toronto Press, 1994.

Laufer, Peter. *A Question of Consent: Innocence and Complicity in the Glen Ridge Rape Case*. San Francisco: Mercury House, 1994.

Lee, Cynthia Kwei Yung. 'Beyond Black and White: Racializing Asian Americans in a Society Obsessed with O.J.' *Hastings Women's Law Journal* 6, no. 2 (Summer 1995): 165–207.

Lewis, Hope. 'Between *Irua* and "Female Genital Mutilation": Feminist Human Rights Discourse and the Cultural Divide.' *Harvard Human Rights Journal* 8 (1995): 1–55.

Lewis, Reina. *Gendering Orientalism: Race, Femininity, and Representation*. London: Routledge, 1996.

Lilles, Heino. 'Some Problems in the Administration of Justice in Remote and Isolated Communities.' *Queen's Law Journal* 15 (1990): 327–44.

– 'A Plea for More Human Values in Our Justice System.' *Queen's Law Journal*, 17 (1992): 328–49.

Liu, Lydia. 'The Female Body and Nationalist Discourse: The Field of Life and Death Revisited.' In *Scattered Hegemonies: Postmodernity and Transnational Feminist Practices*, ed. Inderpal Grewal and Caren Kaplan, 37–62. Minneapolis: University of Minnesota Press, 1995.

Long, Walter C. 'Escape from Wonderland: Implementing Canada's Rational Procedures to Evaluate Women's Gender-Related Asylum Claims.' *UCLA Women's Law Journal* 4, no. 179 (1994): 179–254.

Lorde, Audre. *Sister Outsider*. New York: The Crossing Press, 1984.

Luckasson, Ruth. 'People with Mental Retardation as Victims of Crime.' In *The Criminal Justice System and Mental Retardation: Defendants and Victims*, ed. Ralph W. Conley, Ruth Luckasson, and George Bouthilet, 209–20. Baltimore: Paul H. Brookes Publishing Co., 1992.

Lugones, María. 'Hablando cara a Cara/Speaking Face to Face: An Exploration of Ethocentric Racism.' In *Making Face, Making Soul: Creative and Critical Perspectives by Women of Color*, ed. Gloria Anzaldúa, 46–54. San Francisco: an aunt lute foundation book, 1990.

MacKinnon, Catharine A. *Feminism Unmodified: Discourses on Life and Law*. Cambridge: Harvard University Press, 1987.

- 'Sex and Violence: A Perspective.' In *Feminism Unmodified: Discourses on Life and Law*, 85–92. Cambridge, MA: Harvard University Press, 1987.
- *Toward a Feminist Theory of the State*. Cambridge, MA: Harvard University Press, 1989.
- 'From Practice to Theory, or What Is a White Woman Anyway?' *Yale Journal of Law and Feminism* 4, no. 1 (1991): 13–22.
- 'On Torture: A Feminist Perspective on Human Rights.' In *Human Rights in the Twenty-First Century: A Global Challenge*, ed. Kathleen E. Mahoney and Paul Mahoney, 21–31. The Netherlands: Kluwer Academic Publishers, 1993.
- 'Turning Rape into Pornography: Postmodern Genocide.' *Ms.* 4 (July/August 1993): 24–30.
Macklin, Audrey. 'Refugee Women and the Imperative of Categories.' *Human Rights Quarterly* 17 (1995): 213–77.
Magendzo, Salomón. 'Popular Education in Nongovernmental Organizations: Education for Social Mobilizations?' *Harvard Educational Review* 60, no. 1 (February 1990): 49–61.
Mahboubeh, Katirai. *Assessing the Needs of Alternative Services for Culturally Diverse Assaulted Women*. Hamilton, ON: Interval House of Hamilton-Wentworth, 1991.
Mahoney, Martha. 'Whiteness and Women, in Practice and Theory: A Reply to Catherine MacKinnon.' *Yale Journal of Law and Feminism* 5, no. 2 (1995): 217–51.
Malik, Keenan. 'Universalism and Difference? Race and the Postmodernists.' *Race and Class* 37, no. 3 (Jan–March 1996): 1–18.
Mannette, Joy, ed. *Elusive Justice: Beyond the Marshall Inquiry*. Halifax: Fernwood Publishing, 1992.
Maracle, Lee. *I Am Woman*. North Vancouver: Write-on Publishers, 1988.
Marchak, Patricia. *Racism, Sexism, and the University: The Political Science Affair at UBC*. Montreal: McGill-Queens University Press, 1996.
Marchetti, Gina. *Romance and the 'Yellow Peril': Race, Sex, and Discursive Strategies in Hollywood Fiction*. Berkeley: University of California Press, 1993.
Marcus, Sharon. 'Fighting Bodies, Fighting Words: A Theory and Politics of Rape Prevention.' In *Feminists Theorize the Political*, ed. Judith Butler and Joan Scott, 385–403. New York: Routledge, 1992.
Martin, Biddy. 'Feminism, Criticism and Foucault.' In *Feminism and Foucault: Reflections on Resistance*, ed. Irene Diamond and Lee Quinby, 3–19. Boston: Northeastern University Press, 1988.
Martin, Jane Roland. 'Methodological Essentialism, False Difference and Other Dangerous Traps.' *Signs: Journal of Women in Culture and Society* 19, no. 3 (1994): 630–57.
Massaro, Toni M. 'Empathy, Legal Story-telling, and the Rule of Law: New Words, Old Wounds?' *Michigan Law Review* 87 (August 1989): 2099–127.

Masuda, Shirley, and Jillian Riddington. *Meeting Our Needs: An Access Manual for Transition Houses.* Toronto: DisAbled Women's Network Canada, 1990.

Matsuda, Mari J. 'Looking to the Bottom: Critical Legal Studies and Reparations.' *Harvard Civil Rights–Civil Liberties Law Review* 22 (1987): 323–99.

– 'Public Response to Racist Speech: Considering the Victim's Story.' *Michigan Law Review* 87 (1989): 2320–81.

Mawani, Nurjehan. 'Introduction to the Immigration and Refugee Board Guidelines on Gender-Related Persecution.' *International Journal of Refugee Law* 5, no. 2 (1993): 240–7.

McCarthy, Thomas. 'Doing the Right Thing in Cross-Cultural Representation.' *Ethics* 102, no. 3 (1992): 635–49.

McClintock, Anne. *Imperial Leather: Race, Gender and Sexuality in the Colonial Contest.* New York: Routledge, 1995.

Meadow, Carrie Menkel. 'Portia in a Different Voice: Speculations on a Woman's Lawyering Process.' *Berkeley Women's Law Journal* 1, no. 1 (1985): 39–63.

McLaren, Peter, and Peter Leonard, eds. *Paulo Freire: A Critical Encounter.* London and New York: Routledge, 1993.

Minow, Martha. *Making All the Difference: Inclusion, Exclusion, and American Law.* Ithaca: Cornell University Press, 1990.

– 'Stripped Down like a Runner or Enriched by Experience: Bias and Impartiality of Judges and Jurors.' *William and Mary Law Review* 33 (1992): 1201–18.

Mohanty, Chandra. 'On Race and Voice: Challenges for Liberal Education in the 1990s.' *Cultural Critique* 14 (Winter 1991): 179–208.

Monture-Angus, Patricia. *Thunder in My Soul: A Mohawk Woman Speaks.* Halifax: Fernwood Publishing, 1995.

Moraga, Cherrie. 'La Guera.' In *Race, Class and Gender: An Anthology*, ed. Margaret L. Andersen and Patricia Hill Collins, 15–22. Belmont, CA: Wadsworth, 1992.

Morris, Jenny. *Pride against Prejudice: Transforming Attitudes to Disability.* London: Women's Press, 1991.

Morrison, Toni. *Playing in the Dark: Whiteness and the Literary Imagination.* Cambridge: Harvard University Press, 1992.

Mukherjee, Arun, ed. *Sharing Our Experience.* Ottawa: Canadian Advisory Council on the Status of Women, 1993.

Mulligan, Maureen. 'Obtaining Political Asylum: Classifying Rape as a Well-Founded Fear of Persecution on Account of Political Opinion.' *Boston College Third World Law Journal* 10 (1990): 355–79.

Musisi, Nakanyike, and Fakiha Muktar. *Exploratory Research: Wife Assault in Metropolitan Toronto's African Immigrant and Refugee Community.* Toronto: Canadian African Newcomer Aid Centre of Toronto, 1992.

Nahanee, Teressa. 'Sex and Race in Inuit Rape Cases: Judicial Discretion and the Charter.' 1992. Unpublished.

– 'Sexual Assault of Inuit Females: A Comment on "Cultural Bias."' In *Confronting Sexual Assault: A Decade of Legal and Social Change*, ed. Julian V. Roberts and Renate M. Mohr, 192–204. Toronto: University of Toronto Press, 1994.

Narayan, Uma. 'Working Together Across Differences: Some Considerations on Emotions and Political Practice,' *Hypatia* 3, no. 2 (Summer 1988): 31–47.

National Action Committee on the Status of Women. 'Justice for Women: A Brief on Bill C-49, An Act to Amend the Criminal Code (Sexual Assault).' Toronto: National Action Committee, 1992.

National Association of Women and the Law. 'A Brief on Bill C-49.' Ottawa: NAWL, 1992.

Neal, David L. 'Women as a Social Group: Recognizing Sex-based Persecution as Grounds for Asylum.' *Columbia Human Rights Law Review* 20, no. 1 (1988): 203–57.

Nedelsky, Jennifer. 'Law, Boundaries and the Bounded Self.' *Representations* 30 (Spring 1990): 162–89.

Neely, Barbara. *Blanche on the Lam.* New York: Penguin, 1992.

Nesiah, Vasuki. 'Towards a Feminist Internationality: A Critique of U.S. Feminist Legal Scholarship.' *Harvard Women's Law Journal* 16 (Spring 1993): 189–210.

Nightingale, Margo. 'Judicial Attitudes and Differential Treatment: Native Women in Sexual Assault Cases.' *Ottawa Law Review* 23, no. 1 (1991): 71–98.

Northwest Territories Status of Women Council. 'We Must Take Care of Each Other: Women Talk about Abuse.' Discussion paper, 1990.

Omi, Michael, and Howard Winant. 'On the Theoretical Concept of Race.' In *Race, Identity and Representation in Education*, ed. Cameron McCarthy and Warren Crichlow, 3–10. New York and London: Routledge, 1993.

Ontario Ministry of the Attorney General. *Crown Policy Manual.* No. SO-2. Toronto: Ontario Ministry of the Attorney General, 1994.

Ontario Native Women's Association. *Report on Aboriginal Family Violence.* Thunder Bay, ON: ONWA, 1989.

Oosterveld, Valerie. 'Refugee Status for Female Circumcision Fugitives: Building a Canadian Precedent.' *University of Toronto Faculty of Law Review* 51, no. 2 (1993): 277–303.

Paine, Charles. 'Relativism, Radical Pedagogy and the Ideology of Paralysis.' *College English* 50, no. 6 (1989): 557–70.

Pateman, Carol. *The Sexual Contract.* Stanford: Stanford University Press, 1988.

Potter, Heather. 'Gender-based Persecution: A Challenge to the Canadian Refugee Determination System.' *Dalhousie Journal of Legal Studies* 3 (1994): 81–104.

Pratt, Mary Louise. *Imperial Eyes: Travel Writing and Transculturation*. London and New York: Routledge, 1992.

Rafiq, Fauzia, ed. *Toward Equal Access: A Handbook for Service Providers Working with Survivors of Wife Assault*. Ottawa: Immigrant and Visible Minority Women Against Abuse, 1991.

Razack, Sherene. 'Revolution from Within: Dilemmas of Feminist Jurisprudence.' *Queen's Quarterly* 97, no. 3 (Autumn 1990): 398–413.

– *Canadian Feminism and the Law: The Women's Legal Education and Action Fund and the Pursuit of Equality*. Toronto: Second Story Press, 1991.

– 'Schooling Research on South and East Asian Students: The Perils of Talking about Culture.' *Race, Class and Gender* 2, no. 3 (1995): 67–82.

Razack, Sherene, and Mary Louise Fellows. 'Seeking Relations.' *Signs: Journal of Women in Culture and Society*, 19, no. 4 (1994): 1048–83.

Ross, Rupert. *Dancing with a Ghost: Exploring Indian Reality*. Markham, ON: Octopus Publishing Group, 1992.

– *Returning to the Teachings: Exploring Aboriginal Justice*. Toronto: Penguin, 1996.

Royal Canadian Mounted Police Public Complaints Commission. *Public Hearing into the complaint of Kitty Nowdlok-Reynolds: Commission Report*. Allan Williams, Q.C., S. Jane Evans, Lazarus Arreak. Vancouver, 1992.

Ruttenberg, Miriam H. 'A Feminist Critique of Mandatory Arrest: An Analysis of Race and Gender in Domestic Violence Policy.' *The American Journal of Gender and the Law* 2 (1994): 171–99.

Said, Edward W. *Orientalism*. New York: Vintage Books, 1979.

– *Covering Islam: How the Media and the Experts Determine How We See the Rest of the World*. New York: Pantheon, 1981.

– *Culture and Imperialism*. New York: Alfred Knopf, 1993.

Salter, V., and Women's Mediawatch. 'Jamaica's Position on Domestic Violence.' *Women's Mediawatch*, 29 December 1994.

Schenk, Todd Stewart. 'A Proposal to Improve the Treatment of Women in Asylum Law: Adding a "Gender" Category to the International Definition of "Refugee."' *Indiana Journal of Global Legal Studies* 2, no. 1 (1994): 301–44.

Scheppele, Kim Lane. 'Foreword: Telling Stories.' *Michigan Law Review* 87, no. 8 (August 1989): 2073–98.

Schmidt, Carol. 'Do Something about Your Weight.' In *With the Power of Each Breath: A Disabled Women's Anthology*, ed. Susan E. Browne, Debra Connors, and Nanci Stern, 248–52. Pittsburgh: Cleis Press, 1985.

Schneider, Elizabeth M. 'Describing and Changing: Women's Self-Defence Work and the Problem of Expert Testimony on Battering.' *Women's Rights Law Reporter* 14 (Spring/Fall 1992): 213–41. Originally published as 'The Dialectic of Rights and Politics: Perspectives from the Women's Movement.' *New York University Law Review* 61 (1986): 589–652.

Scott, Elizabeth S. 'Sterilization of Mentally Retarded Persons: Reproductive Rights and Family Privacy.' *Duke Law Journal* (1986): 806–65.

Senn, Charlene Y. *Vulnerable: Sexual Abuse and People with an Intellectual Handicap.* Downsview, ON: The G. Allan Roeher Institute, 1989.

Setarah, Daliah. 'Women Escaping Genital Mutilation–Seeking Asylum in the United States.' *UCLA Women's Law Journal* 6, no. 1 (1995): 123–59.

Sheilds, Rob. *Place on the Margins: Alternative Geographies of Modernity.* New York: Routledge, 1991.

Shone, Margaret A. 'Mental Health-Sterilization of Mentally Retarded Persons-*Psarens Patriae* Power.' In 'Notes of Cases.' *Canadian Bar Review* 66 (1987): 635–46.

Shor, Naomi. 'French Feminism Is a Universalism.' *Differences* 7, no. 1 (Spring 1995): 15–42.

Sivanandan, A. 'U.K. Commentary: Signs of the Times: An Interview with A. Sivanandan by Paul Grant.' *Race and Class* 33, no. 4 (1992): 63–8.

Sleeter, Christine. 'How White Teachers Construct Race.' In *Race, Identity and Representation in Education,* ed. Cameron McCarthy and Warren Crichlow, 157–71. New York and London: Routledge, 1993.

Social Planning Council of Metropolitan Toronto. *A Time for Change: Moving Through Discrimination in Employment.* Toronto: The Council, 1989.

Spivak, Gayatri Chakravorty. 'The Postmodern Condition: The End of Politics?' In *The Post-Colonial Critic: Interviews, Strategies, Dialogues,* ed. Sarah Harasym, 17–34. New York and London: Routledge, 1990.

– 'The Problem of Cultural Self-Representation.' In *The Post-Colonial Critic: Interviews, Strategies, Dialogues,* ed. Sarah Harasym, 50–8. New York and London: Routledge, 1990.

– 'Strategy, Identity, Writing.' In *The Post-Colonial Critic: Interviews, Strategies, Dialogues,* ed. Sarah Harasym, 35–47. New York and London: Routledge, 1990.

– 'Acting Bits/Identity Talk.' *Cultural Inquiry* 18 (Summer 1992): 770–803.

Stairs, Felicité, and Lori Pope. 'No Place Like Home: Assaulted Migrant Women's Claims to Refugee Status and Landings on Humanitarian and Compassionate Grounds.' *Journal of Law and Social Policy* 6 (1990): 148–225.

Steedman, Carolyn. *Landscape for a Good Woman: A Story for Two Lives.* London: Virago, 1986.

Steele, Robbie D. 'Silencing the Deadly Ritual: Efforts to End Female Genital Mutilation.' *Georgetown Immigration Law Journal* 9, no. 1 (1995): 105–35.

Stoler, Ann Laura. 'Carnal Knowledge and Imperial Power: Gender, Race, and Morality in Colonial Asia.' In *Gender at the Crossroads: Feminist Anthropology in the Post-Modern Era,* ed. Micaela di Leonardo, 51–101. Berkeley: University of California Press, 1991.

Suleri, Sara. *The Rhetoric of English India*. Chicago: University of Chicago Press, 1992.

Table de Concertation de Montréal pour les Réfugiés. *Consultation on Refugee Women Claimants. Report*. Montréal: Fulford Hall, 1444 Union, 1993.

Thobani, Sunera. 'There Is a War on Women: A Desh Pradesh Workshop.' *Rungh: A South Asian Quarterly of Culture, Comment and Criticism* Pt. 1, nos. 1/2 (1993): 12–14.

Trinh, Minh-ha T. *Woman, Native, Other: Writing Postcoloniality and Feminism*. Bloomington: Indiana University Press, 1989.

– 'Not You/Like You: Post-Colonial Women and the Interlocking Questions of Identity and Difference.' In *Making Face, Making Soul: Creative and Critical Perspectives of Women of Color*, ed. Gloria Anzaldúa, 371–5. San Francisco: an aunt lute foundation book, 1990.

Uttal, Lynet. 'Nods That Silence.' In *Making Face, Making Soul: Creative and Critical Perspectives by Women of Color*, ed. Gloria Anzaldúa, 317–20. San Francisco: an aunt lute foundation book, 1990.

van Dijk, Teun A. *Elite Discourse and Racism*. Sage Series on Race and Ethnic Relations. Newbury Park, CA: Sage Publications, Inc., 1993.

Wa, Gisday, and Delgam Uukw. *The Spirit in the Land. Statements of the Gitksan and Wet'suwet'en Hereditary Chiefs in the Supreme Court of British Columbia 1987–1990*. Gabriola, B.C.: Reflections, 1992.

Walkerdine, Valerie. 'On the Regulation of Speaking and Silence: Subjectivity, Class and Gender in Contemporary Schooling.' In *Language, Gender and Childhood*, ed. Carolyn Steedman, 203–41. London: Routledge and Kegan Paul, 1985.

– *Schoolgirl Fictions*. London: Verso Press, 1990.

Watney, Simon. 'Missionary Positions: AIDS, "Africa" and Race.' In *Out There: Marginalization and Contemporary Cultures*, ed. Russell Ferguson, Martha Gever, Trinh T. Minh-ha, and Cornel West, 89–106. New York and Boston: The New Museum of Contemporary Art and the MIT Press, 1990.

Weiler, Kathleen. *Women Teaching for Change: Gender, Class and Power*. New York: Bergin and Garvey, 1988.

West, Cornel. 'The New Cultural Politics of Difference.' In *Out There: Marginalization and Contemporary Culture*, ed. Russell Ferguson, Martha Gever, Trinh Minh-ha, and Cornel West, 19–36. New York and Boston: The New Museum of Contemporary Art and the MIT Press, 1990.

West, Robin. 'Jurisprudence and Gender.' *University of Chicago Law Review* 55, no. 1 (Winter 1988): 1–72.

Williams, Joan C. 'Culture and Certainty: Legal History and the Reconstructive Project.' *Virginia Law Review* 76, nos. 1–4 (1990): 713–46.

Williams, Patricia. *The Alchemy of Race and Rights: Diary of a Law Professor.* Cambridge: Harvard University Press, 1991.

Williams, Robert A., Jr. 'Taking Rights Aggressively: The Perils and Promise of Critical Legal Theory for Peoples of Color.' *Law and Inequality* 5 (1987): 103–34.

Wilson, Honourable Bertha. 'Women, the Family, and the Constitutional Protection of Privacy.' *Queen's Law Journal* 17 (1992): 5–30.

Women's Legal Education and Action Fund. 'Submission of LEAF to the Legislative Committee on Bill C-49, An Act Respecting Sexual Assault.' Toronto: Legal Education and Action Fund, 1992.

Wriggins, Jennifer. 'Rape, Racism and the Law.' *Harvard Women's Law Journal* 6 (1983): 103–41.

Young, Iris Marion. *Justice and the Politics of Difference.* Princeton: Princeton University Press, 1990.

Young, Robert. *Colonial Desire: Hybridity in Theory, Culture and Race.* London: Routledge, 1995.

Zuniga, Ricardo. 'La Gestion Amphibie.' *Revue internationale d'action communautaire* 19 (1988): 157–67.

Legal References

A. *(I.E) (Re).*, [1993] C.R.D.D. No. 111. No. T93-03535. Toronto, Ontario. Reasons for decision.

C. *(X.N.)*, [1993] C.R.D.D. No. 28. No. U92-08714. Toronto, Ontario. H. Maraj and M. Shecter. Heard: 11 March 1993. Decision: 4 June 1993. Reasons for decision.

C.R.D.D. A95-00154, A95-00155. Henders, Kagedan. 12 April 1996. C.R.D.D. T95-01010, T95-01011, T95-01012. Kelley, Then. 30 July 1996.

C.R.D.D. A95-00400. Harker, Parris. 8 November 1996.

C.R.D.D. A95-00442. Gilad, Noseworthy. 19 February 1996 (Reasons signed 22 March 1996.)

C.R.D.D. A95-00837. Henders, Gilad. 3 May, 1996. (Reasons signed 23 May, 1996.)

C.R.D.D. A95-01055. Henders, Shawler. 1 May 1996. (Reasons signed 24 May 1996.)

C.R.D.D. A96–00092. McCauley, Maylum. 26 July 1996. C.R.D.D. A93-80785. Harker, Noseworthy. 27 May 1996.

C.R.D.D. C93-00433. Calgary, Alberta. J.E. Wieler and E.T. Lazo. Heard: 28 October 1993. Decision: 3 December 1993. Reasons for decision.

C.R.D.D. M92-13594. Ottawa, Ontario. E. Harker and J. MacPherson. Heard: 20 April and 15 June 1933. Decision: 13 September 1993. Reasons for decision.

C.R.D.D. M93-03388, M93-03391. Montréal, Québec. M. Hébert and D. Raymond. Heard: 7 October 1993. Decision: 2 December 1993. Reasons for decision.

C.R.D.D. M93-09606. Kafaï, Bergeron. 22 May 1996.

C.R.D.D. M95-00474, M95-00475. Singer, Doray. 1 March 1996.

C.R.D.D. M95-02275, M95-02276. Michnick, ven der Buhs. 8 October 1996.

C.R.D.D. T92-07219. 14 February 1994.

C.R.D.D. T89-04608, T89-04609, T89-04611. Sarzotti, Nig. 22 May 1990. *Reflex*: Special issue 1 (September 1992).

C.R.D.D. T93-00104, T93-09539. Toronto, Ontario. J. Davis and M. Qureshi. Heard: 7 July, 1993. Decision: 29 October, 1993. Reasons for decision.

C.R.D.D. T93-07375. Toronto, Ontario. K.S. Desai and N.L. Cheeseman. Heard: 27 September 1993. Decision: 18 January 1994. Reasons for decisions.

C.R.D.D. T93-08347. Toronto, Ontario. E.A. Grice and M.Y. Mouammar. Heard: 26 October 1993. Decision: 19 January 1994. Reasons for decision.

C.R.D.D. T93-12197, T93-12198, T93-12199. Toronto, Ontario. J. Ramirez and J. McCaffrey. Heard: 10 May 1994. Decision: 13 July 1994. Reasons for decision.

C.R.D.D. T94-01325. Bubrin, Eustagmio. 8 March 1996.

C.R.D.D. T94-01904. Keley, Jalaludin. 1 March 1996.

C.R.D.D. T95-04502. Davis, Koulouras. 30 May 1996.

C.R.D.D. T95-05227, T95-05228. Winkler. 2 July 1996. (Reasons signed 8 November 1996.)

C.R.R.D. T95-06805. Davis, Woloschuk. 21 October 1996.

C.R.D.D. U93-00223. (Calgary, Alberta.) (Winnipeg, Manitoba.) J.E. Weiler and H.S. Pawa. Heard: 25 October 1993. Decision: 31 December 1993; 12 January 1994. Reasons for decision.

C.R.D.D. U93-01178, U93-01179, U93-01180. Toronto, Ontario. B.L. Thomas and D.J. Whitfield. Heard: 5 February 1993. Decision: 16 March 1993. Reasons for decision.

C.R.D.D. U93-0607, U93-06513. Thibodeau, Chan. 1 April 1996.

C.R.D.D. U93-07212. Toronto, Ontario. G. Carsen and A. Leistra. Decision: 3 December 1993. Reasons for decision.

C.R.D.D. U93-07891, U93-07892, U93-07893, U93-07894. Toronto, Ontario. Submissions of counsel. 9 December 1993. Counsel: G. Sadoway.

C.R.D.D. U95-03525. Sotto, Nagvi. 25 September 1996.

C.R.R.D. U95-04292. Allmen, Daya. 2 October 1996.

C.R.D.D. U95-04594. Maraj, Clark (dissenting). 14 November 1996.

C.R.D.D. U95-04687. Fraser, Jackson. 16 September 1996. C.R.D.D. U95-02138. Maraj, Sotto (dissenting). 10 September 1996.

C.R.D.D. U95-04832. Nagiv, Turley. 16 August 1996.

C.R.D.D. V94-00024, V94-00025, V94-00026, V94-00027. Whitehead, Kalvin. 9 September 1996.

C.R.D.D. V94-01847. Brison, 21 June 1996. (Reasons signed 20 August 1996.)

C.R.D.D. V95-00374. Whitehead. 21 November 1996.

Cuffy, Loferne Pauline v. M.C.I. (F.C.T.D.), no. IMN-3135-95, McKeown, 16 October 1996.

Delgamuukw v. Her Majesty the Queen. Reasons for Judgment of The Honourable Chief Justice Allan McEachern, British Columbia Supreme Court, no. 0843, March 1991.

FWTAO v. Tomen (1991), 50 O.A.C. 158 (S.C.C.).

Garcia, Rosa Elena Duran v. M.C.I. (F.C.T.D.), no. IMM-2523-95, McKeown, 10 May 1996.

Harper v. The Queen, (Minister of Employment and Immigration). 212(F.C.J), n.d. Unreported decision, Rothstein, J. I. *(G.F.) (Re).,* [1993] C.R.D.D. No. 114. No. T92-09592. Toronto, Ontario. M.V. Toth and A. Dualeh. Heard: 25 March 1993. Decision: 14 September 1993. Reasons for decisions.

Ingrid Harper and The Queen (Minister of Employment and Immigration) Ont. Ct. (G.D.), 11 January 1993, *Affidavit* 47.

K. (T.J.) (Re)., [1992] C.R.D.D. No. 248.

K. (L.M.) (Re)., [1994] C.R.D.D. No 68. T93-08122. Toronto, Ontario. S.G. Flintoff and N.H. Jiwan. Heard: 13 December 1993. Decision: 16 February 1994. Reasons for decision.

M. (X.K.), [1994] C.R.D.D. No. 78. No. U93-09791. Toronto, Ontario. E.R. Smith and B. Menkir. Heard: 20 October 1993 and 13 January 1994. Decision: 13 January 1994. Reasons for decisions.

Mayers, Marcel v. Minister of Employment and Immigration. (F.C.A.) 1992. 97 D.L.R. 4th 729. N. (L.Y.) (Re)., [1993] C.R.D.D. No. 55. No. U93-02026. Toronto, Ontario. E.R. Smith and P. Stratton. Heard: 31 March 1993. Decision: 13 May 1993. Reasons for decision.

Native Women's Association of Canada and Her Majesty the Queen, reasons for judgment. Fed. C.A., June 11 1992, Mahoney, J.A.

Native Women's Association of Canada, Gail Stacey-Moore and Sharon McIvor and Her Majesty the Queen, The Right Honourable Brian Mulroney and the Right Honourable Joe Clark in *RE. the Referendum Act,* applicants' memorandum of fact and law in the Fed. Ct. (Trial Division), 18 September 1992, file No. T 2283-92.

N. (L.Y.) (Re)., [1993] C.R.D.D. No. 55. No. U93-02026. Toronto, Ontario. E.R. Smith and P. Stratton. Heard: 31 March 1993. Decision: 13 May 1993. Reasons for decision.

Pour, Malek Mohammad Nagmeh Abbas v. M.C.I. (F.C.T.D. *Ontario Human Rights Commission et al. v. Ontario Teachers' Federation et al.* Ontario Court (Divisional Court), File No. 271/94, 273/94. Unreported decision, 21 June 1995., no. IMM-3650-95), Gibson, 6 June 1996.

Q. (X.B.) (Re)., [1990] C.R.D.D. No. 216.

R. v. (A.P.). 1992. November 18, file no. T92-03227. C.R.R.D. no. 318.

R. v. Chin. C.A. (B.C.). 1989. February 23, J., file no. CA008543.

R. v. Chin. S.C. (B.C.). 1987. December 4, J., file no. 204/0529.

R. v. Drozdkik. County Ct.(B.C.). 1988. March 31, reasons for sentence, Boyd, J., file no. CC870536.

R. v. Duffney. 1986. *Nfld. & P.E.I.R.* 61: 178

R. v. E. G. C.A.(Ont.). 1987. *Ontario Appeal Cases* 20:379.

R. v. Hoyt. Terr. Ct. (Yukon). 1991. July 18, reasons for sentence, Lilles, C.J.T.C.

R. v. Hoyt. Terr. Ct. (Yukon). 1992. January 17, oral reasons for judgment, Taqqert, Lambert, and Hollinrake.

*R. v. J.(E).*S.C.(Yukon). 1991. March 15, judgment delivered orally, Madison, J., file no. 90–06337.

R. v. J.(H.). Pr. C.(B.C.). 1990. January 17, reasons for sentence, Barrett, J., file no. 1095FC

R. v. Kowch. S.C. (Yukon). 1989. March 20, file no. 87–4661.

R. v. L. (J.C.) 1987. *Canadian Criminal Cases* 36 (3d):

R. v. L.(K). Prov. Ct. (Man.). 1989. September 18, reasons for sentence, Meyers, J.

R. v. M. (G.O). S.C.(NWT). 1990. *Canadian Criminal Cases* 54 (3rd): 81.

R. v. Malbog. 1989. April 28, Edmonton 8803/3048C3 (Alta. Crt. QB) 2-5.

R. v. Mohammed. Prov. Ct. (Ont.). 1992. April 30.

R. v. Moses. 1992. Terr. Ct.(Yukon). *Canadian Criminal Cases* 71(3d): 347–85.

R. v. O'Connor. 1996. B.C.J. No. 1663, Vancouver Registry No. CC920617, British Columbia Supreme Court, Vancouver, British Columbia, Oppal J. Heard: July 3,4,5,8,9,19, 1996, Judgement: filed Juy 25, 1996.

R. v. O'Connor and Aboriginal Women's Council, Canadian Association of Sexual Assault Centers, Disabled Women's Network Canada, the Women's Legal Education and Action Fund and the Canadian Mental Health Association. C.A.(B.C.). 1993. June 30, written reasons for judgment of application for intervenor status, Taylor, J.A., Wood, J.A., Hollinrake, J.A., Rowles, J.A., and Prowse, J.A., concurring.

R. v. O'Connor. S.C.(B.C.). 1992. December 2, excerpts of proceedings at trial.

R. v. Okkuatsiak. *Nfld. & P.E.I.R.* 65 (1987): 234.

R. v. P. (J.A.). 1991. 6 C.R. (4th) 126. R. v. P. (J.A.). *Northwest Territories Reports* [1991].

R. v. Ritchie. County Ct.(B.C.) 1988. March 2, reasons for sentence. Houghton, C.C.J., file no. CC39/87.

R. v. Roach. S.C. (Yukon). 1987. December 8, file no. 523.87.

R. v. S. (D.D.). Prov.Ct.(Ont.) 1988. November 2, reasons for sentence, Langdon, J.

R. v. Shunamen. 1986. November 19, Halifax S.C.C. 01487 (N.S.C.A.)

R. v. T.(J.J.). C.A. (Sask.) 1989. April 26, judgment delivered orally, Tallis, J.A., Vancise, and Gerwing, J.A., concurring.

R. (U.R.) (Re)., [1994] C.R.D.D. No. 69. No. T93-01306. Toronto, Ontario. J. Morrison and S.G. Flintoff. Heard: 31 March 1993. Decision: 13 May 1993. Reasons for decision.

R. v. Vanden. Terr. Ct. (Yukon). 1988. February 1, reasons for sentence, Langdon, J.

R. v. Whitecap (R.T.) and Whitecap (D.M.). C.A. (Sask.) 1989. January 5, judgment delivered orally, Gerwing, J.A., Tallis, J.A., concurring. Wakeling, J.A., in dissent.

Seaboyer v. the Queen: Re Gayme and the Queen. 1991. 2 S.C.R. 577 at 690.

V. (A.P.). 18 November 1992, Court File Number: T92-03227. C.R.D.D. No. 318 at 11.

W. (C.X.) (Re)., [1991] C.R.D.D. No. 483.

W. (Y.J.) (Re)., [1994] C.R.D.D. No 91. Nos. M92-09034, M92-09035, M92-09036. Montréal, Québec. D.N. Doray and L. Dorion. Heard: 15 February and 1 June 1993. Decision: 28 February 1994. Reasons for decision.

W. (Z.D.) (Re)., [1993] C.R.D.D. No. 3. No. U92-06668. Toronto, Ontario. E.R. Smith and N. Daya. Heard: 13 November 1992. Decision: 19 February 1993. Reasons for decision.

X. (W.N.) (Re)., [1991] C.R.D.D. No. 752.

Permissions

I am grateful to the following journals for permission to republish my work. The chapters are revised versions of the following: 'Beyond Universal Women: Reflections on Theorizing Differences Among Women,' *The University of New Brunswick Law Journal* 45 (1996): 209–30; 'Collective Rights and Women: The Cold Game of Equality Staring,' *Journal of Human Justice* 4, no. 1 (1992): 1–11; 'Storytelling for Social Change,' *Gender and Education* 5, no. 1 (1993): 55–70; 'What Is to Be Gained by Looking White People in the Eye? Culture, Race and Gender in Cases of Sexual Violence,' *Signs: A Journal of Women in Culture and Society* 19, no. 4 (1994): 894–923; 'Domestic Violence as Gender Persecution: The Borders of Nation, Race and Gender,' *Canadian Journal of Women and the Law*, 8 no. 1 (1995): 45–88; 'From Pity to Respect, From Consent to Responsibility: Sub-texts in Cases of Sexual Violence Involving Women with Developmental Disabilities,' *Law and Social Inquiry* 19, no. 4 (1994): 891–922.

Index